Controversies in Con

Through Us, With Us, In Us: Relational Theologies in the Twenty-First Century

Edited by

Lisa Isherwood

and

Elaine Bellchambers

scm press

© The Editors and Contributors

Published in 2010 by SCM Press
Editorial office
13–17 Long Lane,
London, EC1A 9PN, UK

SCM Press is an imprint of Hymns Ancient and Modern Ltd
(a registered charity)
St Mary's Works, St Mary's Plain,
Norwich, NR3 3BH, UK
www.scm-canterburypress.co.uk

British Library Cataloguing in Publication data

A catalogue record for this book is available
from the British Library

978 0 334 04366 9

Originated by The Manila Typesetting Company

Printed and bound by

CPI Antony Rowe, Chippenham SN14 6LH

Contents

Contributors

Elaine Bellchambers is Senior Lecturer in Religious Education and Professional Studies at the University of Winchester. She has been involved in the writing of the six Hampshire Religious Education syllabi since 1978 and is co-author of *Primary Religious Education: A New Approach* (Routledge, forthcoming). She was an Ofsted inspector for seven years.

June Boyce-Tillman is Professor of Foundation Music at the University of Winchester and author of many books including *Constructing Musical Healing: The Wounds that Sing* (Jessica Kingsley, 2000); *The Creative Spirit: Harmonious Living with Hildegard of Bingen* (Canterbury Press, 2000); *A Rainbow to Heaven* (Stainer and Bell, 2006) and *Unconventional Wisdom* (Equinox, 2007).

Beverley Clack is Professor of Philosophy of Religion at Oxford Brookes University and author of a number of books including *Misogyny in the Western Philosophical Tradition: A Reader* (Macmillan, 1999); with Pamela Sue Anderson, *Feminist Philosophy of Religion: Critical Readings* (Routledge, 2004); *The Philosophy of Religion: A Critical Introduction*, co-authored with Brian R. Clack (Polity Press, 1998); *Sex and Death: A Reappraisal of Human Mortality* (Polity Press, 2002) and *Embodying Feminist Liberation Theologies: Essays for Lisa Isherwood*, editor (T&T Clark, 2004).

Mary Condren is Director of the Institute of Feminism and Religion in Eire and author of *The Serpent and the Goddess* (HarperCollins, 1989); 'Melting Hearts of Stone: Mercy not Sacrifice', in Lisa Isherwood and Kathleen McPhillips (eds), *Post-Christian Feminisms: A Critical Appraisal* (Ashgate, forthcoming).

Susannah Cornwall is Research Fellow at the University of Exeter and author of *Sex and Uncertainty in the Body of Christ: Intersex Conditions and Christian Theology* (Equinox, forthcoming).

Jenny Daggers is Senior Lecturer in Theology at Liverpool Hope University, She is author of *The British Christian Women's Movement: A Rehabilitation of Eve* (Ashgate, 2002) and has contributed chapters to two collections on feminist theology. With Diana Neal she co-edited *Sex, Gender and Religion: Josephine Butler Revisited* (Peter Lang, 2006).

Mary Grey is Professorial Research Fellow at St Mary's University College Twickenham. She is a past President of the European Society of Women in Theological Research and the author of many books including *Sacred Longings: Ecofeminist Theology and Globalisation* (SCM Press, 2003 and Fortress, 2004); *Introducing Feminist Images of God* (Sheffield Academic Press/Pilgrim, 2001); *The Outrageous Pursuit of Hope: Prophetic Dreams for the 21st Century* (Darton, Longman & Todd, 2000) and *Prophecy and Mysticism: The Heart of the Postmodern Church* (T&T Clark, 1997).

Maaike de Haardt is Professor for Religion and Gender at the Radboud University Nijmegen and Senior Lecturer in Systematic Theology at Tilburg University in the Netherlands.

Carter Heyward is Professor Emerita at the Episcopal Divinity School, Cambridge, MA, a priest and writer. Her latest books include *Flying Changes: Horses as Spiritual Teachers* (Pilgrim, 2005); *God in the Balance: Christian Spirituality in Times of Terror* (Pilgrim, 2002) and *Saving Jesus from Those who are Right* (Fortress, 1999).

Lisa Isherwood is Professor of Feminist Liberation Theologies and Director of Theological Partnerships at the University of Winchester. She is executive editor of the international journal *Feminist Theology* and author, co-author and editor of 18 books, including *The Fat Jesus* (Darton, Longman & Todd, 2008) and *Trans/formations* (SCM Press, 2009).

Catherine Keller is Professor of Constructive Theology at Drew University, USA, and author of many books including *From a Broken Web* (Beacon, 1986); *Apocalypse Now and Then* (Beacon, 1996) and *Face of the Deep: A Theology of Becoming* (Routledge, 2003).

Ursula King is Professor Emerita at the University of Bristol. She is a past President of the European Society of Women in Theological Research and the author of many books, the latest being *The Search for Spirituality* (Canterbury Press, 2009).

Diarmuid O'Murchu is a writer, priest, social psychologist and freelance scholar. He is author of many books including *Evolutionary Faith* (Orbis, 2004); *Quantum Theology* (Crossroad, 1997) and *Reclaiming Spirituality* (Gill and Macmillan, 1997).

Natalie K. Watson is a writer and theologian, based in Peterborough, UK. She is author of *Introducing Feminist Ecclesiology* (Sheffield Academic Press, 2002) and *Feminist Theology* (Eerdmans, 2003). With Stephen Burns, she has co-edited *Exchanges of Grace: Essays in Honour of Ann Loades* (SCM Press, 2008).

Introduction

LISA ISHERWOOD AND ELAINE BELLCHAMBERS

The history of relational theology is a short one, yet it could be argued that it is foundational in the world we live and, in that time, it has shaken the ground on which we have traditionally created theology. Although the history is short, there have been many people and ways of making theology that have and do contribute to its growing momentum. Process theologians who questioned the wisdom of understanding our being as created and therefore fallen from a place of primal innocence helped disrupt the fixed nature of much theological method. In their thinking, the divine was changed from the architect of a fixed, moulded and pre-formed universe to an artist, a poet, who moved within the ever unfolding process with the very stuff of that universe and the people within it. Still guiding, yes, but also grasping along with creatures for the next step, the next unfolding. For some, there still had to be a fixed end, to which this guiding hand was pointing, while, for others, the process was itself enough.

Feminist theologians have engaged with these questions in many different ways. Daphne Hampson points out that a God who holds all the power leaves the feminist question of autonomy out in the cold. Others, such as Rosemary Radford Ruether, have almost approached the question as one of justice: how could it be that what we call Christ could be a once-and-for-all power-packed event, if we too are meant to change the world? There is a basic injustice here, a built-in falling short that Ruether finds intolerable. Carter Heyward argues from the position of love and embodiment: if God is love, then this of itself demands relationality, since love with all the power stacked in one place is nothing short of abuse. The God who is our genesis is the outpouring of that love and empowerment. She tells us that love reaches out to others, and so this is surely the nature of God. Her work has also shown how this

1

divine relationality works between us, and of late she has extended the boundaries to include the non-human world in this divine relating. Love as the relational revolution knows no boundaries. Catherine Keller has taken us to face the deep and it is here that the self-contained and non-relational notions of God really come unstuck, when faced with the deep, such ideas are exposed for the folly they are – they are given nowhere to go except into retreat.

So relational theologies have many starting-points, but they appear to turn traditional Christian theologies on their head, asserting, as they do, that it is between us and through our experiences that we intuit the God we profess to believe in who is within and among us. This is a form of theological thinking that gives agency to all living things and the cosmos itself and by so doing places all existing models of theology and even notions of the divine within a new frame for reflection. Any theoretically formed theologies can be nothing more than starting-points and no longer seen as the assured end-points against which all human experience is measured. Rather, the lived experience of women, men and the cosmos becomes the stuff of ever-emerging and changing forms of theological reflection. Fixed ends and ultimate truths so easy to declare in the light of the Word becoming flesh are transformed in the crucible of the flesh becoming word – an ever-changing word, as the realities of life unfold and spiral. Such relationality questions many of the old traditional certainties and opens up a future of endless possibility, glorious and mundane, filled with the abundance of life spoken of in the Gospels or crushed and broken by the carelessness of human creatures. We would wish to argue that relational theologies enable Christian theologians to face the reality of incarnation, both its awesome transformative power and its ever fragile existence in the lived experience of women and men and the cosmos itself.

Relational theologies call a great deal into question, not least the role of the divine in this process. The Almighty Lord of All is not easily understood as a relational figure, and the whole notion of power is placed under scrutiny. Of course, power when understood within a divine/human frame also brings into question both theological anthropology and the kind and level of power that the divine is believed to have. Christian feminist theologians, such as Carter Heyward, who have attempted to deal with this issue, have often been accused of at one and the same time giving too much power to humans and reducing the power of God in Christ to such a level as to make it not a Christology at all – and indeed barely a theism! This simply illuminates the way in which divine/human power has been framed under patriarchy – a system that has at its heart a scarcity model which exerts its neurosis over many aspects of theological thinking. The idea that power shared may be power increased could not be contemplated under this system and so the power of God has been made absolute and untouchable. In short, placed where relationality is not an option. So despite Christian theology speaking of immanence, this, too, has been ring-fenced by notions of ultimate distance and difference. So, for relational theologies, which work with their inheritance in the tradition, there emerges the question of the meaning of transcendence in a relational world. Lurking as an ever-present threat to real relationality is the heritage of transcendence which is based in being lifted above and beyond a sinful material world; this is part of the concept that needs to be guarded against in all relational thinking. This seems, then, to be a question that relational theologians should be addressing, and it is good to see Heyward begin that in her chapter in this book by placing the notion of transcendence within and between as an ethical materialist question. As we expand our tent to include the whole cosmos in our theological ponderings, we offer ourselves a bigger range of possibilities in which to understand our hitherto rather narrowly configured doctrines and scriptures. Relational theologies through their embrace of lived diversity as a starting-point for the creation of theology allows for a fuller engagement with the deep mystery of incarnation – incarnation not narrowed by anthropocentric thinking and theorizing.

This book looks at three areas where relational theology is pushing the boundaries and asking questions that expand our understanding of the divine between and within us. These are in embodiment, in our cosmological relationality and within the divine itself.

Carter Heyward takes us on an autobiographical journey, in which she identifies what she calls five breaking points in her story of unfolding relational theology – a story that shows the disruptions that needed to occur in her hitherto doctrinal world. Looking back, she is able to say that relational theology 'is not about fully understanding or adequately imagining anything. It is a poetry that sparks and spins us, through our experiences, imaginations, and cognitive faculties' (p. 10).

Susannah Cornwall is keen to explore the theological and Christo-logical implications of the existence of and treatment of physical intersex conditions. She explores the humanity of the body of Christ and its rela-tional potential across all manner of embodied living.

Ursula King takes us on a journey of exploring love, which she believes has been underexplored in feminist theological discussions. Through her development of what she calls pneumatophores, she explores the *via feminina*, which is a third way for mysticism, a radical way, which seeks new ways of engagement and relationality based in embodied love in a world in crisis.

Beverley Clack claims that, if we are to develop subtle and sensitive feminist theologies, we need to identify the projections that can obscure our engagement with the patriarchy. Through an examination of Klein's paranoid-schizoid position, Clack asks why feminists should attempt to understand their own projections onto patriarchy.

Mary Grey explores the concept of relational theology through Pal-estine as a case study. Here she not only demonstrates the tragedy of non-rationality, but also highlights the emerging spirituality from such a place. This is a Palestinian spirituality of *sumud* or steadfastness which grows from the land and the people who stand resolutely upon it. It is a spirituality of peacemaking based in the biblical notion of the bless-edness of peacemakers, where the Greek word *makarios* (blessed) con-notes action.

Catherine Keller takes us on a cosmic journey through tangles of unknowing, a journey that challenges what she names as our ignorant knowing and aims to replace it with knowing ignorance. She highlights for us that we are part of cosmic boundarylessness based in our shared materiality and that such an insight is not one that is beyond Christian understanding as witnessed by the theologian Nicolas Cusa.

Lisa Isherwood begins with incarnation and challenges theologians to continue the rupture that the divine incarnate made in the world rather than setting in place rigid and fixed absolutes. The story of the cosmos challenges these fixed notions and perfect beginnings and rather propels us into constant flux and unfolding.

Diarmuid O'Murchu takes us into the quantum universe where he challenges us to break out of the idea that humanity is self-contained and superior to the rest of the created order. He claims relationality is the primary condition of the cosmos and the way in which collaboration ensures the progress and elegance of the universe.

June Boyce-Tillman re-enchants stones for us in her chapter where she reminds us that the whole cosmos has a resonance. She demonstrates how the pre-patriarchal world understood that music was central to the cosmic schema and that even the Bible mentions that creation makes music to praise its creator. She reminds us that even the instruments we use for making music are themselves made from the very substance of the earth.

Maaike de Haardt reflects on monotheism and relationality from the context of patriarchal paternal power and abuse in families, communities and politics. She encourages us to ask: does monotheism undermine relationality, is relational theology really free of mono-creativity and mono-generativity, and do we need new concepts and practices?

Jenny Daggers wishes to reassert transcendence 'as a radical alterity to the human' as a response to the secular valorization of immanence, and in so doing she believes that relationality will be taken to new depths.

Natalie K. Watson attempts to rethink the cross from a feminist relational point of view. In so doing she examines the way in which pain and bullying can dehumanize and make a person incapable of giving or even receiving love. The ability to love is the most clear expression of being in the image of God, and so, for Watson, we need to find a place where love is possible within a theology of the cross.

Mary Condren escorts us into the world of Bracha Ettinger and the wealth of possibilities that she provides for those engaged in relational theologies. Ettinger challenges the Freudian and phallic assertion that the subject begins in discontinuity and therefore loss. For Ettinger the creation of subjectivity is an ongoing political and ethical process that is situated in the compassionate hospitality of co-emergence – in the matrixial borderspace. Condren highlights the relationship between Ettinger's work and her own on mercy not sacrifice, at the same time as laying before us the vast challenge and range of possibilities that the work of Ettinger offers.

The essays gathered here are challenging and profound and at times they illuminate the edges of one's own engagement and relationality.

So here you are, dear reader, being invited into the relational dance!

Part 1

Embodying Relational Theologies

1

Breaking Points: Shaping a Relational Theology

CARTER HEYWARD

For Alison Cheek, cherished friend, sister priest, and bold sojourner into the Mystery.

These days I spend most of my reading time absorbed in three stories which, to most people, would appear unrelated and non-theological: the story of the unravelling of global capitalism's high finances, thanks to the managers of our political economy; the story of Harry Potter and Hogwarts School for Witchcraft and Wizardry, thanks to the imaginative power of J. K Rowling; and various books and manuals on the care and well-being of horses, thanks to the presence in my life of several equine friends and the humans who love them. What links these three apparently very different realms of fascination for me, is precisely my interest in the Sacred Power, or God, we meet and come to know through our struggles for mutual relation. The motives of advanced global capitalism illustrate the antithesis of mutuality, what happens when we do not love well. Harry Potter, Hermione Granger and Ron Weasley grow into a realization of the redemptive power of vulnerability and become willing to risk everything on behalf of it. And the horses – well, the horses have become my priests, bearers of a Power both fully creaturely and fully divine, which urges us into mutual relation, which is what this presentation is all about.

I must tell you that nearly everyone in the United States whom I told about this conference looked at me quizzically and asked, 'Relational theology? Is there any other kind?' Admittedly, these friends of mine are not, on the whole, theologians. They are farmers, physicians, therapists, teachers, parents . . . and we had a few chuckles about how, certainly, all theology ought to be 'relational', just like all farming and medicine and therapy and teaching and parenting ought to be.

So then, what do I – what do we – mean by 'relational'? We are suggesting, first, that our theologies are formed in the interactions – relationships – between and among various sources. Anglicans, for example, have insisted on the tripod stool of Scripture, tradition and reason as the foundation of theology; not just one source, the Bible, but several in relation to each other. Second – and this is its most radically challenging attribute – relational theologies present as foundational to all God-talk a mutual relationship between God, creation and humankind, each of whom is most fully experienced and understood as intrinsically (ontologically) relational. Thus, not only is our theology shaped in our imaginations and brains by various interactive forces, but moreover God is truly God only in relation to a creation/humankind that is itself only in relation to God.

Does this mean that we can ever fully understand God? Of course not, but let us admit that we cannot fully understand ourselves either. Relational theology is not about fully understanding or adequately imaging anything. It is a poetry that sparks and spins us, through our experiences, imaginations and cognitive faculties, through what we do well, what we do poorly and what we do not do at all, through what we see and what we do not see, what we say and what we do not say. Relational theology is a poetry that invites us to live a little more fully in right-relation with one another in this world at this time.

Autobiography and theology

As a Christian feminist liberation theologian, I have long insisted that the most liberating theologies are relational, grounded in struggles for, and celebrations of, mutuality as a creative dynamic. I have been away from the realms of professional theological discourse for the past several years but have reflected quite a bit on how my experiences and understandings of God, or Sacred Power, have taken shape over the course of my life thus far. In this chapter I want to reflect on the theological process as it has unfolded in my life over six decades. I hope, in this way, to illustrate how my experiences and thinking about God have taken shape in relation to how others experience and think about God and in relation to how I (or we) believe (or imagine) that God is relating to us. My central thesis is that the relational theological process involves movements of many kinds – social, political, psychological, public/collective, private/ personal – including the theologian's experiential and conceptual shifts and changes, imaged as processes of breaking away from certain theological moorings and breaking towards other places in which to ground our lives and work. Whether and how these places, which I now affirm as vibrant relational theological assumptions, actually foundational to my work, are essential to relational theologies in general is a question I will leave with you.

Though I have long employed autobiography as a theological vehicle, I understand my remarkable sister theologian Catherine Keller's resistance to its use or over-use. Relying on autobiography in our theological work can be merely self-indulgent and frankly boring. (Who really cares?) But human lives and stories can be windows into something beyond the realm of the individual. When a personal story, without being presumptuous, opens itself towards the transpersonal, then sharing of one's own spiritual development, one's own religious history, one's own theological questions, one's own ethical commitments, has long seemed to me an honest way of *beginning* theological conversation. In order not to be presumptuous, however, a theologian has to be open to the transcending and transgressing of her own conceptual boundaries, as she breaks out of herself towards that which is often alien to her own experiences, beyond what she can know or understand on her own. In other words, a theologian needs to welcome, even invite, critiques of her theological work which must be understood as an open and ongoing, not a once-and-for-all, project.

For example, in naming the five 'breaking points' in my theological work, in which I have moved away from some spiritual or theological assumption towards something else, I often discover that others have got to these places before me – sometimes generations, sometimes only

11

moments, earlier, or I see later that sometimes they have arrived after me, usually with clearer, better seasoned insights. For example, Francis of Assisi recognized the animals as God-bearers centuries before I did, and Bonhoeffer beckoned us to 'religionless Christianity' approximately 20 years before I would begin to find my way through to the deep wisdom of his conversion, which would confirm my own. Marcella Althaus-Reid's colourful sexual stories of indecency and perversion came along a decade after my efforts to frame a sexual theology – and her bold critique of feminist liberation theologies continues to challenge and clarify my own thoughts about sex, gender, God and religion. So whether before us in time, alongside us now, or coming after us further along, countless theological voices do, and will, urge us to join our voices with theirs – in agreement or argument. Like the story of Jesus, countless voices speak to us through their particular experiences and memories. This they do through fiction, theology, historical narrative and analysis, liturgy, politics, art, music and the daily news. We stand where we do because others have shown us something, or will show us something one day, that will make us more responsive participants in the ongoing communal dance that transcends and transgresses cultural, religious, gender and generational boundaries, and time itself. What may seem to us, both conceptually and emotionally, like a 'personal life' is always more than simply personal. We are all participants in spiralling, transpersonal historical and spiritual movements.

The five breaking points I am about to lay out cannot be understood as simply chronological, although I have become aware of each a little further down the life-path than the one before. Each, however, arcs backwards and forwards in time and space, becoming in the American witch Starhawk's imaginative language a 'spiral dance' in relation to the others. In each, 'experience' – our embodied lives and participation in the world – grounds cognition and concepts.

First breaking point: from humanity to all of us

I knew nothing of Francis of Assisi nor Thoreau and Walden Pond; nothing of deities Diana of the Forest or Neptune of the Sea, nor of any human, other creature, or divine being who valued the whole of creation as much as humanity. Yet growing up in the mountains of western North Carolina, in the United States South, I knew something about the sacredness of all creation. What I knew was shaping my life by the time I was in kindergarten, more than a decade before Rachel Carson would speak out about these matters in *The Silent Spring*. Still, with saints and imaged deities, scientists and artists and other actors in history as well as parents and childhood buddies and my own intuition moving me along pretty much unaware, I knew, long before I could 'think about it', that God was present and active throughout the created world and not just in me and other people. No doubt from many sources, including the realm of apophatic mystery and negative theology so powerfully examined by Catherine Keller (2008a, b), I knew that the Spirit named 'God' in the Bible and in church was far bigger than we could possibly imagine and that he had as much to do with box turtles, raspberry vines and dogwood blossoms as he did with me and other humans. Never have I believed that there was a deity who preferred humankind to other creatures. Notice, however, that once upon a time, I definitely believed that God was a 'He' – a large Man in the Sky. It would be many years before I could break away from him and become more honestly pan-en-theistic.

Trying to be faithful to my Father God, and long before I knew what I was doing intellectually, I broke away as a child from the anthropocentrism fastened in place historically by Christian Fathers who over the millennia had placed humanity at the centre of God's creation, God's life, God's love and God's christic spirit in Jesus. Transcending the borders of human skin and human identity, I found myself transgressing boundaries established in western religious and philosophical history at least in part to coddle our fear of otherness. Years beyond childhood, I would discover that I was by no means the first or only person to reject Christian anthropocentrism, including Christology, as xenophobic – a worldview rooted in fear of the other. Yet even today, as we know, Christian feminists and other earth- and creation-affirming theologians continue to be trivialized by the custodians of the arrogant, unimaginative and fear-based theologies that put humanity at the centre of God's interest and marginalize other creatures and the earth itself as lesser beings, of lesser value, without soul or intrinsic sacred worth. So although I was being raised as an Anglican Christian, I was becoming more universalist in my spiritual sensibilities years before I could read, much less think about, Christian doctrine or engage in theological debate.

Today, looking back over more than half a century of spiritual and theological reflection, I see this early breaking towards universalism as a foundational leap of transcendence in my own theological development – as it has been also in the theological work of many Christians and women and men from other spiritual as well as secular and scientific arenas who have dared to insist that respect for and care of creation – beyond what most of us can even imagine – is vital to understanding anything and everything of real value. More and more, I am aware that, for our salvation as a species, we humans need help – and that, from a Christian perspective, most of the christic help we need will come from creatures other than human. As Sallie McFague has reminded us (1997), we need other creatures far more than either the earth or its non-human creatures need us.

Shortly after the 9/11 attacks, I wrote a small book exploring images of God 'in times of terror' because I had no doubt that our God-images, like those of the terrorist bombers, have everything to do with the violence we perpetuate against those whom we fear as 'other'. In the book, I end the chapter on 'creatures in the images of a morally complex God' with a small prayer: 'Elephant God forgive us/ Holy mountain shelter us/ Sister spirit stream carry us on/ Tiny sparrow sing to us/ your favorite hymn/ Pelican brother Jesus/ cover us with your wings/ Bid us goodnight/ and raise us in the morning/ in your christic power/ to recreate the world' (2002). In breaking away from an anthropocentric God and creation, I break towards a christic body that is as fully elephant as she is fully human.

Second breaking point: from privatized and apathetic spirituality to the struggle for justice

Dietrich Bonhoeffer wrote to his friend Eberhard Bethge of 'religionless Christianity' – a concept, yes, but more basically an experience, that would shake the foundations of my young teenage body-self and spirit almost a decade before I read his *Letters and Papers from Prison* and would begin to wrestle intellectually with his theology. Thinking back to college days in the mid-1960s, I am still grateful for the moral intelligence of several professors and fellow students for whom the study of abstract religion would not do. Why bother to think about the life of Jesus or the Jewish Talmud or different streams of Islam or the Upanishads of Hinduism or the teachings of the Buddha, unless we are thinking about what differences, positively and negatively, these religious traditions have made to the history of the world and, where applicable, to our own communities and cultures, and to our own lives, values and choices? As Christopher Morse, one of my seminary tutors, and later a professor at Union Theological Seminary in New York City, would put it several years later, the most challenging theological question is often not 'What?' but 'So what?'

Like Martin Luther King, a generation later and an ocean away, Bonhoeffer's legacy bears an indictment of the Christian religion ordinarily associated with the large, once popular mainline Protestant and Catholic churches in Europe and North America and their colonialist heritage throughout the world. The problem with these churches, feminist and other liberation theologians would begin to point out decades after Bonhoeffer and King, is that they are man-servants of global capitalism. One of the ways they serve capitalism is by providing a spiritual rationale for private ownership. They do so by marketing 'spirituality' as a personal commodity and 'morality' as a matter of an individual's sexual control, especially men's sexual control of women's bodies, lives and reproductive options. By selling spirituality as a person's private possession, the churches cultivate public apathy – that is, an aversion to suffering for the common good. In this way even the historically liberal churches, such as certain branches of the Anglican, Lutheran, Reformed and Roman Catholic – despite their social justice concerns – play a maintenance role in the perpetuation of structures of injustice and violence. It is hard not to notice this in areas of gender and sexual violence and oppression, a fact central to the rise of Christian feminism over the last four decades. Because Christian churches historically have been less insistent in their struggles against economic oppression than they have been in their efforts to secure gender and sexual justice, it is often more difficult to notice the Church's role in perpetuating global capitalism's obsession with private possession and personal profit.

As Bonhoeffer's and King's lives bear witness, nothing takes the place of personal involvement in the movements for justice as the most powerful impetus for a conversion to 'religionless Christianity'. Their witness invites us to join in working for justice, peace and compassion wherever we can. In these struggles against racism, against war, against sexism and heterosexism, we transcend – cross over – from a primarily private interest in God to a more public journey with others who are committed to particular justice goals. In breaking away from the private, we transgress the seductive boundaries of what one of my life-companions, Beverly Harrison, has named 'capitalist spirituality' (2004). In Harrison's feminist ethical view, capitalist spirituality weakens us by assuring us falsely that the most spiritual voices are the least angry and most easily persuaded by those with spiritual authority over them. By raising our voices and moving our feet in the struggles for justice, we break away from the spiritual seductions and manipulations of capitalism. In so doing we are breaking towards possibilities of deeper spiritual moorings.

Third breaking point: from theistic power-over to our sacred power in mutual relation

The first two breaking points were foundational to all that has followed in my life and work as a teacher and theologian. At the same time, neither was all that unusual for a North American Christian young adult of conscience in the 1960s and 1970s. It was not hard then, and still is not today, to encounter liberal religious leaders in the USA, Christian and other, who are happy advocates of the earth and dedicated disciples of a god who moves the struggle for justice in its many forms. My participation in the movement for women's ordination in the Episcopal/Anglican Church was rooted in this dedication and was well within the boundaries of a liberal feminist justice-centred Christian faith.

The experience of breaking open spiritually became more challenging for me in relation to the matter of power, both divine and human. As I began to study theology and consciously to think about the God of such modern-day saints and martyrs as Dietrich Bonhoeffer, Martin Luther King and Oscar Romero, I found myself uneasy with the dogmatic assumptions underlying the theologies of these men and of the feminist and other liberation theologies I was teaching. On the one hand, like all my saints, I was clear that God is involved in struggles for justice; on the other hand, I was also clear that God's power is seldom 'victorious' in the struggles for racial justice, or for peace, or gender justice, or for bread for the poor, or for the exploited earth and animals.

The Christian theologian who made the most spiritual sense to me, beginning in the 1970s, was Dorothee Soelle, whose questions about God's power were mine as well. If God's power is not effective, if God doesn't win in the struggles for justice, in what sense can we say that God has, or is, 'power'? (1967). At that point in my life, I was also being shaken by the passion of the Jewish writer and Holocaust survivor Elie Wiesel, who shared these questions about God's power and authority in relation to evil. Horrified by Wiesel's experiences and deeply resonant with his interrogations of God, especially in his early works, a series of novels (beginning with the autobiographical *Night*), I began struggling intellectually as well as spiritually with Soelle's and Wiesel's questions about God's power, and our own, in relation to evil, injustice and violence. I found that I agreed with them that there is no God above us, no divine man or woman either watching over us or partnered with us in history. The viability of theism was dead. I understood the subtitle of Dorothee Soelle's 1967 book *Christ the Representative: Christian Identity After the Death of God*. Looking back, I also understood why, as a college senior, I had written a thesis on the 'Death of God' theologians who were being read among college students in the United States during the social turmoil of the late 1960s.

More than a decade after my earlier fascination with the 'death of God', I proposed in my 1980 doctoral dissertation that there is no God with 'power over' us, no God who is 'omnipotent' in any traditional or meaningful sense of that word. Somewhere I had heard a little riddle: 'If

God is good, He is not God. If God is God, He is not good.' The problem with that riddle, I decided, was its implicit definition of an all-powerful, or omnipotent, God. I agreed with Dorothee Soelle that God's power is God's love and vulnerability, not a divine capacity to reign over any world or win any battle; and I agreed with Elie Wiesel that God's power enters our lives through human acts of love, kindness, courage and solidarity. I suggested that God is our power in the struggle for mutuality – right, mutual relation – in the smallest and largest arenas of our life together. God is not 'over' the struggle, nor even 'leading' the struggle. God is *in* the struggle as the power of the struggle itself, so fully that God *is* the struggle for right, mutual relation and God *is* the power in and of mutuality.

This was a more radical break from both liberal and liberation Christian theologies than any theological step I had taken previously, because I was departing from most common understandings not only of an omnipotent God but also of a transcendent God – understood historically – and wrongly, in my judgement – as residing 'over' us, rather than as 'crossing over' among us. I did not fully appreciate the extent to which those few theologians who were attempting to strip God of his omnipotence and transcendence were barely, if at all, recognizable as 'Christian' by most of the men and women authorized to lead the churches and teach Christian theology. Suggesting that God is our own most vibrant creative, liberating power, which we generate and experience together in our struggles for mutuality and justice, was both intellectually – and, more importantly, spiritually – a slap in the face of the Father and his religion. As blasphemous daughters, we could be tried, convicted and destroyed – or we could be simply ignored by church fathers and mothers labouring to hold patriarchal power in place.

God was no longer, for me, a Heavenly Father. God was becoming a spiritual force, not a person at all and not at all personal – except sometimes, and in certain people and other beings that seem to spill over with God. I began to notice how much God there seemed to be, infusing the daily lives and activities of people and creatures everywhere. It didn't seem unreasonable, much less untrue, to image God in human faces and bodies, or for that matter in glaciers and everglades, equine faces and copperhead snakes. It became clear to me, from a christic perspective, that we can indeed see God in Jesus, and also in you and me and each and every person or creature. The breaking away from a 'power-over' Father/Mother God and towards God as our power in mutual relation would cast new spiritual light on everything and raise many more questions – not only about how we experience and view God but also how we live in relation to one another – partners, spouses, children and friends, yes, but also enemies, those whom we fear, that which we do not know or trust, and indeed sometimes that which can really hurt us. Copperheads, after all, are poisonous snakes in the United States!

How in this world do we god (verb) together – in relation to friends and enemies, those who wish us well and those who would destroy us if they could? This is not a question with easy or fixed answers. One of the great theological processes in the last decades has been the movement through various countries and communities of Truth and Reconciliation Commissions, such as that chaired by Desmond Tutu in South Africa during the 1990s. Efforts to build peace, find common ground, forgive without forgetting – that is, without erasing important historical memory – these are foundational ethical and pastoral challenges which we meet at the heart of relational theology. Of course, the struggle for mutuality lures us into even more confounding conundrums: how do we love enemies who have no intention of repenting, people who seriously do wish to harm us or others? Can we imagine that loving our enemies, whether they have repented or not, involves holding space for them in our hearts – so that perhaps someday, somehow, they or those who come after them can love and respect us more fully? Is this the spiritual work of an open, loving heart? Is this how we learn to see all people and creatures through the eyes of God? Is this what it means, to pray for our enemies?

Janet Surrey, one of the founding members of Wellesley College's Stone Center, where 'relational psychology' has had its moorings in the United States, became one of my chief intellectual and spiritual companions in examining 'mutuality' as a theological, psychological, economic and political possibility. Jan's psychological work on 'connection', her spiritual work as a Buddhist on 'mindfulness', and my theological work on 'mutual relation' have cross-fertilized each other for more than

20 years, as she and I have become mentors to each other and devoted friends. It interests me that, from my earliest work as a theologian, and Janet Surrey's as a psychologist, various professional colleagues have charged us both, and other advocates of relational power, with being too idealistic. Indeed, as I have grown more confident in God as our power in struggles for mutual relation, spiralling back into childhood experiences and intuitions of a universal spiritual force in creation, my theological work has been increasingly dismissed by theological and religious peers as being a pathway into a theological and moral fantasyland.

Several months ago, I was sent a paper by an Italian graduate student Gianluigi Gugliermetto, who urged me to consider how much more in common I have with Augustine than I seem to have noticed, given my unequivocal rejection of Augustine's equation of *sexual* desire and sin. Although Gugliermetto, if I read him correctly, seems to think that I do, in fact, realize the pervasiveness of evil in our life together, he is trying to defend my work against its harshest critics by suggesting that I should be more persuasive in presenting the presence and power throughout our lives of evil and tragedy (an absence of good, often without any discernible meaning or reason, and often apparently random and shocking). I perhaps did not notice how similar my views are to Augustine's in other important ways, especially in recognizing the depth and ubiquity of evil.

I appreciate Gugliermetto's careful reading of my work. At the same time, I must say that the presence and power of evil in the world and throughout our lives has been a primary motivating force in my theological work from the beginning. In fact, I often wonder – how can any theologian, or any human being, not think seriously about evil when we look around us, and within ourselves as well? Like Dorothee Soelle's, my recognition of evil in history, and in our lives, was the pivotal impetus for my breaking away from traditional theism. So I do indeed share Augustine's perception of evil's penetration of our world and our lives in the world. But I do not believe its source, or origin, is in our sexual desire. Rather, I believe that evil's roots are in the infectious and cumulative character of our *spiritual ignorance* which takes many shapes – among them, violence directed towards other people and creatures and the earth itself, fear of difference, greed for more, impatience with one another and ourselves and God, lust for sexual and other pleasures at the expense of others, apathy towards the common good, and indifference and cruelty towards persons and creatures that are not like us.

But let me go a little further in response to Gugliermetto. With a number of other professional theologians, ministers and psychotherapists, Gugliermetto has attempted to understand a heated controversy surrounding the publication in 1993 of my book, *When Boundaries Betray Us*. Describing a difficult and hurtful professional relationship with my psychotherapist, I attempted to examine what can happen not only when mutuality is 'toyed with' and disallowed, by the professional, as a resource for healing and liberation, but moreover when a traditionally structured 'power over' relationship runs amok. Gugliermetto suggests that the loud and angry outcry against this book, and against me as the therapy client in the book, had much to do with many of my critics' agenda – their passionate defence of professional boundaries. But he agrees with some of them that, in this book, I failed to communicate adequately a recognition that, because our world is broken by evil, in which our communities and our lives have been shaped by forces of fear, greed, abuse, ignorance, etc., mutual relation is not always possible. Mutual relationships, in which both or all parties are inspired to become more fully who they are at their best, cannot always be built. Our power in mutual relation – because it is a vulnerable and loving, but not omnipotent, God – doesn't always work the way we, even at our best, might yearn for or imagine to be possible.

I had written *When Boundaries Betray Us* as a testimony to the spiritual fact that mutuality is *not* always possible, not in the real world – a lesson I had learned in the tiny, intimate and socially privileged context of a psychotherapeutic relationship. But Gugliermetto has sharpened my awareness that the book did not communicate well to quite a few readers my awareness that our capacities to god are indeed limited by forces within, among and around us that have shaped what we, and others, can or cannot do, despite our, and their, best efforts. Augustine referred to our human situation as a *massa damnata* – translated literally as a 'damned mass' or 'wretched collective', so profoundly messed up are we by our failures to love one another that God's love is our only hope. I

21

imagine Augustine would gladly join in the 'Serenity Prayer', attributed to Reinhold Niebuhr and made famous as the opening prayer in meetings of Alcoholics Anonymous: 'God, grant me the serenity to accept the things I cannot change; courage to change the things I can; and wisdom to know the difference.' Had I been a wiser psychotherapy client, I'd have realized early on the spiritual folly in trying to change my therapist; and had I been a wiser theologian, I would have written the boundaries book as a novel to help readers focus a little more on the story rather than its author.

Fourth breaking point: from dogmatism to mysticism

Catherine Keller writes, 'It is in subverting (and so anachronistically queering) our most convenient binary oppositions, those dualisms that structure our certainties, that divinity opens' (2008a, p. 918). In her article on the negative, or 'unsaying', task of feminist theology, Keller attempts to shake us out of the rigid conceptual and linguistic crates in which even our own identities of race and gender and our justice-commitments have been formed. One of the two most recent and radical breaking points in my work has been more of a turning than actually a breaking. I have only come recently to recognize and name it as a very deep movement away from not only 'identity politics' and its close theological kin 'systematic theology', but also a powerful surge towards what Keller names as the Mystery that is God – 'deeply hidden, intimately present', she is quoting Augustine here. Keller lifts up the contributions of feminist theologian Elizabeth Johnson who affirms more than anything the mystery of God, also citing Augustine's famous declaration, 'If you can comprehend it, it is not God' (2008b, pp. 214–15). Breaking away from dogma and identity, I find myself breaking towards the mystical, which is invariably, from a Christian perspective, always a bit queer.

What do I mean by 'queer'? It can be an adjective (a queer notion) or a verb (to queer). To queer is to transcend boundaries, to cross over from one identity or standpoint to another, often defying established dogma or teachings of organized religion, politics and other traditional associations. To queer is to transgress traditional gender and sexual identities and dogmas and rules. Queering means breaking away, breaking towards, bursting open, spiralling backward and forward, up and down, in and out, in relation to master narratives of Father Gods, gender identities and doctrinal absolutes. Among Christians, queering takes imagination and a willingness to break towards that which we cannot yet see very clearly.

In this Spirit, I met Sister Angela of the Anglican Clare Community in New South Wales, Australia, when I was lecturing there in 1991. Over tea in a tree house in her monastery, Angela and I launched a friendship that would grow over a ten-year period, until her death by stroke in 2002. Looking back, I see that it was Angela's spiritual companionship I was seeking, and really needed personally and professionally, not 'treatment' by the conventionally trained and rule-bound psychiatrist to whom I had turned several years earlier. My transformative relationship with Angela empowered me to break from spiritual, political and even feminist dogmatism – a leap my spirit had been yearning to make since childhood – and to break towards more profoundly relational evolutions of truth. Angela's way of being in life was both mystical and queer. She sparked and spun and sculpted her way along, urging her companions to enjoy imagination as a window into God and not to get bogged down in ecclesiastical politics or academic squabbles.

It became increasingly clear to me, breaking towards the mystery and imagination that stirs at the heart of the Sacred, that the various categories and identities I had found useful over the years, some wonderfully liberating – like woman priest, lesbian, feminist liberation theologian, radical Christian – were each only partially true. These identities were useful tools in building more just and compassionate institutions in the world/Church. But our identities, our ways of labelling ourselves, become less creative and less liberating the tighter and more definitive they become, the less open to change and transformation. I had witnessed this stagnation again and again – white feminists' difficulty opening our feminist theories or theologies to serious engagement with women of colour; US Black and Latin American male liberation theologians setting forth theologies that were almost as categorically rigid – albeit on behalf of social justice – as any Christian dogma they had boldly deconstructed; gay men and lesbians' discomfort with the term 'bisexual', precisely because of its apparent resistance to being categorized as *either* gay *or* straight.

On the basis of an early discomfort with binary categories in my own life, I had written two 'coming out' essays in the late 1970s. In one, I named myself as 'lesbian' and admitted that this was a 'box' into which I was climbing in order to 'come out' for political and ethical reasons ('Christianity and Crisis', June 1979). In the other, I named myself as 'bisexual', because I did not want to box myself into categories that were only partially true ('The Witness', June 1979). The two essays were published in June 1979 in different religious journals. At the time, the 'lesbian' piece was received as an important contribution to the emergent 'coming out' movement among Christian leaders, while the 'bisexual' piece either went unnoticed or was pretty much ignored as irrelevant. Then and now, I viewed the 'lesbian' essay as a strategic contribution to a movement which was being grounded for a critical historical moment in identity politics; but I realized that the 'bisexual' article was more theologically, ethically, psychologically and politically truthful. I read it now also as the more queer piece.

As a five-year-old, I had insisted that Blackie the snake in our yard was my friend and, as a twelve-year-old, along with my two best friends, I had celebrated the Eucharist with Vienna sausages and coconut milk in the backyard under a fig tree. Throughout my life, I had resisted either abiding by or placing tight, categorical restrictions on either God or the world, creator or creation, ourselves or others. Struggling for racial integration of schools and public facilities in the United States in the 1960s and for women's ordination in the Episcopal Church in the 1970s had been strategic collective attempts to break away from oppressive institutional policies and move towards the inclusion of those groups formerly denied 'admission' into the ranks of full personhood. The growing movement towards 'gay marriage' in the United States, Europe and elsewhere around the world is a similar movement for justice. These collective and happily contagious social movements are corrective efforts to transform institutional policies and patterns that diminish our power in mutual relation – patterns that weaken the presence and power of a living, healing, liberating God in our schools, churches, families and other institutions.

But what these justice movements cannot do – because they rely on 'identity politics' to identify primary victims and perpetrators of injustice – is move our societies and mindsets beyond boxes and categories of identity into realms of genuine transcendence. The struggles for social justice do not often invite us to queerly cross over from one identity to another. Perhaps we cling to definitive identities of ourselves (male or female, gay or straight, black or white, victim or perpetrator, etc.) not only so that we can understand who we are struggling for and against, but also because we fear that 'crossing over' would involve breaking down – losing our bearings, our sanity and our values – losing the confidence in ourselves that enables us to get up in the morning and begin again each day to love and work. But perhaps the more queer we become, as we risk stepping across cultural, religious, gender, species and other boundaries in how we think of ourselves and others, the more likely we are to find ourselves at home in the world rather than as insiders and outsiders.

The theologians whose work touches us most deeply realize this. So many of them radiate such spiritual knowledge: Lisa Isherwood, who is truly a soul force, and Mary Grey from whom we have gleaned much wisdom over decades, and June Boyce-Tillman whose musical energy vibrates among us, and Ursula King who continues to plumb theological depths, and Mary Condren, always out there on the edges beckoning to those of us less bold. We do not have to agree on everything theological or even, sometimes, on much of anything, to learn from and with each other.

The politicians whose commitments we applaud are also people whose lives and works bear witness to these things. Barack Obama is a good example. One of President Obama's strongest assets is his moral intelligence. He knows in his bones that our identities and dogmas can carry us only so far, and that we must find ways of transcending our differences and transgressing the boundaries that keep us apart. In this sense, Obama was a queer candidate indeed! It remains to be seen how queer he will be in helping the United States and, because we are so connected, the rest of the world as well, to avert financial, environmental, military and moral collapse.

Marcella Althaus-Reid's death deprives us of one of the most imaginative and stunning queer theologians ever to put pen to paper. I missed knowing her personally. But I celebrate her gifts, especially her calling us to break away from sexual hiddenness towards sexual honesty. I am grateful that she recognized in my work some seeds of the queer, per/verse and indecent elements essential to honest sexual and social transformation. These seeds are, I believe, present in my work – seeds of transcendence and transgression – but they are only the tiniest of seeds which will grow only insofar as they are cultivated by others. *Touching Our Strength: The Erotic as Power and the Love of God* was published 20 years ago as my contribution to the sexual theologies emerging among Christians and other religious thinkers in the West. Breaking away from male-streams of Christian theology and ethics on matters of sex, gender and God, I was breaking towards something I could not yet name. I was breaking away from established sexual dogma not only of Christianity but also of many feminist theologies which, while more woman-affirming than traditional theologies, were also sexually constrictive – largely in response to the historic evil of sexual violence against women and children. In this important but also defensive social and theological context, most Christian feminist presentations on sex and gender in the 1970s and 1980s were reluctant to play with sex for pleasure outside fairly conventional boxes of monogamy, marriage, modesty and monochromatic (sometimes referred to as 'vanilla') sex.

Queer theologies – emerging in the 1990s in the United States, blending feminist liberation theologies and lesbian/gay/bisexual/transgender theologies with postmodern philosophies and queer secular studies – would have been a logical realm of study and work for me had I been interested in continuing to teach and write as a professional Christian theologian. But by the mid-1990s, I was tired of professional religion and the institutional Church. Looking back, I had always been a bit queer for the Church! As Chris Medeiros, a good friend and colleague at the Episcopal Divinity School in Cambridge, MA, had suggested in the early 1990s, speaking of his own experience: 'The church rejected me [for the priesthood] not because I'm gay, but because I'm queer.' By the turn of the millennium, I found myself breaking away from organized religion as the basis of my work not because I was lesbian, but because I was queer. With my brother Chris Medeiros, I had come to realize, in my body and blood, that while the institutional Church may or may not one day accept gay marriage and gay ordination, it does not understand, welcome or want to be bothered by our queerness, his, mine or ours.

And the fact is, queerness marks both the style and substance of my life, my whole life, not just my sexual and gender identities. Queerness marks both the method and content of what I try to communicate about Sacred Power. Queerness reflects not only the shapes of my sexuality but also every dimension of my theology, which began to form three decades ago with my queer musings about God as the struggle for mutual relation. Mindful of the trivialization of women and of all that is queer by even our liberal churches, and empowered by Sister Angela's ongoing spiritual energy, I am breaking queerly towards the apophatic Mystery at the heart of things, which leads me to the horses.

Fifth breaking point: from human priests to the horse as priest

The horses have become my priests, conduits of sacred energy, creatures who bear me through our fears, theirs and mine, and carry me close to the heart of God. It is to the horses that I turn for solace in sad times and courage in challenging times. It is in their company that I become serene and through their grace and whimsy that I find hope and humour. I observe them grazing in pastures and I see them carrying children and adults with special needs who turn to them for therapeutic care. With horses, I experience a Mystery that is simultaneously divine and equine, a powerful Energy pulling me back to beginnings, back to the precocious girl-child who, like J. K. Rowling's Hermione Granger, often knew so much more than she realized, but didn't have the confidence to believe. The horses, and those who love them, have helped me break towards a stronger confidence in mutuality/Sacred Power.

For example, several years ago, my horse trainer and teacher Linda Levy was observing me work with my own horse in a stable outside

Boston: 'As long as you're afraid of that horse, Carter, she's going to scare you.' Even as they were spoken, Linda's words conveyed a powerful spiritual punch. I saw in a flash, and continue to see, other humans a little more fully than ever before in relation to each other, the creation and God. As long as we fear one another, we'll be scared. As long as we're afraid of our power in the struggles for mutual relation, we'll be too scared to love our neighbours or ourselves very much. As long as I fear my enemies, they will scare me, and as long as they scare me, I cannot make much peace with them. But perhaps I can pray for them, and for myself, and move on with an open heart.

I do not know whether it is that I am older now or in some sense less old, more in touch with the ancients or perhaps with the very young. Or maybe it's simply that my spiritual confidence has been seasoned over 60-odd years. I certainly do not know which dimensions of us are 'merely human' and which are divine. And I wonder whether these words serve primarily to camouflage the simplicity of love. Surely love is what it is and, by whatever names we call it, Love is always and invariably 'fully divine and fully human/fully creature'. Even if we don't believe in someone or something called 'God', as my other beloved life companion Sue Sasser shows me, we can believe in the power of love to make a difference and even to generate holiness and beauty and good humour.

Beyond a human-centred theology, can Christianity become a genuinely earth-and-creation affirming religion of celebration? We have learned, some of us, to affirm our Jewishness, but what of our Pagan roots? Is it just too queer to bear?

Why, decades into feminist and womanist theologies, do church fathers and mothers still choke at the very mention of the Goddess or of a Mother God or of the Christa? Is she just too queer?

How seriously can such a fear-based religion wrestle with the possibility of mutual relation not as an idealistic fantasy but as the very heart of the Sacred, the power that moves the struggles for justice and peace, the power that *is* the struggle, *is* the justice, *is* the peace? Is it just too queer to imagine?

If lived into, this Sacred Power would be the spark to transform global capitalism into something more compassionate, a fairer system of economic production and distribution? But held hostage by capitalist spirituality, even most progressive Christian churches in the United States are timid in the struggle, muted in their support of women, gay/lesbian/bisexual/transgender people, immigrants, trade unions, universal health care, and public policies that would protect the environment. Unbelievable as it may seem in this historical moment, most churches in the United States are silent about the need for some regulation of Wall Street practices. How can anyone doubt the Church's bondage to global capitalism?

This is not to minimize the faith and work of many justice-loving Christian leaders, people like Bishop Gene Robinson, the courageous, openly gay Episcopalian bishop, as well as women and men of every colour and culture in the world, wherever the Christian Church has planted itself. I have no intention of washing my hands of the Church, because it has given many people of many cultures and generations much hope and courage over the years, often despite itself. I will always be grateful for the institutional Church's many gifts, especially the Jesus story at its centre and the spiritual mentoring of many of its people as well as its having given me, albeit begrudgingly, a vocational home. I have simply stopped trying to give the organization my best time and energies, which I did for about five decades.

Six years ago, my quarter horse mare, Red, gave birth to a filly – Feather, I named her. Both Red and Feather are stubborn and resistant to being dominated or bossed around. Neither is an easy horse, but each is in her own way a magnificent, sensitive creature who urges me into the struggle for mutual relation. I end here with an adaptation of a passage from my 2005 'horse book', *Flying Changes: Horses as Spiritual Teachers*, a small book with powerful relational pictures by Beverly Hall, a friend, professional photographer, former theological student and horse lover herself:

> Feather has introduced me to God in ways that help me realize more fully than ever before that God – Holy Spirit, Sophia, she and he of many names and faith traditions and none at all – has always been around, through the cosmos and the struggles for justice, through our

yearnings and hopes, through our sad times and happiness, through our loves and losses and gains and more losses. She has always been here with us on the earth, as ancient as the Appalachian mountains and as light and fresh as the Feather who was born in these hills, daughter of Red the quarter horse and Sebastian the Connemara pony. God has been with us in the earth's soil, with the earth's suffering and struggles for better water and air. God has been shaping and shifting the earth and other planets in and beyond the galaxies as we know them or imagine we do. The Most Holy has been with us in our most intimate relationships, in our shared sensualities and sexualities, in our celibacies and celebrations, our friendships and partnerships, our sacred unions and our connections with children and elders and one another and other creatures too. She has reveled with us playfully, leaping in joy, bucking enthusiastically, kicking up her heels when she is human and her hooves when she is horse. The Spirit has been walking us through and leading us beyond the bleakest, hardest times in our lives as communities, as individual creatures, and as the earth. She has been and will always be our power in the struggles against oppression, injustice, violence, and fear-based politics. She has been and will always be our power for right, mutual relationship; for justice, compassion, and peace. She will always be whoever she will be, and she will be our rock, our light, our wisdom, our joy, and the root of our repentance for violence, greed, and the fear in which such evil festers.

All the horses have been my priests much as they are for those who come to Free Rein Center and other places seeking healing in the special connection between horse and human. All the horses teach me. But more than all the rest, Feather and her mom have me by the heart and are prancing with me into the fierce whimsy of a God who surely must be wondering what is taking us so long. (2005)

References

Althaus-Reid, Marcella (2000), *Indecent Theology: Theological Perversions in Sex, Gender and Politics* (London and New York: Routledge).

Bonhoeffer, Dietrich (1972), *Letters and Papers from Prison* (New York: Macmillan).

Buber, Martin (1958, 1968), *I and Thou* (New York: Scribners; 2nd edn Collier).

Ellis, Marc H. (1997), *Unholy Alliance: Religion and Atrocity in Our Time* (Minneapolis: Fortress).

Ellison, Marvin M. and Thorson-Smith, Sylvia, eds. (2003), *Body and Soul: Rethinking Sexuality as Justice–Love* (Cleveland: Pilgrim).

Greenspan, Miriam (1983), *A New Approach to Women and Therapy* (New York: McGraw-Hill).

Grey, Mary (1990), *Feminism, Redemption, and the Christian Tradition* (Mystic, CT: Twenty Third).

Gugliermetto, Gianluigi (2008), 'The Redemption of Desire: A Study on the Understanding and the Use of Desire in Christian Life', Dissertation Submitted to the Faculty of Claremont Graduate University (Claremont, CA).

Harrison, Beverly Wildung (1985), *Making the Connections: Essays in Feminist Social Ethics*, ed. Carol S. Robb (Boston: Beacon).

——(2004), *Justice in the Making: Feminist Social Ethics*, ed. E. M. Bounds, P. K. Brubaker, J. E. Hicks, M. J. Legge, R. T. Peters, T. C. West (Louisville, KY: Westminster John Knox).

Heyward, Carter (1982), *The Redemption of God: A Theology of Mutual Relation* (Lanham, MD: University Press of America).

——(1989), *Touching Our Strength: The Erotic as Power and the Love of God* (San Francisco: Harper Collins).

——(1993), *When Boundaries Betray Us: Beyond Illusions of What is Ethical in Therapy and in Life* (San Francisco: Harper Collins).

——(1999), *Saving Jesus from Those Who Are Right: Rethinking What it Means to be Christian* (Minneapolis: Fortress).

——(2002), *God in the Balance: Christian Spirituality in Times of Terror* (Cleveland, OH: Pilgrim).

——(2005), *Flying Changes: Horses as Spiritual Teachers, with photographs by Beverly Hall* (Cleveland, OH: Pilgrim).

Isherwood, Lisa (1999), *Liberating Christ: Exploring the Christologies of Contemporary Liberation Movements* (Cleveland, OH: Pilgrim).

Jantzen, Grace M. (1995), *Power, Gender, and Christian Mysticism* (Cambridge: Cambridge University Press).

Johnson, Elizabeth (1992), *She Who Is: The Mystery of God in Feminist Discourse* (New York: Crossroad).

Keller, Catherine (2008a), 'The Apophasis of Gender: A Fourfold Unsaying of Feminist Theology', *Journal of the American Academy of Religion* 76. 4 (December 2008), pp. 905–33.

——(2008b), *On the Mystery: Discerning God in Process* (Minneapolis: Fortress).

Kwok, Pui-lan (2005), *Postcolonial Imagination and Feminist Theology* (Louisville, KY: Westminster John Knox).

McFague, Sallie (1993), *The Body of God: An Ecological Theology* (Minneapolis: Fortress).

——(1997), *Super, Natural Christians: How We Should Love Nature* (Minneapolis: Fortress).

——(2001), *Life Abundant: Rethinking Theology and Economy for a Planet in Peril* (Minneapolis: Fortress).

Mollenkott, Virginia Ramey (2001), *Omnigender: A Trans-Religious Approach* (Cleveland, OH: Pilgrim).

Rowling, J. K. (1997–2007), *Harry Potter*, 7 volumes (New York: Scholastic).

Soelle, Dorothee (1967), *Christ the Representative: An Essay in Theology After the 'Death of God'* (Philadelphia: Fortress).

——(1975), *Suffering* (Philadelphia: Fortress).

——(1999), *Against the Wind: Memoir of a Radical Christian* (Minneapolis: Fortress).

——(2001), *The Silent Cry: Mysticism and Resistance* (Minneapolis: Fortress.)

Starhawk (1979), *The Spiral Dance: A Rebirth of the Ancient Religion of the Great Goddess* (San Francisco: Harper and Row).

SteinhoffSmith, Roy Herndon (1999), *The Mutuality of Care* (St Louis, MO: Chalice).

Surrey, Janet L. (2005), 'Relational Psychotherapy, Relational Mindfulness', in *Mindfulness and Psychotherapy*, ed. Christopher K. Germer, Ronald D. Siegel, Paul R. Fulton (New York and London: Guilford).

Wiesel, Elie (1969), *Night* (New York: Avon).

2

'What Religion or Reason Could Drive a Man to Forsake his Lover?' Relational Theology, Co-creativity and the Intersexed Body of Christ

SUSANNAH CORNWALL

To turn one's attention away from human life toward something 'higher' is to help cultivate the soil for another Holocaust, the destruction of humanity by humanity. There can be no religion or doctrine; no ethic or moral suasion; no racial, sexual, class or ethnic pride; no technological feat; no ends or means; nothing in heaven or earth – not even a deity – that is any more valuable, any more important, any better, than human love for humanity.

(Heyward 1982, p. 181)

For I am convinced that neither death, nor life, nor angels, nor rulers, nor things present, nor things to come, nor powers, nor height, nor depth, nor anything else in all creation, will be able to separate us from the love of God in Christ Jesus our Lord.

(Romans 8.38–39 NRSV)

What religion or reason could drive a man to forsake his lover?

(Erasure, 'A Little Respect')[1]

---

1 This song, written by Erasure members Vince Clarke and Andy Bell, appeared on the duo's 1988 album *The Innocents*.

33

The overemphasis on a particular kind of deity, and specifically a particular kind of deity-become-human in Christ, is part of what has driven men, women and others to forsake their lovers and loves: that is, their fellow human beings. Those, in particular, whose sexed and gendered identities have been deemed deviant, difficult or recalcitrant by a largely heteronormative Church, have been further excluded by imagery whereby a male body, that of Christ, is made unproblematically to stand for all humans. Of course, artists, sculptors and others have long explored female bodies-of-Christ through the image of the Christa (see for example Clague 2005a and 2005b; Crawford 1988; Murphy 1990; Raab 1997; Cornwall 2008a), and theologians such as Elisabeth Schüssler Fiorenza have done important work in showing what feminist, and indeed feminine, Christologies might look like. Kwok Pui-lan has suggested that Christ's gender may be more of a stumbling-block for white western women than it has been for women of non-white ethnicities elsewhere in the world (Kwok 2005, p. 24), noting Susannah Heschel's and Eleanor McLaughlin's explorations of Christ as a transvestite figure (Kwok 2005, pp. 179–80; Heschel 1997; McLaughlin 1993). However, I suspect these reframings do not quite go far enough, for while they destabilize binary gender as mapped onto essentialist sex, they still represent *crossing* phenomena rather than truly liminal ones, and do not adequately disrupt sex itself. In fact, to say that we as humans co-make and co-create Christ – through what Heyward and others have called 'godding' (Heyward 1982, p. 16; 1996b) – means something even more devastating for any of our sexed images of Christ's body in particular. This may be a white feminist preoccupation, but I am a white feminist theologian, and I see the legacies of white masculinist Christology reappear time and again in the social-cultural and medical constructions of legitimacy and normality with which my work engages.

I have been particularly keen to explore the theological and Christological implications of the existence and treatment of physical intersex conditions, as in my book, *Sex and Uncertainty in the Body of Christ: Intersex Conditions and Christian Theology* (Cornwall, forthcoming 2010). Approximately 1 in 2,500 individuals is born with a biological intersex condition which, in some cases, manifests in ambiguous genitalia. Other individuals may have unremarkable male-related or female-related genitalia, but the chromosomes or internal organs usually associated with the 'opposite' sex. Children born with ambiguous genitalia, particularly before the mid-1990s, when the intersex activism movement began to challenge the early surgery paradigm, often had 'excessive' or 'inadequate' genitalia surgically altered soon after birth or through childhood and into adolescence. This sometimes involved, for example, removing the penis of an XY child and assigning a feminine gender of rearing (see for example Preves 2003; Dreger 1999; Kessler 1998; Karkazis 2008). Many intersexed individuals identify unproblematically as the gender in which they were raised, but others – including some who underwent surgery to normalize their genitals since the 1960s when this became commonplace – identify themselves differently. Intersex activist Thea Hillman notes that the nebulous 'intersex community' is far from homogenous:

> What many of us have in common are repeated genital displays, often from a young age. Many of us have had medical treatments done to us without our consent to make our sex anatomy conform to someone else's standards. Many of us suffer from intense shame due to treatments that sought to fix or hide our bodies. And many of us have experienced none of the above. (Hillman 2008, p. 149)

Some intersexed individuals report facing exclusion or suspicion from their church communities, which they attribute to a lack of understanding about their conditions (Curry 2006; Gross 1999, p. 70; Gross speaking in van Huyssteen 2003), stemming from assumptions that intersex equals homosexuality or a propensity for paedophilia.

But individuals with intersex conditions, whether or not they have variant gender identities and whether or not they have undergone genital surgery, are members of Christian churches and thereby co-constituents of Christ. Not only is the Body of Christ that we help to constitute not exclusively male, it is not even exclusively unambiguous in its sexed and gendered nature. The existence of intersex conditions means that it is not as simple as redeeming Christ's maleness (cf. Beattie 1996) or saying that Christ is female as well as male. Rather, binary sex and gender are disrupted in their entirety. In fact, they are in some sense entirely *over* in light of Christ's crucifixion and resurrection. Compare Galatians 3.28 and its assertion that in Christ there is no male-and-female – in other words, no exclusive binary of sexed identity.[2] This does not necessarily mean that there is no male *or* female; biological reproduction in its present form is therefore still possible, and some people may continue to identify as males and females (though see Iain Morland's comments below). But what no longer exists in Christ is male-and-female as an all-inclusive, comprehensive programme for humanity. Humanity in Christ exists as far more than gender-coded jigsaw pieces. Humans are not rendered complete via so-called gender complementarity. The Body of Christ is intersexed, because its members (that is, its constituents) include intersexed bodies. The Body as a whole, like some of the individual bodies within it, is ambiguous, recalcitrant, not neatly or unproblematically gendered or sexed. But we have summarily failed to explore what this really means both for the Christ we remember and re-member in worship and liturgy – for 'more creative epistemologies of the divine and a sense of twisted transcendence' (Althaus-Reid 2003, p. 50) – and for the wider human body we make and constitute beyond church walls.

Carter Heyward has suggested that an overemphasis on the difference of Christ from other humans has encouraged an attitude of postponement and penultimacy among Christians, whereby we lose touch with our own 'power in relation' (Heyward 1982, pp. 131, 164) – what Mary Grey terms a 'metaphysic of connectedness' (Grey 1996, p. 141) – and shirk our responsibility as bringers-in of a newly just order. For Heyward, it is in our relation and interaction as human beings that we make and usher in a relational God. She says:

> Without our crying, our yearning, our raging, there is no God. For in the beginning is the relation, and in the relation is the power that creates the world through us, and with us, and by us, you and I, you and we, and none of us alone. (Heyward 1982, p. 172)

---

2 For my more detailed exploration of this point, see Cornwall 2008a.

We thereby make a place for one another. Too much focus on a distant, other God, in this account, denies both God's humanity in Christ and the value and capacity of humanity per se. It makes our lives here and now not matter, and detracts from the imperative to make things better for bodily life just as it is – especially for bodies that are rejected, abjected and wounded. Crucially, and revolutionarily, Heyward argues that there is *nothing* in heaven or earth – *not even a deity* – that is more valuable, important, or better than human love for humans, since it is *in* human love that we meet and make the God who *is* love. In fact, she says: 'Our love of humanity is our love of God; and our love of God is our love of humanity. Simply that' (Heyward 1984, p. 184). There is therefore an imperative here to explore images of Christ's body – and their implications for our own self-understanding – which admit of the uncomfortable truths inhering in human bodies. It is unjustifiable to hold on to images of Christ's body which lead to the denial, marginalizing or devaluing of those human bodies deemed less perfect than others.

We often fixate as Christians on a deity who is above us, beyond us, big and great enough to pull us out of the mire. It is attractive and comforting to suppose that someone else will save us, and that the God in question is eternal, perfect, benevolent as can be. Heyward says: 'The problem is not in our belief in an altogether good . . . God. The problem lies in our tendency to polarize, and thereby make dualistic, human and divine life, ourselves and God' (Heyward 1984, p. 185). This, she believes, stems from guilt, shame and fear. But it erodes our own responsibility – and joy – to build our eschatological present and future all around us. Doing so may not be impressive, dramatic or romantic in the moment, as Heyward reminds us. But the imperative that we should all be mutually messianic – saviours and makers of ourselves, of one another, of God too – means that we must radically reassess the import we ascribe to Christ's body in its sexed and sexless nature. Heyward comments:

> God's incarnations are as many and varied as the persons who are driven by the power in relation to touch and be touched by sisters and brothers. To focus messianically on any *one* person, to try to locate and establish God in any single figure, to insist that relational tension

and ambiguity be broken and that the definition of 'God' be handed to us as a package in the person of a lone messiah, is to deny the movement of power in relation through many incarnations in history. (Heyward 1982, p. 164)

Similarly, Thomas Bohache states,

> A queer sense of incarnation means . . . that God becomes one with humanity through the assurance that God has always been present and that the realization of this presence will give birth to human infusion with divine anointedness as Christ . . . Jesus was so open to receiving God's anointing that his life and ministry can be paradigmatic for all of those who seek to walk the Christ Way, to become Christ themselves and, like our mother Mary, to birth other Christs. (Bohache 2003, p. 28)

If we take Heyward and Bohache seriously, this also means not focusing on a particular body, or a particular *kind* of body as salvific – and therefore to be prized or emulated – either. The danger of focusing messianically on only one body-of-Christ is insidious, and leads to the violation and exclusion of recalcitrant, boundary-blurring human bodies which seem not to match up to the mythic, perfect Christ-body we worship. It is still rare indeed to encounter in the Christian churches a transgender Christ or a Christ whose body is sexually ambivalent, and yet since these are real experiences and body-states of humanness, they are part of Christ's body too. God is not 'above the fray' of the messiness or specificities of embodied human life (Heyward 1994, p. 176). Actually, Jesus' body is *already* a complicated, even an ambiguous one, because of the differences and distinctions held in tension within it; as a result, comments the intersexed ex-priest Sally Gross, Jesus became for her an icon of suffering, since her own pain and confusion surrounding bodiliness and issues of gender seemed to be repeated in his body (Gross, speaking in van Huyssteen 2003).

The irony is that there has historically been space for this within the Christian tradition, which is replete with 'gender-bending' phenomena, including the possible transcending of gender stereotypes in Gregory of Nyssa (as discussed in for example Burrus 2007; Nausner 2002; Harrison 1990, 1996); Bernard of Clairvaux's strikingly corporeal readings of the Song of Songs, including a discussion of the Bridegroom's nurturing breasts in his ninth Sermon; further imagery of Christ as mother in Julian of Norwich and Catherine of Siena (Dearborn 2002; Bynum 1992); and the existence of a Jesus who lactates from his breasts, or gushes milk from the wound in his side, in much medieval art. Caroline Walker Bynum comments,

> Many medieval assumptions linked woman and flesh and the body of God. Not only was Christ enfleshed with flesh from a woman; his own flesh did womanly things: it bled, it bled food, and it gave birth . . . It was women's bodies almost exclusively that bled as Christ bled, and this blood not only purged the woman of her sin but also saved her fellow Christians by substituting for the expiation they owed in purgatory. Holy women imitated Christ in their bodies; and Christ's similar bleeding and feeding body was understood as analogous to theirs. (Bynum 1986, pp. 423–4)

Of course, Bynum is well aware that this tradition trades on stereotypes of the female/mother as sacrificial, tender and nurturing, and that these have been lionized and co-opted by men to talk about themselves rather than urging reflection on real feminine experience. Indeed, the very tension surrounding the use of this trope echoes the ambiguity in what it is and is not possible to say of the human body of Christ, as well as the equivocal attitude towards muliebrity displayed by the twelfth-century Cistercian abbots who particularly enjoyed using Jesus-as-mother imagery to reflect on their own pastoral roles (Bynum 1986). Yet in more recent years we have often ceased to be comfortable with a body-of-Christ which is simultaneously more than one thing, especially if it is this body's unambiguous gender or sexual continence which is at stake. It is likely that this echoes anxieties about sexuality as well as gender – anxieties about phenomena which exceed or transgress the often-apotheosized Christian norms of heteronormativity and conservative gender roles.

Of course, like all humans, Jesus the human is limited by his historical context; Heyward notes: 'Jesus' experiences of God cannot be compre-hended or expounded fully within the limits of any cultural situation – including the patriarchal limits which Jesus shared in his own time and place' (Heyward 1982, p. 11). But it is in this Jesus' human members that the Christ transcends history and is stretched into new semiological and imaginative shapes. Indeed, says Heyward,

> Because of him, we Christians are stretched beyond what we might have been without these stories and images of a radically faithful brother. And because of us, his sisters and brothers, the images of JESUS[3] are stretched way beyond the horizons that we, or those who have gone before us, could have envisioned. In this way, we and all who have preceded us, including authors of the Bible, have shaped JESUS, making him what he is today. (Heyward 1999, p. 3)

The author of Romans 8 tells us that nothing in all creation will be able to separate us from the love of God in Christ. But what if it is something *not* within creation – something which purports to be *beyond* creation, something to do with God Godself – which becomes a barrier to the di-vine? Actually, it is not possible to access God 'directly', unmediated by our own experience, cultural assumptions and bodily limits. It is in our own human ideologies that distortions of God have arisen.

In fact, none of our humanly erroneous images of God can actually separate us forever from God, though they might do a very good job try-ing. Far more effective, however, is their power to separate us from one another as humans. This is why limiting images of Christ's body that

---

3 This typographical representation of JESUS in Heyward's 1999 volume is not insignificant. She says; 'Throughout the book, the name JESUS, as well as his mes-sianic title CHRIST, is printed in small capital letters. This stylistic irregularity is meant to give the reader at least an occasional pause. I am hoping to remind you, along with myself, that the JESUS in these pages – and everywhere his name is spoken – is a deeply human, significant social construction and also a figure of stunning spiritual energy in the lives of countless communities great and small throughout the world' (Heyward 1999, p. 4).

purport to be the *only*, *real* or *exclusively legitimate* ones are so damaging. To assert that Christ is female, intersexed, disabled or of a variant ethnicity is to make a claim not about the historical human body of Christ (for he, like every other human, was limited to being some things to the exclusion of others), but about what Christ (and God in Christ) has become since, in and through the human members of the Body. Christ is not *only* female or *only* intersexed, but is nonetheless *just as much female or intersexed as male*. It is just as Christlike to be intersexed and impaired as it is to be male and able-bodied. Not only Christ*like*, but Christ*ic*. This is devastating. Every time our liturgies and practices fail to acknowledge the diversity and multiplicity of the Body of Christ, they also fail to acknowledge the Christness, the messianic capacity, of everyone whose body is less able or white or unambiguously male than the images of Jesus we are used to. It has almost invariably been a male body of Christ that has been figured as a site of salvation, and this tacitly devalues all bodies which do not reflect Jesus' maleness. Female sexuality, non-maleness, and all modes of bodily excess or ambiguity are often diminished, and the bodies in which they exist are often not deemed suitable to minister to the rest of the community.

It is in this way that our small, narrow religion and reason drives us to forsake our lovers, the other humans in whose reciprocal love we should be 'godding'. We are *all* God-bearers (Heyward 1984, p. 185) but we put limits on the bodies we believe can bear God to and for others. We forsake one another for the sake of bolstering a falsely monolithic image of God. Sally Gross reports being told by fellow Christians that her baptism was invalid since, as she did not fall into either of the categories 'determinately male' or 'determinately female', she also did not fall into the category 'human', and was therefore not 'the kind of thing which could have been baptized validly' (Gross 1999, p. 70). But God is already more complex, in Christ and in creation, than we often permit. We have often made a God whom only unambiguously masculine woman-loving males and unambiguously feminine man-loving females can legitimately reflect – yet, as many of us have begun to realize, this is not the only God it is in our power to make and remake. For Mary Grey, our interconnectedness is the site both of co-creating and of receiving God:

Interconnectedness can claim to be a revelatory paradigm because this is the means, above all, through which Divine power-in-relation is mediated. *Power* in this context means the relational drive and energy which *both* empowers human becoming and ecological growth and is the locus of Divine presence in the universe . . . Seeking to co-create in forming more just patterns of relating, new forms of mutuality, is both actively making God incarnate, and becoming not *passive* but *receptive* to the ways in which God is already active as energizing presence. (Grey 1996, p. 147)

Much theological fear of bodies which do not 'fit' has come from our false conception of Otherness as simple opposition: male/female, clean/unclean, healthy/sick, able/disabled, divine/human. The sexed differences of humans may reflect the difference and dynamism present in the interconnected relations of the Trinity, but to accept that a simple male/female binary does not tell the whole story is not to negate this difference. Human bodies and human beings are different by virtue of more than sex. The uncertainty and ambiguity often read off intersexed bodies forces our reflection back on our own bodies, particularly if they are deemed sexually (or otherwise) *un*remarkable. Katrina Roen notes,

The quest to know about the intersex person through biomedical tests during infancy is disrupted by understandings of *embodied becoming*, whereby intersex people may come into being despite, rather than because of, medical intervention. The understanding that the infant's body is something that can be operated *on* to produce a 'girl' or a 'boy' is challenged through the argument that the body may be understood 'not as an *object* but as an *event*'. (Roen 2008, p. 51)

Christ's body is also an event, a process, produced and reproduced in community rituals, in Eucharist, in relationality, in challenges to unjust social structures and reframing of long-established social norms. Intersex is an issue of justice because people's real experiences in their real lives and bodies reflect something of the human story, therefore of what it means to be a creature made in the image of God and a creature who makes God too.

A 'theology in the key of intersex', then, can remind us that it is in the specificity and particularity of all kinds of bodies that theological truths are experienced and made. If God is love and justice then it is in loving and just behaviour that we incarnate God within and among us. This includes loving and just behaviour to bodies, to all bodies, and necessitates an understanding that a God who is only in the image of some of us is less of a God than is possible. To devalue certain modes of carnality is, in the end, to devalue carnality per se, for it is to deny carnality's excess, its energy, its transcending of what we consciously will. This is unjustifiable in light of our pursuit of a Christ in whose embodiment the potential of all embodiment is symbolically caught up and held, for we are to 'accept our embodiment as incarnation of our Christ-ness' (Bohache 2003, p. 28).

We must therefore throw away religious trappings which make us elevate some bodies over others or leave out bodies that disturb us when we create images of the Christ whose body we build. Thea Hillman, who grew up with the intersex condition Congenital Adrenal Hyperplasia, writes about normality, atypical bodies and the experience of being different. In her recent memoir *Intersex (For Lack of a Better Word)* she comments,

> Last year, a woman in Texas bashed in the head of her four-day-old baby who was born with ambiguous genitalia. I think of her in those four days. Why did she wait? . . . How will she ever be forgiven for all her sins? And why do I think she already lives in fear of a strict and unbending God? . . . Some gods have made us in their image and then there are other gods that give us permission to maim and kill, operate and murder, all in the name of maintaining the fiction of happy, procreating males and females forever after. (Hillman 2008, pp. 116–17)

Some gods have made us in their image; the God in whose name we maim and kill, for whose sake children's genitals which are deemed to threaten the status quo are still cut off, is a God that we ourselves have helped to make. However, our power-in-relation means that this small, petty, jealous picture of God is not the last word. As Heyward says:

> Love of brothers and sisters as self is . . . the place in which we begin to realize that this loving of humanity and of our other creature-partners on the earth constitutes and is the substance of our love of God. (Heyward 1984, p. 186)

In an exchange of letters with Carter Heyward, Katie Cannon, the black womanist theologian, describes the phenomenon whereby 'women of color often need to test and retest the authenticity of white women's willingness to relate' (Cannon and Heyward 1994, p. 62). Having repeatedly encountered racism and an attitude of withdrawal from ostensibly liberal white women, Cannon suggests that relationality for those who are in a position of privilege involves ceding this privilege. She continues:

> I only know the essential nature of God when I as an individual, and my people as a race, are not permitted – but command by the respect of our very being – space to engage in the most rigorously honest confrontation. (In Cannon and Heyward 1994, p. 62)

Similarly, as I have argued elsewhere (Cornwall 2008b, p. 189) after Iain Morland (Morland 2005, pp. 129–31; Morland forthcoming 2009), in the new creation it may well be that it is those who are unambiguously sexed who must relinquish their related privilege, rather than expecting that those who are transgender or intersexed will be 'healed' of their ambiguity. For Morland, this means non-intersexed people should consider 'a deliberate repudiation of male and female identities' (Morland forthcoming 2009) because of the concomitant oppression of non-males-and-females bound up in these identities and in sex descriptivism itself. As Cannon hints, it is the very being of the less-privileged as persons that demands such ethical praxis. Although Morland does not do so, as theologians we might figure it as prophetic. This will certainly mean a conscious refusal to say that the unambiguous, unremarkably sexed bodies of Christ disseminated in many of our churches and theologies are markers of how good, decent human bodies 'should' be. To see and hear and encounter unfamiliar-to-discourse yet familiar-to-us bodies in worship and liturgy might be a profoundly healing experience for those whose bodies continue to be despised and rejected by society at large, including the Church. Discussing her childhood longing for a black-skinned baby doll, Cannon writes to Heyward,

> I always got white dolls because they were more plentiful and cheaper. But my sister, Doris . . . got a beautiful black doll one Christmas, and the next year we used it for Jesus in the Christmas play at the church. Back in 1956–57 that was a revolutionary, radical thing to do, but we did it, and it felt so good to me, to know that this little black female doll symbolized the boy Jesus. After that I didn't care whether I got a black doll, because if the baby Jesus was black, then the boy Jesus and the grownup Jesus could also be black, and it all started to make sense in my little ever-churched Sunday school mind. (In Cannon and Heyward 1994, p. 75)

My journey of working through what Morland's imperative to cede un-remarkably sexed privilege would mean for me, a heterosexual female who also identifies as broadly feminine, is still in process. It does not cost me much to take small steps such as refusing to disclose my gender on application forms and documents where, as almost always, it is not relevant; it might cost me a great deal more to stop wearing make-up or recognizably feminine clothing. I happen to have a markedly femi-nine given name; I enjoy publishing under it, but coupled with other aspects of my identity perhaps it is too conveniently 'sexed'. In these outer things inhere more than I usually care to admit of my confidence, self-projection as capable and adult, and personal and professional personae.

It is a community project, then, to explore what co-creative theologies that are positive about intersex in particular, and otherwise unexpected embodiment in general, might look like. They will be many things; they will not be monolithic. They will continue the feminist project of em-phasizing the immense inadequacy of male-only language for God, and of hierarchies where only heterosexual masculine males are deemed worthy of authority and power. They will centre the experience and self-understanding of a range of different bodies without forcing them to conform to particular standards of normality. In their commissioning and crafting of art, poetry, song and sculpture for use in worship, they will endorse imagery which pushes boundaries, which is disturbing or subversive, which expands the borders of how we understand God in Christ and creation. They will speak out in support of socio-political movements calling for the protection of the continence of intersexed bodies, and for medical treatments which go beyond crudely heteronormalizing surgeries. They will recognize the inadequacy of accounts of anthropology grounded in the complementarity of two mythic genders overlaid on two mythic opposite sexes. Accordingly, they will reject stereotypical accounts of 'biblical manhood and womanhood' and of the conservative social norms that are perpetuated through them.[4] They will not privilege only certain authorized states of embodiment or identity as being desirable for those who teach and minister to Christian communities; nor will they negate people's own understandings of their identities or the particular needs of their bodily situations. They will promote an awareness that God-making and God-reflecting are goods to which all humans should have access, and will seek out hidden or silenced talk about God from the margins even where this threatens cherished or established

---

4 Such accounts are by no means limited to what is taught to adults. In 2007, the publisher Thomas Nelson marketed two new über-gendered books for 4–8-year-olds, the blue *God's Mighty Warrior Devotional Bible* for boys and the pink *God's Little Princess Devotional Bible* for girls. The features in the boys' book are based around the imagery of the Armour of God in Ephesians 6, designed 'to help a budding warrior earn his armor', since 'He [i.e. God] created little boys to be mighty warriors . . . even when they feel small.' The cover features a large silver sword. By contrast, the girls' book (the cover of which prominently features a jewelled tiara) contains sections called 'Beauty Secrets', 'Bible Princesses' and 'Princess Charming'. According to the publisher's blurb, 'Girls long to be loved and adored, and give their heart to their hero. God is that hero! The characteristics focused on in this Bible storybook will help your little girl blossom into the princess she was created to be . . . The perfect format for girls to learn about their destiny as a daughter of their King.'

beliefs about the nature of God. They will value discussion and debate, positively encouraging dissent as a fruitful means to working out what a group or community believes about God and valuing all the questions and uncertainties that remain.

Marcella Althaus-Reid, who died much too soon, suggested that one image for refiguring Jesus might be that of the Bi/Christ, that is, a Christ who makes space to be imagined beyond binary boundaries (Althaus-Reid 2000, p. 117). This Christ is simultaneously sexual/non-sexual, homosexual/heterosexual, and so on, also existing *between* the either/ors. We could also say that this Christ is clearly sexed/liminally sexed, which further destabilizes heteronormativity by questioning the reality of the sex categories on which gender norms supervene. This image chimes with the beginnings of a queer Christology undertaken by Thomas Bohache, who says that to recognize that the Christ-presence of anointedness dwells in all people (Bohache 2003, p. 21) means to recognize that this Christness, this anointing, also dwells in all kinds of bodies. He comments:

> God is male, female, intersexual, transgendered; God is gay, lesbian, straight, bisexual and non-sexual; God is strong and weak, old and young, abled and differently abled. And yet God is greater than all of this and more than all of this, for God has not stopped creating. (Bohache 2003, p. 22)

Indeed, God has not stopped creating; moreover, God has not stopped being created by, in and through our responses to and interactions with one another's bodily experience. This is profoundly democratic; as Althaus-Reid says: 'The concept of participation in the Trinity means that the Queer strangers can now . . . talk of God from hidden experiences and distrusted knowledge' (Althaus-Reid 2003, pp. 74-5). This is 'true kenosis . . . where God does not grant Godself privileges and thus discovers the meaning of incarnation' (Althaus-Reid 2003, p. 75). By dis/covering Christ's intersexed body we help destabilize the heteronormative body which keeps God small. The boundaries between redeemer and redeemed are blurred (Althaus-Reid 2003, p. 138); indeed, this is crucial, for perhaps the God who in Althaus-Reid's terms remains closeted in strictures of heteronormative decency really is not at liberty to remake the Body of Christ alone. Human love for humanity, which tenaciously refuses to be stripped of hope, will continue to be the veritable site of God's coming-into-being.

Making love in the world is making justice (Heyward 1984, pp. 194, 199): let us not forsake our lovers, but let all our interactions in and through the Body of Christ be a love-making of creative embodying and the breaking down of walls.

References

Althaus-Reid, Marcella (2000), *Indecent Theology* (London and New York: Routledge).

—— (2003), *The Queer God* (London and New York: Routledge).

Beattie, Tina (1996), 'Sexuality and the Resurrection of the Body: Reflections in a Hall of Mirrors', in D'Costa, Gavin (ed.) (1996), *Resurrection Reconsidered* (Oxford: Oneworld), pp. 135–49.

Bohache, Thomas (2003), 'Embodiment as Incarnation: An Incipient Queer Christology', *Theology and Sexuality* 10.1 (September), pp. 9–29.

Burrus, Virginia (2007), 'Queer Father: Gregory of Nyssa and the Subversion of Identity', in Gerard Loughlin (ed.), *Queer Theology: Rethinking the Western Body* (Oxford: Blackwell), pp. 147–62.

Bynum, Caroline Walker (1986), 'The Body of Christ in the Later Middle Ages: A Reply to Leo Steinberg', *Renaissance Quarterly* 39.3 (Autumn), pp. 399–439.

—— (1992), *Fragmentation and Redemption: Essays on Gender and the Human Body in Medieval Religion* (New York: Zone Books).

Cannon, Katie G. and Carter Heyward (1994), 'Can We Be Different But Not Alienated? An Exchange of Letters', in Daly, Lois K. (ed.) (1994), *Feminist Theological Ethics: A Reader* (Louisville, KY: Westminster John Knox Press), pp. 59–76.

Clague, Julie (2005a), 'The Christa: Symbolizing My Humanity and My Pain', *Feminist Theology* 14.1 (September), pp. 83–108.

Clague, Julie (2005b), 'Divine Transgressions: The Female Christ-Form in Art', *Critical Quarterly* 47.3 (Autumn), pp. 47–63.

Cornwall, Susannah (2008a), 'Ambiguous Bodies, Ambiguous Readings: Reflections on James M. Murphy's "Christine on the Cross"', in Zowie Davy et al. (eds), *Bound and Unbound: Interdisciplinary Approaches to Genders and Sexualities* (Newcastle: CSP), pp. 93–111.

—— (2008b), 'The *Kenosis* of Unambiguous Sex in the Body of Christ: Intersex, Theology and Existing "for the Other"', *Theology and Sexuality* 14.2 (January), pp. 181–200.

—— (forthcoming 2010), *Sex and Uncertainty in the Body of Christ: Intersex Conditions and Christian Theology* (London: Equinox).

Crawford, Bobbie (1988), 'A Female Crucifix?', *Daughters of Sarah* 14.6, pp. 24–7.

Curry, Mike [aka Michael/JoAnn, aka JoAnn Michelle] (2006), personal communication (19 February).

Daly, Lois K. (ed.) (1994), *Feminist Theological Ethics: A Reader* (Louisville, KY: Westminster John Knox Press).

Dearborn, Kerry (2002), 'The Crucified Christ as the Motherly God: The Theology of Julian of Norwich', *Scottish Journal of Theology* 55.3, pp. 283–302.

Dreger, Alice Domurat (ed.) (1999), *Intersex in the Age of Ethics* (Hagerstown, MD: University Publishing Group).

Grey, Mary (1996), 'Claiming Power-in-Relation: Exploring the Ethics of Connection', in Adrian Thatcher and Elizabeth Stuart (eds), *Christian Perspectives on Sexuality and Gender* (Leominster: Gracewing).

Gross, Sally (1999), 'Intersexuality and Scripture', *Theology and Sexuality* 11, pp. 65–74.

Harrison, Verna E. F. (1990), 'Male and Female in Cappadocian Theology', *Journal of Theological Studies* 41, pp. 441–71.

—— (1996), 'Gender, Generation and Virginity', *Journal of Theological Studies* 47, pp. 38–68.

Heschel, Susannah (1997), 'Jesus as a Theological Transvestite', in Miriam Peskowitz and Laura Levitt (eds), *Judaism Since Gender* (New York: Routledge), pp. 188–97.

Heyward, [Isabel] Carter (1982), *The Redemption of God: A Theology of Mutual Relation* (Lanham, MD: University Press of America).

Heyward, Carter (1984), *Our Passion for Justice: Images of Power, Sexuality, and Liberation* (New York: Pilgrim Press).

—— (1994), 'Heterosexist Theology: Being Above It All', in Lois K. Daly (ed.), *Feminist Theological Ethics: A Reader* (Louisville, KY: Westminster John Knox Press), pp. 172–80.

—— (1996a), 'Empowerment', in Lisa Isherwood and Dorothea McEwan (eds), *An A to Z of Feminist Theology* (Sheffield: Sheffield Academic Press), pp. 52–3.

—— (1996b), 'Godding', in Lisa Isherwood and Dorothea McEwan (eds), *An A to Z of Feminist Theology* (Sheffield: Sheffield Academic Press), p. 85.

—— (1996c), 'Mutuality', in Lisa Isherwood and Dorothea McEwan (eds), *An A to Z of Feminist Theology* (Sheffield: Sheffield Academic Press), pp. 155–6.

—— (1999), *Saving Jesus From Those Who Are Right: Rethinking What It Means To Be Christian* (Minneapolis, MN: Augsburg Fortress).

Hillman, Thea (2008), *Intersex (For Lack of a Better Word)* (San Francisco: Manic D Press).

van Huyssteen, Wessel (producer/director) (2003), *The 3rd Sex*, broadcast SABC (South Africa), November.

Isherwood, Lisa and Dorothea McEwan (eds), *An A to Z of Feminist Theology* (Sheffield: Sheffield Academic Press).

Karkazis, Katrina (2008), *Fixing Sex: Intersex, Medical Authority, and Lived Experience* (Durham, NC and London: Duke University Press).

Kessler, Suzanne J. (1998), *Lessons from the Intersexed* (New Brunswick, NJ and London: Rutgers University Press).

Kwok, Pui-lan (2005), *Postcolonial Imagination and Feminist Theology* (London: SCM Press).

McLaughlin, Eleanor (1993), 'Feminist Christologies: Re-Dressing the Tradition', in Maryanne Stevens (ed.), *Reconstructing the Christ Symbol: Essays in Christology* (New York: Paulist Press), pp. 138–42.

Morland, Iain (2005), 'Narrating Intersex: On the Ethical Critique of the Medical Management of Intersexuality, 1985–2005', unpublished PhD thesis, Royal Holloway: University of London.

—— (2009), 'Why Five Sexes Are Not Enough', in Noreen Giffney and Michael O'Rourke (eds), *The Ashgate Research Companion to Queer Theory* (Aldershot: Ashgate).

Murphy, James M. (1990), *A Female Christ for Men and Women*, unpublished document.

Nausner, Michael (2002), 'Toward Community Beyond Gender Binaries: Gregory of Nyssa's Transgendering as Part of his Transformative Eschatology', *Theology and Sexuality* 16 (March), pp. 55–65.

Preves, Sharon E. (2003), *Intersex and Identity: The Contested Self* (New Brunswick, NJ and London: Rutgers University Press).

Raab, Kelley Ann (1997), 'Christology Crossing Boundaries: The Threat of Imaging Christ as Other than a White Male', *Pastoral Psychology* 45.5 (May), pp. 389–99.

Roen, Katrina (2008), ' "But We Have To *Do Something*": Surgical "Correction" of Atypical Genitalia', *Body and Society* 14.1 (March), pp. 47–66.

3

Pneumatophores for Nurturing
a Different Kind of Love

URSULA KING

The words 'relational' or 'relationality' used in feminist theological writing seem to me far too abstract to capture the myriad forms of human connectedness, relationships and mutual caring, much of which we associate with love. But have we enough words and ideas to embrace the many kinds of love that humans can experience and are capable of? Have we ever explored or reached the limits of love?

But what is love and its meaning? That question was already poignantly asked by Julian of Norwich in the fourteenth century. To her, the answer seemed more simple and straightforward than to us, since for her 'love was our Lord's meaning'. But what is love's meaning for us in the twenty-first century? The letter to the Romans says that nothing 'in all creation, will be able to separate us from the love of God' (Rom. 8.39). This is such an extraordinary, all-encompassing affirmation that, if taken seriously, it should suffuse us with the greatest of joys and an invincible trust in all that is.

Looking for love

But have theologians, especially feminist theologians, really wrestled with such a foundational, all-encompassing understanding of love? Have they taken the immense powers of love seriously, perceived all its possibilities, reflected on all its challenges?

I don't think so. In fact, I have been surprised how little love has been included in feminist theological discussions. A quick check of feminist theological dictionaries confirms this impression. Although the first dictionary in feminist theology, produced in Germany in 1991, does contain just over five pages on 'Liebe' in the Old and New Testament followed by a 'feminist discussion' contributed by Elisabeth Moltmann-Wendel, to my surprise this entry on love was not carried over into the new and considerably larger second edition of this reference work when it was published again in 2002 (Moltmann-Wendel 1991). Nor does Letty Russell's and Shannon Clarkson's *Dictionary of Feminist Theologies* make any reference to 'love', whereas Lisa Isherwood's and Dorothea McEwan's *An A to Z of Feminist Theology*, published in the same year, carries a one and a half page entry on 'Love' by Julie Clague, who deals with 'Love and Language', 'Love, Relationships and Sexuality' and 'Self-Sacrificing Love', but also admits that '[t]he vastness of this topic precludes any comprehensive and systematic treatment of issues' (Clague 1996, p. 122). While Christian sacrificial love has been much criticized by feminist thinkers, love has played its part in discussions on sisterhood and friendship and acquired new significance in feminist reflections on eros, desire and maternality. Yet I would argue that love invites a still larger share of attention; it needs to be re-examined from new perspectives and become embodied in new practices in a world in crisis and in need of profound transformation,

Numerous socially and spiritually sensitive observers of the contemporary world have commented that we need a global spiritual awakening on a much larger scale than exists at present. To extend our sensibilities, nurture spiritual awakening and foster a greater spiritual literacy in contemporary society, I suggest to introduce here the word '*pneumatophore*' into our discussion. This is a term drawn from the taxonomy of the plant kingdom which carries a profound ecological meaning. Botanists use it to refer to the air roots of plants growing in swampy waters. Such roots, sticking out into the air, are carriers of *pneuma*, of air or spirit, if this word is translated literally. When I used it before, one of the people present pronounced this word simply as 'new metaphor'. This is a very clever reading, since this word is meant to be used metaphorically in my reflections, in the sense that I understand it as referring to those transformative, empowering ideas and inspirations that can serve as bearers of spirit and channels for new life of individuals and communities today.

Within the secularity of modern society we need many such pneumatophores: ideas that are vibrant bearers of spirit, ideas that can literally 'inspire' and guide us to generate new life. Such ideas may be drawn from traditional religions, secular society, the sciences or the arts; they may arise from the sacred or the secular, from national, transnational or global contexts – it does not matter where they come from as long as they lead us to a heightened awareness and sensibility, a sense of global responsibility, and a new kind of spiritual literacy that can help people to live a life of dignity on the planet without destroying the life-support system of the earth or killing each other.

A striking example of a powerful pneumatophore is the remarkable idea about the great capacity of 'love energy' for the transformation of people and planet found in the writings of several contemporaries to which I shall refer later. Given the extraordinary critical situation we are in, it seems imperative to reflect on what love is and can do, and what difference it can make to our world and our lives. Since so many efforts in exercising love and charity have so dismally failed, the question arises whether we need an altogether different kind of love?

Learning to love differently

The transformative power of love is well captured in one of the sayings of Pierre Teilhard de Chardin: 'Love is the free and imaginative outpouring of the spirit over all unexplored paths' (Teilhard de Chardin 1959, p. 55). This pregnant phrase provides an inspiring leitmotif. It anchors love in the dynamic action of spirit while proclaiming that there are still many completely unexplored paths for humans to discover by following the way of love in their lives.

For many religious people, it is ultimately God, the Divine or the Ultimate Ground of all beings, who is the very source and fountain of love, whatever this divine Ground is named or experienced as. What can believers and non-believers, as well as secular scientists, find in the notion of love in the complex world of the twenty-first century? Can religious and scientific understandings of love find a common ground or pole? Can they share a much enlarged lens that helps us to discover a new landscape of love, a qualitatively different kind of love?

This requires detailed investigation and much research, for we have to gather in the many strands that past experience and traditions can provide us with, but these rich, diverse strands need weaving together with our present knowledge and experience to form a new, much stronger, more developed pattern. Julian of Norwich affirms in her famous writing *Showings of Love* that love *is* God's meaning. Her vision of divine motherly love, passionate and compassionate, accepting and supporting, helping and healing, can be a tremendous inspiration when meditating on the nature of love, especially from a woman's point of view. In a very affirming, positive way Julian expresses particularly well what many other religious sources proclaim. Love is always there, it always accompanies us, surrounds, upholds and comforts us. But how to access and partake in this inexhaustible ocean of love? Love is a fire, both human and divine. How can we spread it effectively today in a world so torn apart?

We need to awaken the energies of love to stir and transform the people on our planet. For this, the old ways of understanding and practising love are no longer enough. While making use of all the resources of knowledge and wisdom available to us, we have to push the boundaries of our understanding of love, find love in a new land, on new roads still to be mapped out and established. It is no longer enough to think simply about love in the way our forebears did, or search in sacred Scriptures, world philosophies and literature for the established meanings of love. We live in such a different world and have such a nuanced awareness of our own becoming within the cosmic epic of evolution, and the grand web of life, that all our assumptions need to be examined and assessed anew. In Thomas Berry's words, we are called to 'a great work' in the world and in ourselves (Berry 1999). The centre of this work is fired by the powers and energies of inexhaustible love.

The energies of love reach out to everybody and touch on everything. They cannot be seen as something only personal and inward; they radiate outward; leap forward; overcome obstacles; move onward and upward. We can dream of *the ways and energies of love as new ways of living.*

It is a dream that links up with so many other dreams; it goes beyond
what existed and was possible in the past. It is the discovery of a new
road, the seeding of seminal ideas, the crossing of a new threshold in the
long history of our human species and the history of life, the revelation
of a communal heart.

Pneumatophores for a different kind of love

My own thinking on nurturing a different kind of love – a love deeper,
richer, more inclusive and accepting of differences, a love that empowers, transforms and creates new possibilities – has been much influenced
by the ideas of four different people who have given us new metaphors
and ideas about love for our time. Two are women, two are men. Other
examples can no doubt be found, but I want to refer especially to these
four, since they possess considerable originality and have been particularly important for me.

The first is the American scholar, artist and spiritual director Beverly
J. Lanzetta, who published in 2005 a daring, innovative book, *Radical
Wisdom: A Feminist Mystical Theology* (Lanzetta 2005), and two years
later another study, *Emerging Heart: Global Spirituality and the Sacred*,
of particular interest for interfaith relations (Lanzetta 2007).[1]

Beverly Lanzetta is convinced of the importance of gender implications for the spiritual life. She invites us to a rereading of mystical
theology from a feminist angle to discover new spiritual lineages and
revelatory traditions. Just as Sara Maitland argued over 20 years ago that
we need women map-makers of the interior country (Maitland 1983), so
Lanzetta, too, speaks of women standing on the borders of a new country as map-makers of uncharted spiritual territory. Her reflections are
grounded in a deep love of God and the world, and a profound sense of
belonging and trust that make her challenge many aspects of traditional
spirituality from a strong feminist perspective. It is impossible to do this

---

1 For more information on Lanzetta's work in spiritual direction see her home
page on Schola Divina www.scholadivina.net.

rich book justice here; I hope feminist theological discussions will in due course take note of its original thinking.

Lanzetta points to a new *via feminina* in mystical spirituality, a feminine way not restricted to women but open to both women and men, although it expresses itself differently in females from in males. She means by this feminine way a quality of religious consciousness and a mystical path that treads new ground. Thus she redefines the spiritual journey from the perspective of women, but not in an exclusive sense. Instead of seeking union with God through either a *via positiva* or a *via negativa*, she sees the *via feminina*, the feminine mystical way, as a 'third way', unveiling to us 'the feminine heart of divinity and the spiritual equality of women' (Lanzetta 2005, p. 13). The *via feminina* is presented as a 'radical mysticism' which seeks new forms of expression and engagement, while recognizing at the same time that some features of traditional mysticism reveal themselves as products of patriarchy that have to be dismantled and replaced by something new for the present world.[2] This means transforming and in some cases even subverting the traditional spiritual journey, by turning into two directions, 'inward toward the divine center of the self, and outward toward the world' (Lanzetta 2005, p. 63). This must include the naming and eliminating of spiritual oppression as well as eradicating the many forms of violence and of economic, sexual and social abuse of women.

Turning inward, Lanzetta subtly traces the deep longing to love in the great women mystics of the past, especially in Julian of Norwich and Teresa of Avila:

Julian and Teresa felt that the soul is so close to the divine nature, so attuned to the rivers of longing that flow between the divine and human heart, that a woman only knows herself when she knows God. By seeing the divine reflected in the mirror of her own longing, Teresa

---

2 I have discussed these and the following ideas of Lanzetta in more detail in my Julian Lecture 'Inspired by Julian: Seeking a Feminine Mystical Way for the 21st Century', The 27th Annual Julian Lecture, Norwich, 12 May 2007, on which I have partly drawn here.

realizes the limitations of human interpretations of women and recognizes that God alone can assist her in true self-knowledge. (Lanzetta 2005, p. 87)

The central metaphor and spiritual matrix of the female mystics' lives is 'the mutuality of passion flowing between God and the human person' which not only 'inspires the journey but also is the very process that heals and restores. Longing for God reciprocates God's longing for the soul. In this mutuality of love rests a microcosm of the whole macrocosmic universe' (Lanzetta 2005, p. 88).

Lanzetta's discussion of 'a feminism of the inner way' and her daring thought on 'embodied and engaged contemplation' which includes a whole chapter on 'Women's Body as Mystical Text' (Lanzetta 2005, pp. 155–73) deserve an extensive analysis, which I cannot pursue here. Embodied contemplation invites us to see all experiences and reality through God's eyes while engaging in an all-embracing love of the world in all its concreteness, with all its pains and suffering as well as its intoxicating beauty, joys and glory.

Lanzetta comes up with the excellent idea of 'women's spiritual rights' but extends the distinct notion of *spiritual rights*, building on international human rights, to all people. This brings a new perspective to global suffering, including women's suffering, since spiritual rights ask us to see each other and all creation from a divine perspective. She writes:

Because the highest calling of the person is to have fullness of being, spiritual rights address what prevents or violates this pursuit.

As the common element in all human cultures and traditions, the spiritual dimension of life is intertwined with and underlies all other rights . . . It recognizes that spirituality is life itself; thus, a life of dignity is inconceivable without spiritual integrity and freedom . . .

Derived from 'a belief that recognizes within other people the presence of the divine through which a person attains full humanity', spiritual rights place the expressly spiritual as a recognized right interdependent with and interrelated to civil and political rights, and economic and social rights. (Lanzetta 2005, p. 183)

I find the notion of 'spiritual rights' a very helpful one, although it needs further elaboration and discussion. The inclusion of spiritual rights into the vocabulary of rights encourages us to think about human dignity from a different perspective while reminding us that mental and spiritual violence as well as physical violence can destroy not only the body, but also the human spirit. In Lanzetta's words, spiritual rights are 'attentive to a certain quality of consciousness and a certain depth of heart that heal and transform. An indivisible relationship exists between the attainment of planetary responsibility and the necessity for spiritual practices, prayer, and meditative solitude' (Lanzetta 2005, p. 184).

The distinctiveness of spiritual rights leads Lanzetta to an 'ethic of ultimate concern', an embodied engagement that moves out of contemplation into action in the human social sphere, thereby expanding into a deeply caring and transforming *love* for the world. She calls this a 'mystical ethic' described as

> in essence, a mothering one; it embraces the world as a mother's body surrounds and nurtures life within her womb. Metaphors of pregnancy and birth help convey how each day we bear – lay our bodies down for – the spiritual renewal of life. (Lanzetta 2005, p. 201)

Much more could be said about Lanzetta's book *Radical Wisdom*, which celebrates the powers of a different kind of love by seeking the love of God through the transformation of the self, of women's lives and of the world. Her work presents us with intriguing and entrancing pneumatophores, with challenging perspectives on feminism and mysticism that are refreshingly new and daring. Her vision of the organic wholeness and spiritual unity of humanity is strengthened by her comparative perspective in acknowledging the mystical richness of different faiths. Her reflections on sexual love as a type of contemplation, of embodiment as a writing of divinity into the world, and her critical stance on our material culture, 'blinded to the unseen', are also very challenging (Lanzetta 2005, p. 183).

While many feminist theologians have written on women's struggle with a male God and patriarchal religious language, Beverly Lanzetta's meditative study explores with deep sensitivity and urgent social concern the innermost spiritual oppression of women's souls and bodies. She attempts to draw a new map of an active mystical spirituality anchored in love that can energize women's struggles for spiritual equality and agency, and can inspire both men and women to foster a deeply caring and nurturing love.

My second example of finding more pneumatophores for a different kind of love is provided by another American writer, Anne Hillman, whose book *Awakening the Energies of Love: Discovering Fire for the Second Time* (Hillman 2008) provides an extraordinary inspiration for learning to love in a new and different way. Steeped in rich personal experience as a musician, singer, poet and professional consultant on organizational development, Hillman is deeply interested in the internal aspects of social change, and how interior personal development can contribute to fundamental changes in our culture. Drawing on deep insights from mystics of all cultures, she traces the process of awakening – whether as gradual transformation or sudden mystical epiphany – to the ever present powers of love that run like a current of fire through all of life. Full of passionate wisdom and a great love of life, her book invites everyone to the great adventure of harnessing the energies of love for the transformation of the world and ourselves.

Hillman's pioneering work deserves another essay by itself, but I can only provide a few key ideas and quotations here. Her emphasis is very much on the need for a new awakening now. She traces this process in an evolutionary framework by following the rise of consciousness within the development of humanity, and within each person. We each carry two beginnings in ourselves, that of a child, and as a child of the human race. Reflecting on the evolution of our mind and the foundations of our soul, we discover a profound capacity for relatedness and for a qualitatively different love that can embrace differences. We need to discover our fundamental relatedness to everything that exists, not only to other persons, but to the whole natural world. Awakening the energies of love and learning to live with fire inside, 'we learn to live in relationship – all relationship – in wholly new ways: to live as the greater community of life' (Hillman 2008, p. 236). For Hillman, those whose awakening makes them increasingly transparent to the mystery of love are lights, carriers of fire and conduits of power. She traces the different changes and learning curves that accompany this profound transformation into practising a different kind of love. At this evolutionary juncture of the human species, we are all called to awaken to a new kind of love, a love that is not a feeling, but a great power. Awakening to this radically different love may be gradual or come in a flash:

> The awakening impulse – this Love moving through the entire human species like an evolutionary wave – is a *huge energy* . . . At issue at every turn, is your whole bodymind's ability to adjust to its increase. Learning to tolerate and to accommodate the energy without becoming exhausted becomes paramount. You may find that there seem be a series of learning curves: an influx of energy, then a period of discovering how to adapt, followed by a plateau; then, a new influx of energy. It hardly seems to be the benign bliss promised by the new-age spiritualities! (Hillman 2008, pp. 240f.)

Animated and motivated by that tremendous evolutionary energy wave we begin to see and hear things differently, learn to access life in a new way. Our sense of identity begins to change and we learn to live in a conscious communion with life, to live as relationship, and to be motivated in all things by love. To use Meister Eckhart's term, it is a 'one-ing' in a deep mystical sense that helps us to overcome our misunderstanding of love, a 'one-ing' lived in community. Hillman writes: 'To put it another way, we experience the difference between having a relationship to *thoughts* about love . . . or to *feelings* of love . . . or *sensations* we associate with love – *and come into a quality of deep relatedness with Love, Itself*' (Hillman 2008, p. 267). It means living in conscious communion with the larger Life.

Early in her book she quotes Meister Eckhart's words, 'Nothing that knowledge can grasp, or desire can want, is God. Where knowledge and desire end, there is darkness, and there God shines.' Yet she also knows that it 'is a long journey into the shining' (Hillman 2008, p. 25). Her book flows over with amazing insights, deep wisdom and an energy of light and fire that can kindle a new kind of love if we are attentive and willing to receive its sparks. It means that we live our lives in a great Presence. But this Presence also lies inside us:

> In the heart of you lies Love. Without your opposition, it shines through you. You have only to let yourself be held in the larger embrace, let yourself be loved, let yourself be known as you are – *and you will be lit up*. (Hillman 2008, p. 346)

Thus the book appropriately ends with 'The Song of Love':

> You are a shining.
>> You are not only the small being who wants to be safe.
>> You are Love.
>> You are Life.
>> You are Light.
>> You are Fire.
>> Go shining.
>> (Hillman 2008, p. 346)

Hillman's journey into 'awakening the energies of love' was originally inspired by the saying of Pierre Teilhard de Chardin: 'Someday, after mastering the winds, the waves, the tides, and gravity, we shall harness for God the energies of love, and then, for a second time in the history of the world, humanity will have discovered fire.'[3]

This makes me turn to my next example, Pierre Teilhard de Chardin (1881–1955), and because of the striking parallels in his thinking on a new kind of love with that of the Russian-American Pitirim A. Sorokin (1889–1968), I consider both men at the same time.

---

3 Quoted at the beginning of her book, p. 7, this passage is a slightly reworked translation of the final passage of an essay on 'The Evolution of Chastity' written by Teilhard in February 1934. See Teilhard de Chardin 1975, pp. 86f.

Teilhard de Chardin was a Jesuit scientist and mystic who spent half his working life as a geologist and palaeontologist in China, whereas Sorokin was the first fully trained Russian sociologist who fled from Russia to the West after the revolution. His childhood as the son of an alcoholic icon painter consisted of accompanying his father during his restoration work of Orthodox churches around different parts of the country. After his studies, he first worked in Russia, then in Western Europe. From there he went to the USA, where he finished up as founding professor of sociology at Harvard University. An original thinker and productive writer, Sorokin spent his last ten years (1949–59) at Harvard University at his Research Center in Creative Altruism. In 1954, he published a magisterial study on *The Ways and Powers of Love*. This book was almost completely ignored if not to say scorned by fellow sociologists, until it was republished in 2002 (Sorokin [1954] 2002). Only then the parallelisms with Teilhard's ideas on love energy – relating to one's family, friends, nation, religion, humanity and the whole universe – which are scattered throughout his many essays, became apparent and received attention (see King 2004).

Both thinkers agree that humans at present know less about 'love energy' than about light, heat, electricity and other forms of physical energy, so that the transformative power of love must be studied in all its different dimensions, whether cosmic, physical, biological, psychological, social, personal, religious or ethical.

Teilhard assigned the greatest significance to love in the whole universe and in human life. He wanted to trace the evolution of the phenomenon of love, but criticized the traditional concept of love as too static and too narrow. Our understanding of love is too 'spiritualized' and too divorced from its cosmic roots, from natural passion, in which all love, including the love of God, has its starting-point. Thus Teilhard spoke of 'the transformation of love', whereby love itself is undergoing a change of state which we have to study as systematically as any other aspect of the human phenomenon, for love not only makes possible and deepens personal growth, but is equally necessary for the further development of society.

The most comprehensive study of Teilhard de Chardin's all-embracing, dynamic vision of love has been undertaken by the German theologian Mathias Trennert-Hellwig. His book *Die Urkraft des Kosmos: Dimensionen der Liebe im Werk Teilhard de Chardins* (Trennert-Hellwig 1993) discusses Teilhard's reflections on love in relation to 'physics, metaphysics and mysticism'. These three terms refer in his work to the overall areas of science, philosophical thought and religious practice. In other words, Teilhard de Chardin's worldview, and in particular his approach to love, involve empirical investigations, theoretical conceptualizations and practical applications.

Teilhard experienced the tension between human and divine love, and reflected on the need for the further growth of love in an evolving universe. From a modern evolutionary perspective, he considered love as a cosmic energy, a universal form of attraction linked to the inwardness of all things. Love is the most universal, the most powerful, the most mysterious of cosmic energies working towards the attraction, unification and convergence of divergent elements and forces, a primordial energy that runs through all becoming. We may only think of 'love' in a rudimentary sense when considering the fusion of atoms, molecules and cells into greater units of combination on their way towards the growth of life. The use of the word 'love' in this context might be regarded as most inappropriate and imprecise by those who want to restrict it to something uniquely human.

For Teilhard, however, the 'physical structure of the universe is love' and 'the manifestation of this fundamental power' reveals itself 'to our consciousness in three successive stages: in woman (for man), in society, in the All – by the sense of sex, of humanity and of the cosmos' (Teilhard de Chardin 1969, p. 72). In his great visionary essay, 'The Spirit of the Earth' (Teilhard de Chardin 1969, pp. 19–52) written in 1931, Teilhard said:

> Love is the most universal, the most tremendous and the most mysterious of the cosmic forces. After centuries of tentative effort, social institutions have externally dyked and canalized it . . . the moralists have tried to submit it to rules . . . Socially, in science, business and public affairs, men pretend not to know it, though under the surface it is everywhere. Huge, ubiquitous and always unsubdued – this wild

force seems to have defeated all hopes of understanding and govern-
ing it. It is therefore allowed to run everywhere beneath our civilization. We are conscious of it, but all we ask of it is to amuse us, or not
to harm us. Is it truly possible for humanity to continue to live and
grow without asking itself how much truth and energy it is losing by
neglecting its incredible power of love? (Teilhard de Chardin 1969,
pp. 32f.)

The 'rediscovery of fire' mentioned earlier requires the analysis of the
powerful and transformative energies of love and the channelling of 'this
wild force' for the good of individuals and communities. But is this possible in our contemporary global situation torn by warring conflicts,
competitive individualism and the rationalistic cynicism of many academic minds? Teilhard was convinced that far from being a spent force,
love has incredible power for bringing humanity more closely together,
but the full extent of this power has not yet been sufficiently developed
and tested.[4]

Like Teilhard, Sorokin also speaks of love as one of the highest energies known and argues in a similar way that the production and distribution of love has until now been given little systematic thought in
practically all societies. It still remains 'in the most rudimentary form,
corresponding to the primitive manual technology of material production in preliterate tribes' (Sorokin 2002, p. 37). Until now, little effort
has been made in the human community to produce love deliberately
beyond what is produced 'naturally'. Just as Teilhard was interested in
'the technicians and engineers of the spirit' to calculate and attend to

---

4 Teilhard's understanding of the energies of love is far too large a topic for
brief reference in one essay. I have written on it extensively elsewhere. See among
others my earlier book *The Spirit of One Earth: Reflections on Teilhard de Chardin
and Global Spirituality* (New York: Paragon House, 1989), especially pp. 175–84
on 'Love: The Spirit of One Earth', and the more recent essay on 'Love Cosmic,
Human and Divine: Pierre Teilhard de Chardin's Thoughts on the Phenomenon
of Love', in T. W. Bartel (ed.) (2003), *Comparative Theology: Essays for Keith
Ward* (London: SPCK), pp. 177–87.

our 'spiritual energy resources',[5] Sorokin pointed to the 'inventors and engineers of love production' (Sorokin 2002, p. 38), who have helped to produce love in groups or in humanity at large, but this has happened spontaneously and haphazardly rather than as a result of planned action. This shows an astounding lack of organized effort on the part of humanity which now threatens its very future. Throughout human history, the family has been one of the most efficient agencies in producing altruistic love, and so have small religious communities. But altruistic love must now be extended beyond these small groups and developed 'for the human "world market"' (Sorokin 2002, p. 39). Sorokin paints a bold picture of the transformative power of love, and the systematic possibility of developing, accumulating and storing its energy for the benefit of individuals and communities. The great geniuses, heroes or apostles of love throughout history are like 'great power stations producing love for generations of human beings'. But their example alone is not enough. What is needed now is an increase of love production by ordinary people and groups, in fact, by the whole culture, so that 'love, radiated by culture and by social institutions, would form a permanent atmosphere that would pervade all human beings from the cradle to the grave' (Sorokin 2002, p. 45).

In discussing the 'techniques of altruistic transformation of persons and groups', Pitirim Sorokin argues for the extension of love over the whole of humankind, a vision also implicit in Teilhard de Chardin's work. Sorokin wrote in the preface of his book in 1954:

Unselfish love has enormous creative and therapeutic potentialities, far greater than most people think. Love is a life-giving force, necessary for physical, mental, and moral health . . .
Love is the most powerful antidote against criminal, morbid, and suicidal tendencies; against hate, fear, and psychoneuroses.
It is an indispensable condition for deep and lasting happiness.

---

5 On this theme, Teilhard's whole essay 'The Zest for Living'. Given as a talk to an interfaith group in Paris on 9 December 1950, the text is found in Pierre Teilhard de Chardin, *Activation of Energy* (London: Collins, 1970), pp. 229–43.

It is goodness and freedom at their loftiest.

It is the finest and most powerful educational force for the ennoblement of humanity.

Finally, only the power of unbounded love practiced in regard to *all human* beings can defeat the forces of interhuman strife, and can prevent the pending extermination of man by man on this planet. Without love, no armament, no war, no diplomatic machinations, no coercive police force, no school education, no economic or political measures, not even hydrogen bombs can prevent the pending catastrophe. Only love can accomplish this miracle, providing, however, we know well the nature of love and the efficient ways of its production, accumulation, and use. (Sorokin 2002, pp. xi, xiii)

Sorokin writes movingly on the power of creative, altruistic love as the mainspring of life in individuals and social movements. He examines different types of altruists, different ways of altruistic growth, and different techniques of the altruistic transformation of persons and groups. The practical examples he describes include Hindu Yoga, spiritual practices of early Christian monasticism and those of modern free brotherhoods, especially the Hutterites in the United States. He concludes with a passionate plea for the transcendence of tribal egoism through an immense extension of love, the deliberate, planned creation of a universal altruism. He argues that the extension of love beyond tribal solidarity to all of humanity 'does not require elimination of all interpersonal and intergroup dissimilarities. It requires only a thorough cleaning of individuals and groups from the poison of exclusive selfishness.' Such a universal extension of love initially means three things:

first, that *everyone* loves the members of his family and the limited circle of his friends and acquaintances . . . Second, universal love means that *everyone* must abstain from all actions harmful to any human being . . . Third, it means that *everyone*, within his capacity, extends his loving hand beyond his special group to *everybody* who is in need to help and give warm sympathy – first of all, in one's immediate community and second, in the whole human universe . . . If each community does the same in regard to other communities in need of help, then the whole human population will be blessed by, at least the minimum of love and vital help . . . This extension of love can be done privately and publicly, in individual and social forms. (Sorokin 2002, pp. 463f.)

I hope this brief essay shows what daringly original thinkers both Sorokin and Teilhard were, and how much their soaring visions and challenging ideas deserve further in-depth study and development. Their thoughts about love energy display a remarkable parallelism and convergence in spite of some distinctive differences. In his wide-ranging comparative study of the power of love Sorokin skilfully draws on the work of social scientists, historians, philosophers and scholars of religion, but not on natural scientists, where Teilhard is fully at home. Although little concerned with historical details, Teilhard has greater strength in showing the cosmic and biological roots of the universal powers of attraction, unification and complexification within the evolutionary epic of life, culminating in a radiant vision, a 'fire', of unifying love as the highest form of human energy. He has also more to say about the spiritual nature and mystical power of love in human–divine union. By contrast, Sorokin's understanding of the socio-psychological aspects of love are much greater than Teilhard's, and he proposes far more detailed suggestions for the systematic cultivation of love energy at the socio-cultural level.

For Teilhard, love – divine, cosmic and human – is an inexhaustible source of energy which creates all worlds, whether cosmic, social or personal. For him, the fire of Christianity burned most ardently in a mysticism of love and union centred on the love of God in Christ, but expressed and practised in a new way, in a 'new mysticism'. He developed his thinking on love by bringing together the insights of his Christian faith with those of mysticism and modern science. The emergence of the great cosmic event of consciousness and of the self-reflexivity of the human species enables humanity to take its own further self-evolution now in hand. This has to be complemented by a 'break-through in *amorization*', by which Teilhard means the activation of love within the framework of evolution. 'To amorize' means to energize *to a maximum*.

Sorokin spoke, similarly, of the need for a new 'amitology'. Both thinkers have made tremendous efforts to articulate the necessary steps to nurture new ways of creating and finding more love and thereby achieve both personal and social transformation on a planetary scale.

Concluding reflections

Even from the little I have written, it is clear that Teilhard's integral understanding of the phenomenon of love and Sorokin's appeal to the immense potentialities of creative, altruistic, all-transforming love contain very powerful invitations for further work and thought. They, together with the other two authors I discussed, provide inspiring examples of how to do this, how to nurture and increase these extraordinary love energies to a new degree of intensity for the benefit of the whole human community. All four examples present us with a range of dynamic pneumatophores to lead and guide creative thought and action by drawing on the amazingly rich energies of love. They open up immense vistas and reveal to us previously unknown spaces for living a fuller, richer, more interrelated life. They make us realize that the old ways of understanding love, including mystical love, are no longer enough. They are too static for what we need; we have to catch a new dynamic, have to become more fully alive. While making use of all the previous wisdom resources, we now have to push the boundaries of our understanding of love and lay new foundations. This is a gigantic and arduous task. Yet we should take hope, inspiration and empowerment from the realization that we can discover and draw on so many compelling pneumatophores for nurturing a new, all-embracing and healing fire of love if only we make the effort to find it and learn to weave its energizing dynamic into our lives.

References

Berry, Thomas (1999), *The Great Work: Our Way into the Future* (New York: Bell Tower).

Clague, Julie (1996), 'Love', in Lisa Isherwood and Dorothea McEwan (eds), *An A to Z of Feminist Theology* (Sheffield: Sheffield Academic Press), pp. 122–4.

Hillman, Anne (2008), *Awakening the Energies of Love: Discovering Fire for the Second Time* (Putney, VT: Bramble Books).

King, Ursula (2004), 'Love – A Higher Form of Human Energy in the Work of Teilhard de Chardin and Sorokin', *Zygon: Journal of Religion and Science* 39.1 (March), pp. 77–102.

Lanzetta, Beverly J. (2005), *Radical Wisdom: A Feminist Mystical Theology* (Minneapolis: Fortress Press).

——(2007), *Emerging Heart: Global Spirituality and the Sacred* (Minneapolis: Fortress Press).

Maitland, Sara (1983), *A Map of the New Country: Women and Christianity* (London: Routledge and Kegan Paul).

Moltmann-Wendel, Elisabeth (1991), 'Liebe', in Elisabeth Gössmann, Elisabeth Moltmann-Wendel, Herlinde Pissarek-Hudelist, Ina Praetorius, Luise Schottroff, Helen Schüngel-Straumann (eds), *Wörterbuch der feministischen Theologie* (Gütersloh: Gütersloher Verlagshaus).

Russell, Letty M. and J. Shannon Clarkson (eds) (1996), *Dictionary of Feminist Theologies* (Louisville, KY: Westminster John Knox Press, and London: Mowbray).

Sorokin, Pitirim A. ([1954] 2002), *The Ways and Power of Love: Types, Factors and Techniques of Moral Transformation* (Radnor, PA: Templeton Foundation Press).

Teilhard de Chardin, Pierre (1959), *The Future of Man* (London: Collins).

——(1969), *Human Energy* (London: Collins).

——(1975), *Toward the Future* (London: Collins).

Trennert-Hellwig, Matthias (1993), *Die Urkraft des Kosmos: Dimensionen der Liebe im Werk Teilhard de Chardins*, Freiburger theologische Studien 153 (Freiburg, Basle and Vienna: Herder).

4

Knowing Thyself: Psychoanalysis and Feminist Philosophy of Religion

BEVERLEY CLACK

Introduction

In the ancient world, someone seeking an answer to their problems would send to the oracle at Delphi. Arriving, they or their messenger would be confronted with the legend 'know thyself' inscribed above the entrance to the temple. Self-knowledge, according to this tradition, would go some way to providing a solution to any problem that one had. No doubt it is significant that these words demanding self-knowledge were also attributed to the law-giver Solon, the philosopher Socrates and the mathematician Pythagoras.

In this chapter, I shall explore the importance of self-knowledge for feminists engaged with the critique of patriarchal forms of religion. The ability to know one's self is far from a straightforward task, and it is considerably more complicated if one takes seriously the psychoanalytic claim that the self is not transparent, only located in consciousness, but also consists of *un*conscious fears and desires. I shall consider the implications of this contention alongside an investigation of some of the psychic processes associated with the unconscious; processes that need to be taken seriously, I shall argue, by feminists seeking to challenge patriarchal ways of thinking and acting.

Delving the depths: Delphi and beyond

Before we consider specifically psychoanalytic theories, it is worth staying in Delphi a little longer, for the stories surrounding it fit rather well with the psychoanalytic perspective I wish to advocate: not least because Freud was himself fascinated by classical themes and many of his key concepts relate to ideas derived from the ancient world.[1]

The legend of Delphi's founding as a place for prophecy and knowledge offers a powerful dramatization of the process required in order to 'discover' the self. According to legend, a herd of goats came across a deep perforation in the ground out of which was issuing steam. They started to behave strangely, and the goatherd who was accompanying them, following their example, peered into the hole. Immediately, he was gripped by a kind of ecstasy and began to prophesy. The temple of Apollo was subsequently founded over this fissure, and Delphi was seen as the place which lay at the centre of the earth, called, appropriately, '*terrae umbilicus*' ('the navel of the world').

The idea of something which comes out of the depths, which challenges the self and which leads to something new resonates with Freud's comment on the limits of dream interpretation. For Freud, 'the interpretation of dreams is the royal road to the knowledge of the unconscious activities of the mind' (Freud 1900, p. 608). Dreams provide the opportunity, through interpretation, of accessing deeper knowledge about the self, its unconscious fears and desires. Yet there is a limit to this self-knowledge, for no dream can ever be fully interpreted: 'there is at least one spot in every dream at which it is unplumbable – a navel, as it were, that is its point of contact with the unknown' (Freud 1900, p. 111). In this sense, the self is ultimately mysterious,[2] for its desires and fears can never be fully known.

Self-knowledge, according to this view, is never final but is always in process, constantly evolving. Knowing oneself is no simple matter: it involves a process akin to a plumbing of the depths. Hence Paul Tillich's view that self-knowledge is something flimsy and fragile, constantly open

---

1 For a detailed examination of this aspect of Freud's thought, see R. H. Armstrong (2005), *A Compulsion for Antiquity: Freud and the Ancient World* (Ithaca and London: Cornell University Press); also Victoria Hamilton ([1982] 1993), *Narcissus and Oedipus: The Children of Psychoanalysis* (London: Karnac) for a discussion of Freud's use of classical stories in the development of his theory.

2 As the title of one of Julia Kristeva's works puts it, we are ultimately 'strangers to ourselves' (New York: Columbia University Press, 1991).

to challenge. Yet for Tillich this disruption presents us with an opportunity, for it is only when we are challenged that it is possible to move into a deeper form of existence. Here's Tillich describing this process:

> It is only when the picture that we have of ourselves breaks down completely, only when we find ourselves acting against all expectations we had derived from that picture, and only when an earthquake shakes and disrupts the surface of our self-knowledge, that we are willing to look into a deeper level of our being. (Tillich [1949] 1962, pp. 62–3)

To use Paul Tillich is, for some feminists, highly problematic. He has been castigated for his wife's allegations, after his death, of promiscuity and use of pornography (see Daly [1979] 1991, pp. 94–5). These allegations have been challenged, but what if this picture is correct? Even if true, I am not sure that we need reject his theology of the depths, for what Tillich provides is an example of the struggle involved in the attempt to shape a life of integrity and goodness. The kind of subtlety and sensitivity found in his theological works does not mean that one's actions will automatically be thoughtful and ethical. The self is not transparent or simple: it is multilayered and complex. If psychoanalysis is correct, we best understand ourselves as psychosexual beings. Our selves are the result of a complex developmental process as we move from our earliest, symbiotic relationship with the mother out into the broader external world. The complexity of such a process – with all the ways in which it might go astray or become stuck in one set of experiences – means that we cannot escape an engagement with our more primitive and (perhaps) dark desires.[3] Against such a backdrop, there is always the possibility to which Saint Paul alludes: that which I know I should do I do not do, and that which I should not do I do! Considered thus, Tillich's example

---

3 For the psychoanalytic account of the processes/stages/positions that determine human development see Sigmund Freud (1905), *Three Essays on the Theory of Sexuality*, SE 7, pp. 135–243; Anna Freud ([1936] 1995), *The Ego and the Mechanisms of Defence* (London: Karnac); Melanie Klein ([1946] 1997), 'Notes on Some Schizoid Mechanisms', in *Envy and Gratitude and Other Works 1946–1963* (London: Vintage), pp. 1–24.

exhorts us to consider our own selfhood, whether we are really so 'without sin' that we can condemn without also considering our own desires, manipulations and failings.

There is a medieval image that sums up perfectly the terrors that we might discover if we delve deeper into ourselves: a procession of rich people, sumptuously dressed, are going to a banquet. Suddenly, the paving stones beneath their feet give way, plunging them into hell. Again, we are presented with an image of the depths, only this time they are seen for what they are: perilous. After all, we may not like what we find if we look beneath the surface of our behaviours and attitudes. To move beneath the surface can be a frightening experience, and not surprisingly psychoanalytic theory talks of resistance when confronted with the harsh facts of our desires and fears. It is no easy thing to move beneath the surface of our being, but we have to take that risk if we want to come to a better understanding of who we are and the things that we do.

The unconscious and self-discovery

The images we have considered thus far suggest something of the difficulties of seeking that deeper self. While I have touched upon psychoanalysis, I want to offer a more sustained analysis of the complex, multilayered self with which the psychoanalyst works. If much of western philosophy since Descartes has tended to formulate the self as transparent, identified with consciousness and thus relatively easy to access,[4] Freud's 'discovery' of the unconscious suggests a very different picture of subjectivity. Now, the individual is opaque, conflicted between the surface ego that emerges as the result of our earliest repressions, and the id that lies

---

4 For the classic picture of the thinking, conscious self, see Rene Descartes (1984), *Meditations on First Philosophy* in *The Philosophical Writings of Descartes*, vol. 2, trans. John Cottingham, Robert Stoothof and Dugald Murdoch (Cambridge: Cambridge University Press). For impact of this idea, see for example the existentialist philosophies of Jean-Paul Sartre (1969), *Being and Nothingness*, trans. Hazel Barnes (London: Methuen); and Martin Heidegger (1962), *Being and Time* (Oxford: Blackwell).

beneath the ego and which Freud describes as the repository of our earliest desires and fears, loves and hates (Freud 1915, p. 1923).

To take this picture seriously means that human action can no longer be understood simply as the result of rational decision-making. For the psychoanalyst, we are not reducible to our conscious thoughts, feelings and experiences. To accept this claim necessitates a different relationship to the self. It is not just that considerable weight is to be given to the role that past events and emotions have had in shaping individual character. According to psychoanalytic theory, many of these events or emotions have been driven from consciousness by the processes of repression. In particular, the repressed fears and desires associated with our parents shape to a significant extent the way we think about love, hate and the values by which we live. The superego, Freud's conscience, is the internalized voice of parental and societal norms, and the form that this takes – based upon our experience of our parents/carers – influences the extent to which we are able to make moral decisions and judgements about what is right and wrong. Accessing our deepest selves becomes, under this model, a work of considerable patience. For the psychoanalyst, it involves cultivating a certain kind of reflection, initially in dialogue with another, and then through learning to become an analyst to one's self. Analysing dreams and forms of parapraxis such as losing, forgetting and slips of the tongue, enables us to enter to some degree the forgotten and hidden world of our earliest desires. Through reflection we can come to know more about ourselves and our behaviours.

In many ways, this kind of critical reflection mirrors ideas considered at the beginning of this essay about the difficult task of acquiring self-knowledge. But we might wonder whether psychoanalytic ideas can sit comfortably with feminist ideals: after all, I have claimed that this essay will consider the relationship between psychoanalysis and feminist philosophy of religion. Freud's ideas have been subjected to considerable criticism by feminists who have drawn attention to the implicit – and sometimes explicit - misogyny of his ideas and those of later psychoanalysts. Having been equally critical at one time (Clack 1999), I am no longer convinced that such readings are the only ones open to us. This has come largely through a committed reading of Freud's many works.

Yes, one reading of his ideas about the distinction between the sexes can be read as affirming the doctrine that 'biology is destiny'. He is, after all, a man of his time. But Freud can never be reduced to a biologist, and his interest is always with understanding the psychology that develops out of our earliest experiences. Thus, Juliet Mitchell argued that psycho-analysis does not *support* but rather *reveals* the workings of patriarchy (Mitchell 1975, p. xv). In similar vein, I want to suggest that psychoana-lytic theory provides a useful framework for feminists seeking to critique patriarchal constructions of religion. Freud's theories, along with those developed by later analysts are important not least because they con-front us with an account of the processes that form our psychosexual development, alerting us to the way in which some of these can become overactive, limiting the extent to which we are able to become self-aware. This process of analysis is useful for identifying the fears and desires that drive patriarchal discourse.[5] But it can also be applied when attempting to develop a self-critical and self-reflexive feminist method.

Feminist method in theology and the study of religion has moved a long way since Angela West's critical account of a tendency in some feminist thinking to portray women as wholly innocent victims of pa-triarchal machinations (West 1995). West was concerned to show that no one is devoid of the capacity for sin, and that women have played their part in the history of violence and the oppression of others. And in recent years feminists have sought a more critical engagement with their ideals: thus Ellen Armour challenged 'whitefeminists' to engage with their racial bias (Armour 1999); while Tina Beattie has challenged the unacknowledged Protestant character of much feminist philosophy of religion (Beattie 2004). My aim is to continue this process of self-criticism, not as an end in itself, but as a way of developing subtler forms of critique with a view to better forms of relationship. In developing an analysis of the psychological processes that hinder self-knowledge, my

---

5 See Grace Jantzen's use of psychoanalytic theory as a way of identifying the fears and desires driving much contemporary philosophy of religion. In particu-lar, Jantzen identifies the obsession with death through an analysis of the work of philosophers in this area (Jantzen 1998).

aim is to enable better, deeper forms of relationship. None of what follows is intended to get the patriarchs 'off the hook', so to speak. While writing this, areas of Pakistan are increasingly coming under the control of the Taliban, who are destroying schools in order that girls should not be educated. Considerable fear of the female lies behind such actions: a fear that has a long history and which cannot be limited to one historical period or set of social conditions.[6] The sheer range and historical prevalence of ideologies that malign the female should not, however, blind us to the uncomfortable truth that women have historically been complicit in their own oppression. Women are not immune from repressive and oppressive tendencies: hence the role of women in the genital mutilation of their daughters. What I want to investigate in the remainder of this essay is the psychological process of projection. A process crucial in the establishment of the self, if it is overused and not identified it can contribute to distorted views of self, others and the world. Understanding our own projections can help us identify and engage with the projections of others. In this way, I believe that psychoanalytic theory can be useful for feminists attempting to understand the sources of oppression and the barriers to relationship.

The process of projection

We are perhaps most familiar with the idea of projection as it arises in Ludwig Feuerbach's analysis of the essence of Christianity. According to Feuerbach, the concept of God can be shown to be a projection of human values. Freud's critique of religion employs a similar model, and, indeed, for both men the concept of God is located in the psychological

---

6 For examples of the historical scope and prevailing power of misogyny, see Alcuin Blamires (1992), *Woman Defamed and Woman Defended: An Anthology of Medieval Texts* (Oxford: Clarendon Press); Clack 1999; Mary Daly ([1979] 1991), *Gyn/Ecology* (London: Women's Press); Marilyn French (1992), *The War Against Women* (London: Hamish Hamilton); Mary Lefkowitz and Maureen Fant (1992), *Women's Life in Greece and Rome* (London: Duckworth); Joan Smith (1989), *Misogynies* (London: Faber & Faber).

processes of the human mind.[7] Initially, Feuerbach places a positive significance upon this process for establishing consciousness. The ability to project out of one's self into the external world is a fundamental
building-block in the establishment of human selfhood. The notion of
God is crucial to this development, for human self-consciousness can
only develop in the presence of an external conversation partner who
enables the creation of an internal dialogue. Religion is thus what makes
us different from other animals: as he colourfully puts it, 'the brutes have
no religion' (Feuerbach [1841] 1957, p. 24). Having identified this crucial process Feuerbach's concern is to expose this projection, for, if it is
left unchecked, it leads to alienation: 'To enrich God, man must become
poor; that God may be all, man must be nothing' (Feuerbach [1841] 1957,
p. 26). All that is best about human being is located elsewhere and we are
left with the feeling that we are miserable sinners. Feuerbach's primary
aim, then, is to enable his reader to recognize the process of projection at
work in their life in order that they might take these 'divine' values back
into themselves, thus living lives that are not in thrall to God, that are not
based upon an illusion.

Such claims presage aspects of Freud's early work: the work of analysis
is to 'cure' the patient of that which ails him by uncovering the phantasies
that support the neurotic illness.[8] The later Freud is less optimistic. He
argues that it is misleading to talk of a 'cure' for what ails the human soul.
The phantasies that inform our development and behaviour are never
truly eradicated. As he notes in one of his last works, 'one feels inclined

---

7 This similarity is not altogether surprising: as William McGrath notes, as a
student Freud read Feuerbach and was influenced by his brand of atheism (see
William McGrath (1986), *Freud's Discovery of Psychoanalysis* (Ithaca: Cornell
University Press), pp. 95, 101–7).

8 This notion of a 'cure' is to be found in the *Studies in Hysteria* (1893–5, SE 2),
written with Joseph Breuer. The narrative of each of these case studies moves from
a discussion of the hysterical symptoms, the tracing of their source, and the return
to good health. Yet even in this early work there is the sense that 'cure' is rather too
definite and positive a word for what psychoanalytic therapy can achieve. Freud concludes: 'much will be gained if we succeed in transforming your hysterical misery
into common unhappiness. With a mental life that has been restored to health you
will be better armed against that unhappiness' (Freud and Breuer 1893–5, p. 305).

to doubt sometimes whether the dragons of primaeval days are really extinct' (Freud 1937, p. 229). We are always at the mercy of events that may reactivate or remake the neurosis of which we seem to be cured. As an example, he presents the case of a woman whose illness seems to have been cured. As time passed, she was forced to confront a range of difficult and disappointing circumstances, yet she 'stood up to all this valiantly' (Freud 1937, p. 222). Then a gynaecological complaint leads her to meet a doctor with whom she falls in love. Her love is unreciprocated, and a complete reversal of her apparent cure occurs: she 'wallow[ed] in masochistic phantasies about the fearful changes in her inside – phantasies with which she concealed her romance – and proved inaccessible to a further attempt at analysis' (SE 23, p. 222).

Applying a limit to the idea of a 'successful' analysis suggests something of the developments in psychoanalytic theory made by later analysts. Foremost in these developments is the idea of a fluid, overlapping depiction of psychosexual development. Where Freud might have described the 'stages' of psychosexual development, suggesting progress,[9] Melanie Klein denotes 'positions' of development between which the human subject is constantly moving. Crucial to this psychic theory is Klein's concept of projective identification. Like Feuerbach, Klein suggests that the work of projection is intimately connected to the way in which humanity establishes its difference from other animals. Yet there is a radical difference in the role that projection plays in their respective theories: for Feuerbach, once the projection is recognized, the values that were projected outwards can be taken back into one's life. Klein's account suggests a more complex interplay of factors, where our relationship to the external world is not just consciously constructed, and thus open to conscious manipulation, but where reality is also structured according to the less certain, more ambiguous forces of the unconscious.

According to Klein and her followers, the earliest stage of child development – what she terms 'the paranoid-schizoid position' – is characterized by the child's attempt to project outwards its feelings – predominantly

---

9 Although it should be noted that Freud himself sees the stages as overlapping rather than straightforwardly consecutive (Freud 1905).

hostile – on to the parental object or part-object: usually the mother's breast. This leads to phantasies of the good (satisfying) breast and the bad (absent) breast (Klein 1946). But the projection of such feelings also involves identification (Klein 1955). The child may seek to distance itself from the unsettling feelings of love and hate, yet it also identifies with the object on to which such feelings are projected. There is thus an intimate connection between the way the child views the breast/mother, and, most importantly, the phantasies that it constructs about both.

In the 'depressive' position that follows the paranoid-schizoid position, the feelings projected outwards are taken back into the developing psyche. At the same time, the parental object is integrated, recognized as embodying *both* good and bad qualities. Yet there is little sense that the process of projection could ever be eradicated once and for all. Indeed, throughout life the subject will shift between these two positions: when the paranoid-schizoid position is in the ascendancy, the subject will be engaged in projecting its concerns outwards; when in the depressive position, the work of integration will be to the fore. In this sense, Klein grounds projective identification in the ongoing process of becoming human. To project is not necessarily bad: indeed, Priscilla Roth describes it as 'a psychological achievement' (Roth 2001, p. 41). In making a division between good and what is evil, the child takes its first steps towards thought.

Projective identification and feminist philosophy of religion

Why should feminists engage with the process that Klein describes? We might readily see how such a process applies to patriarchal systems of thought; so, for example, the projection of sexuality on to the female allows the male to define himself as immune from such messy natural forces, for he (not she) is more spiritual, innately rational. And there is much to commend this kind of analysis. Yet my concern is with the implications that the process of projection has for self-understanding: moreover, with how a greater degree of self-awareness might lead to a more self-reflexive feminist philosophy of religion. If we are to create subtle and sensitive theologies we need to identify the projections that can obscure our engagement with the forces of patriarchy.

We might, for example, consider the way in which feminist and patri-archal concerns have meshed around the image of the mother. A staple of patriarchal views of the 'good' woman, feminist ideas of natality and the maternal have sometimes used the image of the mother to connect women with all that is good, eliding that which is bad.[10] Nel Noddings' 'ethic of care' has also tended towards a straightforward connection between wom-en's reproductive function and a natural ability to care (Noddings 1984). Anna Motz, a clinical and forensic psychologist, has identified some of the problems with this idealization. Motz notes the considerable hostil-ity directed towards women who fail to be appropriately self-sacrificing, especially when they abuse or kill their children. The collective societal response suggests an inability to believe that women could behave so badly.[11] As Motz suggests, this inability to countenance the image of the 'bad' mother means that women are less likely to express their concerns when they feel that they might be failing as mothers, or when they feel ambivalent about their children and motherhood itself.[12] At the same

10 Grace Jantzen's postulation of natality as leading to a better model of human-ity than that derived from mortality tends to a rather simplistic dualistic division between values derived from the female and values derived from the male (see Jant-zen 1998). Similarly, the feminist movement to reinstate the Goddess has at times suggested a simple connection between the maternal and the good: see Carol Christ (2003). This is not always the case: see Raphael 1996, which includes an explicit engagement with the chaotic and destructive powers associated with the crone.

11 For an analysis of how stereotypes of female caring impact upon women's treatment in the courts, see Kennedy 2005.

12 Adrienne Rich's reflections on this ambivalence stand out in the literature: 'The bad and good moments are inseparable for me. I recall the times when, suck-ling each of my children, I saw his eyes open full to mine, and realized each of us was fastened to the other, not only by mouth and breast, but through our mutual gaze . . . I recall the physical pleasure of having my full breast suckled at a time when I had no other physical pleasure in the world except the guilt-ridden pleasure of ad-dictive eating . . . I remember being uprooted from already meagre sleep to answer a childish nightmare, pull up a blanket, warm a consoling bottle, lead a half-asleep child to the toilet. I remember going back to bed starkly awake, brittle with anger, knowing that my broken sleep would make next day a hell, that there would be more nightmares, more need for consolation, because out of my weariness I would rage at those children for no reason they could understand. I remember thinking I would never dream again' (Rich 1977, p. 31; quoted in Gerhardt 2004, pp. 16–17).

81

time, social workers and other professionals, immersed in the same idealizing culture, are, Motz suggests, less likely to identify the abusive mother, having difficulty thinking that women could do such dreadful things (Motz 2008, pp. 71–109).

The examples that Motz catalogues, while extreme, suggest a peculiar conjunction between patriarchal and feminist idealizations of the mother. In such a context, it seems appropriate to interrogate the emotions and phantasies that drive these idealizations. What projections lie beneath such constructions, and how do they relate to theorizing about religion?

We might, for example, consider the religious formulation of Mary the Mother of Christ. Feminists have been concerned to expose how patriarchal constructions of the Madonna have presented women with the impossible ideal: the virgin who is also a mother.[13] But we should not forget the power that this image has bestowed upon women, giving them status in contexts where otherwise there would be none. And perhaps feminists have not been entirely immune to the power of this model of female perfection, for read as an image of womanhood Mary's example of self-giving love can lead us to suppose a form of femaleness that excludes anger, aggression, loathing and fear.

Valerie Saiving's famous analysis of 'the human condition' can be read as defining distinctively male and female faults. Saiving argued that the Christian tradition had constructed the notion of sin from male experience: hence the idea that sin arose from selfishness. Saiving argued that this notion ignored specifically female forms of sin which she categorized as arising from an underdeveloped sense of self (Saiving 1960). She lists the following female failings: 'triviality, distractibility, and diffuseness; lack of an organizing center or focus; dependence on others for one's own self-definition; tolerance at the expense of standards of excellence; inability to respect the boundaries of privacy; sentimentality, gossipy sociability, and mistrust of reason – in short, underdevelopment or negation of the self' (Saiving 1960, pp. 13–14).

---

13 For the classic account of the varied constructions of Mary, see Warner 1990.

There is much to commend this analysis: nearly 50 years on from the time of this article there remains a tendency for many women to live through the lives of others, be they the men or women with whom they live, or the children they look after. But I wonder if identifying self-assertion as the source of male sin and selflessness as the source of female sin blinds us to the intricate and interwoven complexity of human behaviour. In recent years psychotherapists like Motz and also Estela Welldon have taken this discussion in a darker direction, drawing upon their clinical work to present us with the narcissistic mother who refuses to accept the individuality of her children and uses them and their bodies as an extension of her own (Welldon 1988). And such controlling behaviour should not be identified only in women who are mothers: we all know (perhaps intimately) women who seek to control the lives of those among whom they live and work.

Religion can play a powerful role in such behaviours. In *The Second Sex*, Simone de Beauvoir alerted us to the dangers religion poses for women. Part of her analysis considered the way women can use religion as 'a pretext for satisfying [their] own desires' (Beauvoir [1949] 1972, p. 634). Negative emotions and attitudes can be sanctified through belief in God: frigidity can become holiness in following an ascetic path; hatred of one's child can be transformed into righteous anger against the sinner, and so on. All of which suggests that we should be wary of investing too heavily in images of 'natural' female caring. Demonizing the male may blind us to the conflicts that lie in our own hearts.

Klein's theory of projection demands that we acknowledge the connection between what is projected and the one doing the projecting. What I hate is often connected with what I am most fearful of in myself. Acknowledging our own projections need not lead to passivity or the acceptance of that which is unacceptable. If anything, identifying our projections can lead to a more mature engagement with patriarchal forces. Being prepared to examine our own weaknesses and failings enables us to engage with the failings of others in a more compassionate way: it enables a more nuanced judgement.

Identifying and acknowledging our failings and our projections does not mean that we are no longer able to name what is shameful,

oppressive or brutal. Mary Midgley's writings on wickedness are useful here. Midgley resists the idea that if we recognize our own failings
we will be rendered incapable of judging the failings of others (Midgley
1984, ch. 3). Quite the contrary: it is only by judging the actions of others that we are able to make moral judgements about our own lives. If
we are to know how to live we must be able to discriminate between different forms of life, and we can only do that if we are prepared to judge.
Midgley's analysis demands that we consider the relationship between
judgements about the lives of others and the moral structure of our lives.
My intention is not dissimilar, albeit with a different emphasis. If we investigate our own failings – the desire for power, the attempt to crush our
rivals, and so forth – we find ourselves in a better place to challenge the
oppressive demands of others.

Conclusion: relationship and feminism: philosophical and theological practice

Considering the psychoanalytic account of projective identification enables us to attain a greater degree of self-knowledge for our philosophical and theological practice. In considering psychoanalytic theory I
have paid little attention to the practice of psychoanalysis, and in many
ways it is the *practice* of psychoanalysis that proves useful for forging a
way forward. At the heart of psychoanalytic practice is the therapeutic
relationship. Ideas are not worked out in isolation, but through *dialogue*.
It is through the conversation between analyst and analysand that the
unconscious phantasies, fears and desires that shape the analysand's life
can be brought out into the open, discussed and possibly challenged.
Making one's self vulnerable to the other, allowing them to enter into the
world of one's deepest hopes and fears, is not for the fainthearted. Yet
it is through precisely such an encounter that acceptance of who one is
might become possible.

Applied to philosophical debate, such a method could be extremely
valuable, exposing not just the differences, but also the similarities, between apparently polarized positions. At the same time, the study of

religion provides a highly useful context for an exploration of the hopes and fears that drive human life and discourse. Religious narratives provide us with creative accounts of the hopes and fears of every life. Such stories provide a space in which to explore our relationships, the things that we wish for and the things that we fear. Developing a greater sense of who we are, the forces that have contributed to the person we are now, arises from the willingness to challenge our own phantasies and beliefs, not just those of others. Taking seriously the oracle's injunction is important not just for the internal dialogue that can be cultivated through religious practice. Achieving a greater degree of self-awareness – being prepared to face the dragons that inhabit the deeper reaches of our psyche – offers the possibility of relationships that move beyond the surface and towards the depths. Through understanding ourselves, we can come to a better understanding of the desires and fears that motivate us all.

References

Armour, Ellen (1999), *Deconstruction, Feminist Theology and the Problem of Difference: Subverting the Race/Gender Divide* (Chicago: University of Chicago Press).

Beattie, Tina (2004), 'Redeeming Mary: The Potential of Marian Symbolism for Feminist Philosophy of Religion', in Pamela Sue Anderson and Beverley Clack (eds), *Feminist Philosophy of Religion: Critical Readings* (London: Routledge), pp. 107–22.

Beauvoir, Simone de ([1949] 1972), *The Second Sex* (Harmondsworth: Penguin).

Christ, Carol (2003), *She Who Changes: Re-imagining the Divine in the World* (New York: Palgrave Macmillan).

Clack, Beverley (1999), *Misogyny in the Western Philosophical Tradition: A Reader* (Basingstoke: Macmillan).

Daly, Mary ([1979] 1991), *Gyn/Ecology: The Metaethics of Radical Feminism* (London: Women's Press).

Feuerbach, Ludwig ([1841] 1957), *The Essence of Christianity* (New York: Harper & Row).

Freud, Sigmund (1900), *The Interpretation of Dreams* (First Part), SE 5.

——(1905), *Three Essays on the Theory of Sexuality*, SE 7, pp. 135–243.

——(1915), 'The Unconscious', SE 14, pp. 32–54.

——(1923), 'The Ego and the Id', SE 19, pp. 12–66.

——(1937), 'Analysis Terminable and Interminable', SE 23, p. 216–53.

Freud, Sigmund and Josef Breuer (1893–5), *Studies on Hysteria*, SE 2.

Gerhardt, Sue (2004), *Why Love Matters: How Affection Shapes a Baby's Brain* (London: Routledge).

Jantzen, Grace (1998), *Becoming Divine: Towards a Feminist Philosophy of Religion* (Manchester: Manchester University Press).

Kennedy, Helena (2005), *Eve was Framed: Women and British Justice* (London: Vintage).

Klein, Melanie ([1946] 1997), 'Notes on Some Schizoid Mechanisms', in *Envy and Gratitude and Other Works 1946–1963* (London: Vintage), pp.1–24.

——([1955] 1997), 'On Identification', in *Envy and Gratitude and Other Works 1946–1963* (London: Vintage), pp. 141–75.

Midgley, Mary (1984), *Wickedness: A Philosophical Essay* (London: Ark).

Mitchell, Juliet (1975), *Psychoanalysis and Feminism* (Harmondsworth: Penguin).

Motz, Anna (2008), *The Psychology of Female Violence: Crimes against the Body* (London: Routledge, 2nd edition).

Noddings, Nel (1984), *Caring: A Feminine Approach to Ethics and Moral Education* (Berkeley: University of California Press).

Raphael, Melissa (1996), *Thealogy and Embodiment: Post-Patriarchal Reconstructions of Female Sacrality* (Sheffield: Sheffield Academic Press).

Roth, Prisilla (2001), 'The Paranoid-Schizoid Position', in C. Bronstein (ed.), *Kleinian Theory: A Contemporary Perspective* (London: Whurr), pp. 32–46.

Saiving, Valerie (1960), 'The Human Situation: A Feminine View', in Mary Heather MacKinnon and Moni McIntyre (eds), *Readings in Ecology and Feminist Theology* (Kansas City: Sheed & Ward), pp. 3–18.

Tillich, Paul ([1949] 1962), *The Shaking of the Foundations* (Harmondsworth: Pelican).

Warner, Marina (1990), *Alone of All Her Sex: The Myth and Cult of the Virgin Mary* (London: Picador).

Welldon, Estela (1988), *Mother, Madonna, Whore: The Idealization and Denigration of Motherhood* (London: Karnac).

West, Angela (1995), *Deadly Innocence: Feminism and the Mythology of Sin* (London: Mowbray).

5

Sustaining Hope when Relationality Fails: Reflecting on Palestine – a Case Study

MARY GREY

I would like to begin by remembering gratefully someone who was for me a jumping-off point for relational theology. In 1972 the then Bishop of Winchester, John Taylor, wrote a book called *The Go-Between God* (Taylor 1972). In an inspirational way, he developed a theology of the Holy Spirit as the energy or force field drawing people together in relation. He used the word *annunciation* to express the relational encounter of mutuality – inspired by the New Testament annunciation story. (Later I changed this idea to 'epiphanies of connection' because I think this better captures the idea of mutual encounter). But it was Taylor who first drew me to the Jewish thinker Martin Buber as inspiration for 'I and Thou' mutuality, and his insistence on 'In the beginning was the Relation' – a leitmotif that Carter Heyward has developed in her inspirational book *The Redemption of God* (Heyward 1982). Since these early days there has been a great cloud of witnesses as to the empowering dynamics of relational theology in feminist theology – and beyond. The ideas of mutuality, connection, compassion, wisdom, relation and relational justice have continued to inspire and sustain us all. A key connection to state is that God, our passion for justice is at the heart of relational theology. Justice is at the heart of faith because our concern for justice is fuelled by God's very self. It is not an optional add-on. Justice is the very heartbeat of God, wrote Philip Newell of the Iona Community. And, to cite Carter Heyward from *In the beginning*,

Long before there was any idea of God, something stirred. In that cosmic moment, pulsating with possibilities, God breathed into space, and groaning in passion and pain and hope, gave birth to creation. We cannot remember this easily, for we cannot easily bear to remember the pain and hope of our own beginning. But it was good. (Heyward 1984, p. 25)

In the beginning was God. In the beginning was relation, because God *is* the power and energy of our relating, our yearning for justice and right relation. Whether we speak about God's creation of the universe, the embodying of Jesus to heal the broken connections, or the wind and flame of the Spirit at Pentecost, birthing communities of connection, we are speaking of God's passion for justice, for healed relationships among all people, all earth creatures and life forms. If the divine purpose for creation is the remaking of broken connections (traditional theology calls it reconciliation), a healed and restored universe, justice and peace are the way to achieving this. Our passion for justice confronts the fact that though we yearn for mutuality and connectedness, broken relation is in fact what surrounds, even overwhelms us on personal, community and international levels.

Whose justice? What kind of relation?

I argue that it is *restorative justice* that seeks to transform the corrupt systems that are in place to find breakthroughs in interpersonal and intergroup conflict. Rooted in older traditions of community justice, it is continually inspired by the Sermon on the Mount, and by earlier biblical concepts like jubilee (a year of freedom, restoration and forgiveness) and *shalom* (from Hebrew) or *salaam* (from Arabic), meaning 'peace with justice'. Seeking right relationships, not vengeance, restorative justice refocuses our gaze. Is it the state or the person whose body, soul or property was violated? What is real accountability? Is it 'taking your punishment', or 'taking responsibility for restoring right relation as far as possible'? Can a people who have been violated and oppressed 'forgive and forget'? Or does true healing and reconciliation require remembering, truth-telling, repenting and forgiving? For restorative justice, the key is to move away from an adversarial approach and through truth-telling, mutual repentance, a reconciling process, aim for healing for all parties in a given situation. On an international level this comes into play strikingly where governments tell the truth about atrocities carried out in the name of the state. So, during the past 25 years, there have been more than 20 truth commissions around the world with perhaps the best known example being the Truth and Reconciliation Commission (TRC) of South Africa in which Archbishop Tutu played such a prominent part, and said, 'Without memory, there is no healing. Without forgiveness, there is no future.' But I want to look at something far more complex than one-to-one restoration of right relation between individuals, or even on a national basis, namely justice for the Holy Lands, the Bible Lands, close to all our hearts as Christians, Jews and Muslims. And I would like to begin this with brief extracts from a diary narrative.

Restorative justice and Palestine

Sabeel is an organization working for the liberation of Christians in the Holy Lands, founded by Cain Naim Ateek. Travelling with Sabeel to Jerusalem, to the West Bank villages – Bethlehem, Ramallah, Jericho – and then to Nazareth in Israel, is a profound experience and raises many questions about the sheer possibility for justice and the restoration of right relation amid the severity of the suffering, oppression and violence.

Tel Aviv, 3 November 2006

What strikes the traveller most of all on leaving Tel Aviv airport are the barren, rocky hills, with forlorn-looking olive trees on the terraces. Land that had been worked for 10,000 years now rendered unfertile, unworkable, because the people who carefully tended the terraces had been evicted from land and villages. A tragic broken connection. And the olive tree is much loved in Palestine (as is the *neem* tree in India), celebrated in myth and poetry. This poem, 'My Olive Tree', expresses something of the love of this tree:

> The olive oil that feeds the Sacred flame;
> Your light in temple lanterns pure, divine,
> Endures – Thine consecration to proclaim.
> Thou noble spirit of the ancient heights,
> The breath of Jesus in your shade transpires;
> Apollo of the ages, firm and stout,
> Your vespers Allah from His throne inspires.
> High on that lovely Hill top that commands,
> The sun-rise and the sun-set far beyond;
> The crest of joy, the fusion of delight,
> To thee my heart for ever shall respond.
> Ramallah – «Hill of God» thy name was given,
> Your crown, the Tireh Sector shall adorn;
> My olive tree, a jewel on your brow,
> Fed by the angels, was an angel born.

Farmers evicted from this land are a prominent theme of the film, *The Land Speaks Arabic*, shown to us recently in Nazareth and Jerusalem. A farmer in anguish is dragged away from his land, screaming 'My mother, my olives, my father, my olives.' Abandoned olive groves were a grim introduction to the theme of Sabeel's conference, titled 'The Forgotten Faithful', referring to the Christians of Palestine, tragically diminishing in number through emigration and the hardship of Israeli occupation. (There are now 400,000 Palestinian Christians with about half a million worldwide. More than 269,000 Palestinians have left their homes and gone abroad (Raheb 1995, p. 7).) As I mentioned, Sabeel was founded in 1989 by Canon Naim Ateek, an Anglican priest from Galilee, whose family was evicted from the town of Beisan in 1948. It is his book, *Justice, Only Justice*, that began to tell the world that there is a Palestinian liberation theology, a story that still needs to be told.

East Jerusalem, 3 November

Here we were confronted by the day-to-day realities and hardships of the Palestinian people. Patriarchs, bishops and other church representatives revealed the complexities of their lives. Two facts stood out for me: the number of speakers who spoke of how Christians lived in harmony with Muslims – 'We are Palestinian first, and Christian or Muslim second,' they all said. Second, the question of 'Where do we look for hope?' was central. For example, the cry of Jean Zaru, a Quaker peace activist and theologian from Ramallah, was: *'How do we bear the pain? Where do we look for hope and continually fan the embers of life?'* His question has to be taken with utmost seriousness by relational theology.

Bethlehem, 4 November: from grotto to ghetto

It was a bright sunny morning the following day when we set off for the West Bank of Palestine, apprehensive for what we might see. This poem I wrote after a more recent visit captures something of the injustice of checkpoints and the humiliations that Palestinians suffer on a daily basis.

How will you go to Bethlehem this year?
Will you take the road the Arabs take?
Catch the 124 bus by Damascus Gate,
just by the City Walls? So far, so good.
But don't expect an easy ride.
You may be stopped, jolted from your dreaming thoughts
of the 'little town'.
For, look! Israeli soldiers halt the bus, and now,
at gunpoint, demand IDs and permits . . .
Maybe you too must share some sense of humiliation,
the daily fare of Palestinians – bread of affliction.
And don't expect to revel in the hillsides of your Bible texts!
Those hills where 'shepherds watched their flocks'.
These hills are covered now in 'settlements',

that snake illegally across the hillsides,
where Jewish settlers enjoy a quality of life
denied to Palestinians.
And once you're there, how will you enter?
This town denies you access.
The Wall has done its work.
This barrier keeps its people in a tomb.
Israel has made this town a prison,
and you, like Bethlehem's people must brave the checkpoint.
And should you come in early morning,
you'll see the truth, the pain of Bethlehemites.
You'll see the faces of the 'lucky ones',
with permits for Jerusalem,
who queue for hours each morning,
faces deep-lined with suffering, suppressing anger,
as they wait to cross the checkpoint,
to earn their daily bread.
Yes, you'll get to Manger Square.
Yes, you'll view the Holy Places where the Child was born.
But what nativity do you seek?

Another birth? – of justice for the land?

In fact, on that day of my first visit, none of us got to Manger Square
and the Church of the Nativity. The Israeli army, with 40 tanks, had made
an unexpected incursion into Bethlehem, surrounded an area and started
to destroy a house which was home to six or eight families. The soldiers
shot dead two young men and injured a few more, including an elderly
woman of 86 who is now brain-damaged. The people of Bethlehem were
angry and upset: there had been no provocation. Nor did it reach the
outside press – but its truth was made very clear by the mayor of Bethlehem who addressed us later in the afternoon. Welcome to Bethlehem,
this most sacred place for Christians housing 22 churches – where the
Word became flesh, but now in reality a great prison in the West Bank.

To begin with, the historic entrance road to Bethlehem, where Joseph and Mary would have travelled, used to pass by Rachel's tomb, a holy site for both Jews and Christians, but is now blocked off for the Christians of Bethlehem as the great 'Separation Wall' (now more than 700 kilometres long), officially built for Israeli 'security', now encircles the old city, cutting off the access of the ancient pathway, and effectively allowing only two entrances to Bethlehem. Israelis control who will be allowed in and out. Some of the families suffering the effects of the path of this huge wall were present at our meeting.

Khalid is cut off from his grocery shop, and therefore his livelihood. Claire Anastas's family have lost their garden and now the Wall dominates the view from every room. The effect on business and economic life has been devastating, as acres of olive groves lie outside the Wall and the farmers have no right of access. Out of 80 businesses, 72 have closed along the Jerusalem road; 14,000 people still live in the refugee camps. But this is not the worst element: the gradual encroachment of Israeli settlements on Palestinian land is threatening the very existence and survival of the Palestinian people – in Bethlehem now only 1.5 per cent is Christian. Such is the effect of emigration. There are many Bethlehemites in Chile, for example. In Bethlehem district there are 27 settlements and 73,000 settlers on Bethlehem's land. The huge settlement of Har Homa towers over the old city. (Har Homa plans to take over the tourism industry.) To travel along the Jerusalem to Jericho road today, as we did for the next few days, is a grim experience, as the reality of the encroachment becomes so clear. The beginning is an innocuous-looking observation tower at the top of a hill, we were told. This then expands – eventually into the huge settlements that we could see on every horizon. There are 217 settlements on the West Bank, we were told. I saw no hill without a watchtower. I also saw many Bedouin 'encampments' – poor tin shacks, where people and animals were crowded. Because these people have lost their land, they can no longer follow their nomadic lifestyle. But an enforced sedentary lifestyle has meant that the Bedouins now suffer from previously unknown illnesses for them, such as diabetes. The encroachment still continues relentlessly: on 28 February 2006, the *Guardian* reported more Bedouin shacks being bulldozed. And everywhere the

Wall cuts off access to their land for the Palestinian people, as well as access to Jerusalem. (That affects people coming together for Christmas and Easter.) Permits are not easy to obtain. Nor are these checkpoints predictable: 'flying checkpoints' appear without notice. Harassment of the people is an increasing reality. At one point in our journey, at a checkpoint, where a Palestinian Christian was discovered on our coach, we were forbidden access and had to make a long detour to find a checkpoint that let us through. A new checkpoint – 'Qallandia' – outside Jerusalem, is being constructed to operate more as a border control. This is only to speak of one town. The story can be repeated with varying degrees of harshness in Hebron, Ramallah, Nablus.

Background to the 'broken connections'

The year 2008 was the 60th anniversary of the expulsion of the Palestinians from their ancestral villages in Israel and the Gaza strip and the beginning of the Occupation. In this time we have seen the end of apartheid in South Africa (which began roughly contemporaneously with Al Nakba), but the struggle of the Bible Lands bleeds remorselessly on. It seems that the world lacks both political will and moral strength to act effectively, defeated by the complexities. And it *is* complex.

It is not the place here for a long history and I'm omitting how we got from Pentecost to the present century. There were broken connections all along the way and tensions continue between Christians of the Holy Land themselves – as the stories frequently emerging from events at the Church of the Holy Sepulchre tell us. Here, to give a snapshot of broken connections *now* is the focus. Repeatedly, Palestinians tells us that they have a history of peaceful coexistence with Muslim and Jewish neighbours. As Naim Ateek writes in his new book, *A Palestinian Cry for Reconciliation*:

At the beginning of the 20th century . . . according to a 1921 census, Palestine was largely populated by Muslims (590,000), and marginally by Christians (89,000) and Jews (84,000). All were called

'Palestinians' and all lived together. In some places people tended to congregate around their religious groupings, yet oftentimes they lived as neighbours within the same neighbourhoods. As far as we know, the level of violence varied, but most of it centred on interpersonal matters, interfamily feuds, or interreligious issues. Most of the time, the feuds were dealt with through communal intermediaries, who at least brought about uneasy peace between the antagonists or even succeeded in bringing reconciliation among adversaries. (Ateek 2008, pp. 37–8)

The three groups – including the small Jewish community – shared the joys and sorrows of daily living, experiencing together the domination of the Ottoman empire. An ancient connection that would soon be shattered. If we make the link with Serbs and Croats before the Balkan wars, there is a connection to be made with the fact that different ethnic groups here lived as neighbours, until Serbian expansion and dreams of empire forced them into implacable hostility. As Miroslav Volf told us: neighbours like the Serbs and Croats do not turn into enemies overnight! (Volf 1996).

Second, British responsibility cannot be avoided or denied: Palestinians cannot forget the cruelty of British domination – some say it was worse than the Ottoman empire. It was also the Balfour Declaration in 1917 that began the process of giving the land of Palestine to the Jewish people, for the creation of the State of Israel, ignoring the fact that there were other people in the land already. 'A land without people for a people without a land', so the famous slogan went, disguising the fact that this became a Zionist colonialist project ignoring indigenous people who had been there for millennia.

Third, we have to factor in a broken connection with tragic consequences. The history of anti-Semitism in Christianity and especially in Western Europe, and the continuing fresh outbreaks of anti-Semitism in many parts of the world, together with Christian culpability in the horror of the Holocaust, still sharp in our collective memories – and how much more sharp and anguished in Jewish memory – continue to fuel the alleged justification for the actions of the Zionist government in

Israel. Whereas after the Second World War there was a general feeling that restitution must be made to the Jewish people for a long history of discrimination, massacres and expulsions, culminating in the Shoah, and that it was right for Israel to have a home, this been exploited by Zionism as pretext for expelling Palestinians from their land and denying them fundamental human rights.

Fourth, specific Christian responsibility goes further. The Bible is continually appealed to as justification for conquest and annexation. Certain books – Joshua and the chronicling of taking possession of the land, slaughter of Philistines and Amalekites are continually read out in Christian churches as part of our annual cycles of readings, with total neglect as to the way they are being used, day by day, year by year, to deny the rights of Palestinians to their own land. The second area of our responsibility is the way Christian Zionism has become the ally of Jewish Zionism, both encouraging a superficial and literal understanding of Scripture. In fact Christian Zionism pre-dated Jewish Zionism. Both use each other for their own purposes – but in fact the goal of Christian Zionism is ultimately anti-Judaistic. Christian Zionists want Jews to return to the Holy Land, to bring about God's purpose, namely the second coming of Christ, through a violent end – Armageddon, when Jews must either convert to Christianity or die. Christian Zionists are growing – especially in the USA, where they have been politically influential in fashioning US policies in the Middle East. When travelling in the Bible Lands we are all very aware of the growing numbers of Christian Zionist pilgrimages – who gain almost no firsthand knowledge of life and reality on the West Bank. (They are told it is too dangerous to go there.)

I cannot forget the words of the former Latin patriarch in Jerusalem, Michel Sabbah, words that still ring in my ears. 'Every Christian has a vocation for the Holy Land', he told us. 'A vocation to keep it holy and keep it as a place of redemption.' He sees it as an obligation for every Christian and every church, and I add, all biblical faiths, *to help Israel make peace*. In fact many church leaders, activists and NGOs plead for international solidarity and action. So, what is the way forward, the Sabeel to restorative justice and peace?

Towards the healing of broken connections

First, we need to be clear about Palestinian relationship with the land. Land is at the heart of the conflict. Jewish love and passion for *ha'arets Israel* is rightly a powerful motif. But Islam too has a theology of the land, and within the general Palestinian culture, trusteeship of the land is very important. Elias Chacour, Melkite Archbishop of Galilee, in his book *We Belong to the Land*, probably expresses the relationship between Palestinians and the land in the most evocative way:

> Mobile Western people have difficulty comprehending the significance of the land for Palestinians. We belong to the land. We identify with the land, which has been treasured, cultivated and nurtured by countless generations of ancestors. As a child I joined my family in moving large rocks from the fields. We lay with our backs on the ground, our feet on the rock and pushed, pushed, all together. Little by little . . . the rock was moved to the side of the field. Perspiration rolled off our bodies, and blood often streamed from our feet, soaking into the ground. It took months to clear the stones from just a small field. The land is holy, so sacred to us, because we have given it our sweat and blood. (Chacour 2001, p. 80)

Further, he adds the story of his family's expulsion from their village of Biram in 1948; yet in 1950, his father obtained permission from the new Jewish owner to care for his olive, fig and almond orchards: 'Father persuaded us that we, the true owners, would care properly for our beautiful trees and keep them safe for the next year' (Chacour 2001, p. 79).

This is the first broken connection to be healed. Some of the NGOs now working in Palestine focus exactly on this, from accompanying farmers to their land across the checkpoints (like the Ecumenical Accompaniment Programme (EAPPI) of the WCC), to fighting for land rights, struggling against the demolition of Palestinian homes, for return to the villages of 1948 and the return of the refugees to their homes.

Second, everyone knows that the real solution is political: end the occupation and work for a just sharing of the land between two peoples.

Even if the two-state solution is not thought of as an ideal by many, at the moment it is the only practical, viable means to peace. It involves Palestine recognizing the right of Israel exist, and Israel ending the occupation and recognizing the human rights of the Palestinians. Already, as Naim Ateek writes, after numerous failed peace processes, Palestinians are offering peace on generous terms:

> Today the Palestinians seek to build their own independent Palestinian state, not on the 45% land agreed to by the United Nations, but on the remaining 22% that Israel occupied in the war of 1967. (Ateek 2008, p. 33)

It is this offer that is being refused as Israel continues to annex further land for settlements.

Third, Sabeel, and other groups like it in Palestine and Israel, have deliberately chosen to seek non-violently for peace and justice, explicitly rejecting the violent option. Healing the broken connections, restorative justice and developing a spirituality that sustains the Palestinian spirit, are elements in this. In this deliberately chosen Sabeel, there are elements where relational theology and non-violent resistance are mutually supportive. Non-violent theology and spirituality have rejected the violent opposition of groups like Hamas, while understanding the reasons why they have resorted to violence. (Jesus faced a similar choice in his rejection of the violent resistance of the Zealots, whom he had even included among his followers.) Such a choice allows for being open to the pain and wounded memories of the other (in this case Jewish) and the fact that innocent Jewish people have been victims of suicide bombers and the rockets that Hamas sends off from Gaza.

Cynics will no doubt say that efforts so far are a ripple in the pond, in the face of the might of the Israeli Defence Force (IDF) backed by the United States. Catherine Keller has remarked that relational power is fragile in the face of the horsemen of the Apocalypse! But please reserve judgement!

Actions on the ground include relating to people and groups of good will across the divide on a faith basis or on a restorative justice basis:

Sabeel has good relationships with B't Selem (Jewish human rights group); Rabbis for Human Rights; ICAHD (the Campaign against Housing Demolition); many Jewish peace groups; soldiers speaking out against the occupation; peace groups bringing together young people from the three biblical faiths. MEND – a Palestinian group 'Middle East Non-violent Democracy' – also works with young people in this way. There is also a humanitarian task to enable people to survive and to keep alive the sinking Palestinian economy.

On an international basis Christians are beginning to take seriously the task of enabling reading biblical texts differently. Relational theology can inspire a liberating reading of the Bible with different understandings of texts. For example, we can highlight God's love of many peoples:

> Are you not like the Ethiopians to me,
> O people of Israel? says the LORD.
> Did I not bring Israel up from the land of Egypt,
> And the Philistines from Caphtor, and the Arameans from Kir?
> (Amos 9.7)

It is of vital importance to read the conquest narratives in a different light, namely as a post-event attempt to justify the dominant position of the Israelites vis-à-vis the neighbouring tribes. As the Palestinian historian Nur Masalha has written recently:

> Archaeology gives no record of Exodus, of forty years of wandering in the desert, of Joshua's conquest of the land: even the Davidic Kingdom becomes reduced to the fiefdom of a small tribal chieftain. Israelites and Canaanites are more closely related, the Israelites being mostly Canaanites with a distinctive development path. So the textual narratives as we know them would have developed after the Babylonian exile (587–535) to express the experience of returning from exile and idealising myths of origin. (Masalha 2003, p. 262)

The strength of the philosophy of groups like Sabeel and linked peace groups, in the face of military might and vested interests of different countries, is the integrity of non-violent resistance. Ultimately it draws on the inspiration of the New Testament. Like the ideas of relational justice in feminist liberation theology as God's purpose for the world, it offers a new and transforming way to live:

> When He called His society together Jesus gave its members a new way of life to live. He gave them a new way to deal with offenders by forgiving them. He gave them a new way to deal with money – by sharing it . . . He gave them a new way to deal with a corrupt society – by building a new order, not smashing the old. He gave them a new pattern of relationship between parent and child, between master and slave, in which he made concrete a radical vision of what it means to be a human person. He gave them a new attitude toward the state and to the 'enemy nation'. At the heart of all this novelty is what Jesus did about the fundamental temptation: power. (Rynne 2008, p. 102, citing John Howard Yoder)

It is all about power, but what kind of power. Relational power, I observed, is fragile. But Gandhi's life and development of non-violent resistance show that relational power has the power of truth. In his *satyagraha* movement (*satyagraha* literally means the power of truth, speaking truth to power), he attempted to reach the heart of his opponent:

> Let my friend understand the implications of non-violence. It is a process of conversion . . . But there is no such thing as compulsion in the scheme of non-violence. Reliance has to be placed on the ability to reach the intellect and the heart . . . Its secret lies in bearing anything that may be inflicted on us. We want to win, not by striking terror into the heart of the ruler, but by awakening their sense of justice. (Rynne 2008, p. 71, John Chathanatt (1991), 'Two Paradigms of Liberative Transformation: Gandhi and Gutierrez', PhD Diss., University of Chicago, p. 165)

This message is inspired by the Sermon the Mount (the genealogy goes – Tolstoy, Gandhi, Luther King, Desmond Tutu), but even if Palestinian theologians are inspired by Gandhi and all of these, theirs is a specific contextual interpretation. Justice, mercy and loving-kindness go alongside the way to reconciliation and forgiveness. For Elias Chacour, whose village is very close to the Mountain where the Sermon is thought to have taken place, and who, since childhood, has taken refuge there in search of inspiration, the words 'Blessed are the peacemakers should be understood in a very active way.' He says that the word 'blessed', 'makarioi', is derived from the Aramaic 'ashray, verb yashar'. This has an active meaning:

Set yourself on the right way for the right goal; to turn around, repent.[1]

Sabeel does not separate forgiveness from justice. At its most recent conference on 'Al-Nakba', participants heard the remarkable story of Joseph Ben Eleazar, present with his son and daughter-in-law. Himself a Holocaust survivor, he had fled to Israel, and joined the Irgun, one of the groups responsible for the early massacres dispossessing Palestinians from their villages. He was involved in the rounding-up of the men of the village of Al-Tantura, and suddenly experienced a moment of déjà vu, as he remembered his own experience of being rounded up in a square in Germany. Years of seeking his own pathway ended in conversion to Christianity and his joining the Bruderhof, a Peace Group.[2] Later, searching the internet, he discovered the names of the sons of the men killed at Al-Tantura and made a journey to Israel to beg forgiveness. His journey seeking forgiveness and reconciliation carries on. It is easy to dismiss one incident. What does it mean, in the face of intransigent violent policies? Does it stop the expansion of settlements, or harassment of Palestinian schoolchildren trying to get to school?

Mitri Raheb gives an example of non-violent resistance undertaken by a whole village, namely Beit Sahour (near Bethlehem – the site of the

---

1 Cited in *Reflections in the Galilee* (Jerusalem: Sabeel Ecumenical Liberation Theology Centre, 2008), p. 7. Quoting from Chacour 2001, pp. 143–4.
2 See Joseph Ben-Eleazar, *The Search*, www.ploughbooks.com.

Shepherds' Fields). The villages wanted to join in Palestinian resistance during the Intifada by refusing to pay their taxes. (There were no social services, not a single benefit from doing so.) The IDF decided to 'teach them a lesson' and completely surrounded the village, cutting them off from the rest of the world. Then the soldiers began to cart off material goods from their houses – TV sets, fridges, washing machines and so on. One story is extremely poignant. The soldiers removed everything from the living room of one house:

> Each piece of furniture called up stories, reminiscences and the memory of the sweat it had cost them. After a few hours, the living room was totally empty. The soldiers, having robbed her of all her possessions, turned to bid farewell to the elderly owner, a Christian. The old woman looked at the young soldier sadly. Her glance contained suffering, pain and rage. Her lips moved, but not to curse, not to cry out, not even to scold. 'You forgot the curtains. Please do not forget to take them down too and remove them.' An eerie silence descended on the room. Shamed and guilty the soldiers left. They took everything except the curtains. (Raheb 1995, p. 111)

The elderly woman had retained her dignity. This was the kind of non-violent resistance the Sermon on the Mount speaks about in saying,

> 'And if anyone wants to sue you and take your cloak, give your cloak as well.' (Matthew 5.40)

If such non-violent resistance is for the long haul, without apparent political success in the short term (we cannot judge its moral success), how do the people retain courage and hope? There is a remarkable spirituality developing, the spirituality of *sumud*, or steadfastness. Jean Zaru writes of its importance:

> To practice *sumud* is to remain steadfast on one's own land . . . to remain steadfast in service to one's homeland to the struggle for freedom. (Zaru 2008, p. 72)

Her book, *A Palestinian Woman Speaks*, gives a remarkable example of women's resistance in the refugee camps in Ramallah. Punished by having gas and electricity supplies cut off, the women tried to find ways of baking bread by collecting wood and rubbish and making a communal fire. But the soldiers came and tried to put the fire out and destroy the dough. The women resisted, shouting:

> 'Go tell your leaders that no matter what you do, no matter what kind of restrictions you impose on us, we will not allow our children to starve. We will find a way to bake bread, and all your efforts to destroy our spirits are not going to succeed. What God has created no one can destroy!' (Zaru 2008, pp. 72–3)

This is *sumud*, she concludes.

The spirituality of *sumud* brings together many of the aspects of a praxis of reconciliation, of living out a relational theology seeking justice. Spirituality in its simplest meaning is the life of the Spirit, embracing the human spirit, human dynamism for life, human *zeitgeist* (spirit of the times), the energy grounding hope, itself linking with the divine, the universal spirit of life, which is shared by all faiths, and people of no official faith. But the meaning of spirit that unites us in the most literal way of all, is the Spirit as breath of life grounding hope. Taking a deep breath, in this, the dark night of the Palestinian people, means connecting with this spirit, calling on resources for the long haul and refusing to give way to the suffocating effects of daily violence and humiliation. No easy option. Yet the most ancient meaning of 'taking a deep breath' is drawing deep on the Spirit, breath of life, keeping hope alive and energizing hope of new life.

Second, taking a deep breath brings the gift of *living peacefully when there is no peace*: this means calling on a type of imagination that is prophetic in remembering and seeing differently, an imagination that summons us to live out of a new reality that does not yet exist – but can be embodied in every act of non-violent resistance, of giving thanks, giving God praise, in acts of simple kindness, moments of joy, beauty, singing and dancing. In so doing we draw strength from ancient traditions that form Palestinian identity, such as hospitality, love of the beauty of the land – the olive trees, the fruit trees in blossom, the myths and poems that celebrate this, the stories that we want our children to remember. More than ever, in times of persecution, tensions and daily harassment, it is important to draw strength from cherished traditions (Grey 2008, pp. 9–10).

Mitri Raheb stresses the importance of culture for Palestinian contextual theology as well as for a spirituality of *sumud*:

> Culture thus becomes the space where people can meet others and themselves, where they can discover a language that is local yet universal, and where they realise that in order to breathe, one has to keep the windows wide open to new winds and fresh air that blow in from across the seas and oceans. (Raheb 2008, p. 10)

Toine van Teeffelen and Fuad Giacaman (from the Arab Educational Institute in Bethlehem) see the importance of *sumud* for a theology and spirituality of resistance. Historically in 1978 the term was given to a fund in Jordan that collected contributions from Arab countries to support the conditions of Palestinians in the occupied territories. Since then it has passed through several meanings and come to symbolize the value of staying put while confronting an overwhelmingly stronger military and political force. They cite the lawyer from Ramallah, Raja Shehadeh, as giving the concept two important meanings – roughly speaking, an exterior and interior interpretation. On the one hand the *samid* or steadfast one, refuses to accept being dominated by the occupation; on the other hand he or she refuses to become dominated by feelings of revenge and hatred of the enemy. The writers themselves use '*sumud*' as an umbrella term for stories of daily life under the occupation, stories that emphasize their love of the land and its beauty. Yet 'staying put' should be seen as more than imaginative resistance, challenging the spirit to move on, 'crossing boundaries along alternate routes, despite pains and sacrifices' (Raheb 2008, p. 30). And is this not reminiscent of the Lukan Jesus, who, in the context of warning his followers of the great persecutions that are to come, yet tells them not to fear:

'Not a hair of your head will perish. *By your endurance* you will gain your lives.' (Luke 21.18–19 RSV)

The final dimension of the spirituality of *sumud*, and a non-violent theology of resistance (and here we link again with feminist relational justice theology), is the dimension of vision. All writers cited are eloquent in their hopes for a land shared peacefully between two peoples and an end to occupation and the sharing of Jerusalem. They call on a vision of the Holy Spirit as beauty to sustain this hope and the reality of struggle. Beauty is linked with the holy, the truthful, and possesses a unique power to move hearts. The challenge for the moral imagination of a theology of non-violence is to transcend narrow, limited and deadlocked views, while still living amid cycles of violence, building on people's participation, and the creating of spaces for authentic renewed relationships of trust. The need for a spiritual practice is crucial (as Gandhi saw) – one that respects both the depth of woundedness but the need for daily strength just to survive. Deep in all faith traditions there are in fact resources for coping with poverty, pain and the trauma of violence. It is also through the Spirit that we are enabled *to inhabit the truth of the other* ... And to respect difference in the formation of community across the boundaries of faith and nation, the valuing of particularity and specificity. The Spirit is a great *boundary-crosser* ... This disruptive Spirit, keeping chaos and spontaneous prophetic activity alive, fuels a compassion that crosses rigid boundaries. Through God's Holy Spirit comes the strength to live peace when there is no peace: this means living out of a new reality that does not yet exist – in every act of non-violent resistance, of giving thanks, giving God glory, acts of simple kindness, moments of joy, beauty, singing. So, taking a long breath – in the Spirit – means turning round the notion of salvation – salvation is now, not the future. We do believe the kingdom will come – but we anticipate its reality in simple acts of feeding people, being fed. (Bethlehem = house of bread.) In taking the long breath of *sumud*, we share God's own *hesed*, steadfastness, compassion ... and God's vulnerability. Keeping God's presence alive when God does not seem to be able to do much to help us. Except to be *Emmanuel*, God with us. And a breath of hope: the *Sabeel* of Christ, means witness, faithfulness and for all of us in solidarity to accept the invitation to be the 'salt of the earth' that transforms an unjust society. That's what restorative justice – *God's passion for justice* – means in the Holy Lands today.

References

Ateek, Naim Stifan (2008), *A Palestinian Cry for Reconciliation* (Maryknoll: Orbis).

Chacour, Elias (2001), *We Belong to the Land* (Notre Dame, IN: University of Notre Dame Press).

Grey, Mary (2008), 'Deep Breath – Taking a Deep Breath: Spiritual Resources for a Pedagogy of Hope', in Toine van Teeffelen and Fuad Giacaman (eds), *Challenging the Wall: Toward a Pedagogy of Hope*, Culture and Palestine Series (Bethlehem: Arab Educational Institute).

Heyward, Isobel Carter (1982), *The Redemption of God: A Theology of Relation* (Washington: Square Press).

—— (1984), *Our Passion for Justice* (New York: Pilgrim Press).

Masalha, Nur (2003), *The Bible and Zionism: Invented Traditions, Archaeology, and Post- Colonialism in Israel–Palestine* (London and New York: Zed Books).

Raheb, Mitri (1995), *I am a Palestinian Christian* (Minneapolis: Fortress).

—— (2008), 'Culture – Culture as the Art of Breathing', in Toine van Teeffelen and Fuad Giacaman (eds), *Challenging the Wall: Toward a Pedagogy of Hope*, Culture and Palestine Series (Bethlehem: Arab Educational Institute).

Rynne, Terence J. (2008), *Gandhi and Jesus: The Saving Power of Non-Violence* (Maryknoll: Orbis).

Taylor, John V. (1972), *The Go-Between God* (London: Collins).

Volf, Miroslav (1996), *Exclusion and Embrace* (Nashville: Abingdon).

Zaru, Jean (2008), *Occupied with Non-Violence: A Palestinian Woman Speaks* (Minneapolis: Fortress).

Part 2

Relationality and the Cosmos

6

Tangles of Unknowing: Cosmology, Christianity and Climate

CATHERINE KELLER

The argument for constitutive relationality – for the idea that we are constituted in and through our relations to one another, that in our differences we are not merely externally related, that we are members one of another – has a complex ancestry. But qua radical relationalism it is a feminist theological idea from the start. It may be that I have never really thought about anything else – whether the metaphor is of web or braid, network or fractal or rhizome, the politics of love or, at this moment, entanglement. But for some time it is the relation of relationality to an apparently unrelated idea that persistently provokes and eludes me. That other idea always threatens to cancel itself out. That other idea is *unknowing*. The 'tangle of unknowing' signals an internal relation between relationality and unknowing. If our relations as they unfold and multiply entangle us in an expanse beyond our knowing, we come from the start entangled in our unknowing; we come ignorant of the extent of our specific entanglements.

Within the theological force field of this pair, cosmology, Christianity and climate provide for the present meditation three primary and mutually embedded instances. *Cosmology* reflects on the creation as our boundlessly shared material reality; I will echo an argument for the creation from chaos as a more relational theology than creation from nothing. *Christianity* as a conflictual but communally materialized discourse will be represented by the mystical heritage of the *knowing ignorance*. And *climate* provides the apocalyptic test of any living theology.

Let's start there. Our tangled web of material relations is precisely what is at stake in the looming catastrophe of global warming. As Anna Primavesi shows in *Gaia and Climate Change*, a theology of life on earth as a gift event stirs a boundless new relationalism; this gift that is not a mere 'present' discloses the unpresentable, the excess beyond what we can ever grasp, know or commodify (Primavesi 2008). We can no longer think about our own bodily relationality without reference to the earth's bodily interdependence – or that of all creatures within *hashamayim we haeretz*, the atmosphere and the earth. We are now in a manner of speaking obstructing the breath, *ruach*, of the earth, as the greenhouse gases create a mirror of the upper atmosphere, bouncing back rather than exhaling the excess heat. It is as though carbonization forges of our interdependence an artificial partition, choking the earth's own atmosphere off from its porous relation to its outer cosmos.

This warming process, we hear, may be proceeding faster than the predictions of the last IPCC (Intergovernmental Panel on Climate Change) report . . . given the melting of the late summer arctic ice – it may be gone, not by the turn of the half-century or century but by the turn of the decade.[1] We *know* this stuff. There is scientific consensus now on manmade [*sic*] causes, on the global damage to be expected . . . The problem is inaction, not unknowing, isn't it? What's not to know?

Yet it seems that what is known easily comes unknown.

Two days after Barack Obama was sworn in as president of the United States, the Pew Research Center released a poll ranking the issues that Americans said were the most important priorities for this year. At the top of the list were several concerns – jobs and the economy – related to the current recession. Farther down, well after terrorism . . . was climate change. It was priority No. 20. That was last place. (Gertner 2009)

There are many explanations for this shortsightedness. But one of them recently became manifest as a *New York Times* headline, 'Industry Ignored Its Scientists on Climate':

---

1 June 2008 http://www.ipcc.ch/ipccreports/tp-climate-change-water.htm

For more than a decade the Global Climate Coalition, a group representing [oil, coal, auto and other] industries with profits tied to fossil fuels, led an aggressive lobbying and public relations campaign against the idea that emissions of heat-trapping gases could lead to global warming. 'The role of greenhouse gases in climate change is not well understood,' the coalition said in a scientific 'backgrounder' provided to lawmakers and journalists through the early 1990s, adding that 'scientists differ' on the issue. But a document filed in a federal lawsuit demonstrates that even as the coalition worked to sway opinion, *its own scientific and technical experts were advising that the science . . . of global warming could not be refuted.*

'The scientific basis for the Greenhouse Effect and the potential impact of human emissions of greenhouse gases such as CO_2 on climate is well established and cannot be denied,' the experts wrote in an internal report compiled for the coalition in 1995. (Revkin 2009, my emphasis)

As environmentalists have long charged, industry did know early on that the science demonstrated a human influence on rising temperatures. 'By questioning the science on global warming . . . groups like the Global Climate Coalition were able to sow enough doubt to blunt public concern . . . and delay government action.' The article cites George Monbiot, who writes that 'by promoting doubt, industry had taken advantage of news media norms requiring so called neutral coverage of issues, just as the tobacco industry once had. "They didn't have to win the argument to succeed, Monbiot said," only to cause as much confusion as possible."'

This sort of confusion is interesting. Recently I came across a word coined by a couple of historians of science. '*Agnotology*' is a neologism based on the Greek αγνώσιζ, 'not knowing' (Proctor and Schiebinger 2008). Rather than epistemology, as the study of how we know what we know, agnotology studies how we don't know what we don't know. It 'designates the study of culturally-induced ignorance or doubt, particularly the publication of inaccurate or misleading scientific data'. 'A prime example is the tobacco industry's conspiracy to manufacture doubt about the cancer risks of tobacco use.' Under the banner of scientific certainty, the shadow of uncertainty is systematically exploited.

The manipulation of uncertainty lies at the heart of climate confusion. There is real uncertainty at every level of the modelling – this is a system of complex systems, processes taking place by definition at the edge of chaos, in which fractal probabilities and not linear outcomes are calculated. The greenhouse effects are now impressively knowable: but not so as to expunge uncertainty. The *New York Times* piece verifies that the repression of knowledge was itself knowledgeable. The industries' *own* scientists were silenced. This knowing production of ignorance about the climate counts then as the prime instance, in our time, of what I will call '*ignorant knowing*'. The perpetrators not only produce ignorance among the truly unknowing, they choose to ignore the knowable consequences of their own actions. They use and disguise knowledge with wilful ignorance. And they subordinate environmental knowledge to the transcendent certainty of the self-regulating hand of the global market. The globe now reaps its fruits.

Agnotology however seems to imply that the only answer to such ignorant knowing and the unknowing ignorance it manipulates is – *knowledge*: we can only cry out for more facts, objectivity, science. All the more indignant at the collusion of the US religious right with the imperial state economy in the manufacture of an anti-scientific, anti-environmentalist spirit, progressive Christians may join in the Dawkinsian chant: *sola scientia!* In the US we have witnessed the 'wise use' theology of the Acton Institute and Cornwall Document throughout the critical period (Kearns 2007). When worrisome facts have broken through the opiate haze, the religious right has countered with 'dominion!' 'prosperity gospel!' And now more than ever, 'jobs'. Believing in an omnipotent Father with the whole world in His hands, even moderate Christians can in the name of faith pull down a convenient cloud of cluelessness.

Under such circumstances, won't any mystical cloud of unknowing, of the Christian apophasis (unsaying), at best obscure the glaring clarity of the present emergency? At worst, the appeal to ineffable mystery deploys the disembodied Neoplatonic One for cultural mystification. In a recent paper on decolonizing epistemology, the philosopher Eduardo

Mendieta used the language of the *knowing ignorance* indistinguishably from ignorant knowing, the *agnosis* of a culpable ignorance – when it ignores for instance the realities of *la migra*, of the neocolonial injustices that structure the global economy (Mendieta 1997, pp. 253–72). I agree with his language of *ignorant knowledge* – but only as distinguished from, indeed opposed to, *knowing ignorance*.

If agnotology defines itself against all teachings of unknowing, it will only exemplify, I fear, the ignorant knowledge it deconstructs. For it will lose track of its own margin of uncertainty. The *docta ignorantia* was the transforming realization of Cardinal Nicholas of Cusa in 1440. 'No person,' he wrote, 'even the most learned in his discipline, can progress farther along the road to perfection than the point where he is found most knowing in the very ignorance that characterizes him; and he will be the more learned, the more he comes to know himself for ignorant.'[2] Here we find a stumbling-block to the know-it-alls of any field, above all of the Church, inasmuch as they convert the contents of revelation and faith into the certainties of 'belief'. The practice of negative theology does not silence the affirmative proliferation of language. But it knows that when it comes to the infinite our knowledge is ostentatiously finite. But because the finite unfolds from and is enfolded in the infinite, all knowledge casts an apophatic shadow.

If anachronistically displaced for example to *la migra*, the knowing ignorance would recognize how little I know about the struggles of the immigrants, who also do much more than I know to make my lifestyle possible. By contrast to ignorant knowledge, which thinks it already knows enough about these people, it commits me to learning more. What I learn will be real knowledge; just never complete.

2 Nicholas of Cusa, *De docta ignorantia*, 1440, in *Nicholas of Cusa: Selected Spiritual Writings*, trans. H. Lawrence Bond (Mahwah, NJ: Paulist Press, 1997), p. 84. Cf. also my article, 'The Apophasis of Gender: A Fourfold Unsaying of Feminist Theology', *Journal of the American Academy of Religion* 76 (2008), pp. 934–69, and Chris Boesel and Catherine Keller (eds), *Apophatic Bodies: Negative Theology, Incarnation, and Relationality* (New York: Fordham University Press, 2009).

The implications for the uncertainty management so key to climate science are clear: uncertainty cannot be extinguished. Environmentalists worry about how risky it is to admit publicly to the actual uncertainties of the science. Complex systems involve nonlinear loops of feedback, making mechanical prediction impossible. 'Climate feedbacks', I read, 'are the central source of scientific . . . uncertainty in climate projections.' The cloud of unknowing – that fourteenth-century English trope – shadows not only divinity but creation. In a charming irony, it turns out that 'the dominant source of uncertainty are cloud feedbacks, which are incompletely understood' (Schneider 2008).

In the face of uncertainty, the science theorist Bruno Latour tells us that two attitudes become possible: 'we can wait for the sciences to come up with additional proofs that will put an end to the uncertainties, or we can consider uncertainty as the inevitable ingredient of crises in the environment and in public health'. Uncertainty becomes the condition of a postmodern collectivity, collected from the 'associations of humans and nonhumans'. He would shift a democratized scientific discourse from objectivizing 'matters of fact' to interdependent 'matters of concern'. 'The risk-free objects, the smooth objects to which we had been accustomed up to now, are giving way to *risky attachments*, tangled objects' (Latour 2004, p. 22).

Such risky attachments may in the face of ecological crisis mentor us in the entanglement of unknowing and relationality.

Speaking of risky attachments: let us loop back through feminist theory and its destabilization of interhuman relations. For is it not in the attempt to pin down as some sort of knowable essence a gender, a sex, that old and new objectifications kick in – jamming the emancipatory associations that we seek to form? Thus in resistance to feminist identity politics, coalitions between straight and lesbian turned fortunately queer – yielding even the Queerly Trinitarian God (in whose articulation we grieve Marcella Althaus Reid). Similarly, in resistance to the ignorant knowing of white women, feminism showed itself multicoloured and hybrid; and the anthropocentric social justice of feminism blossomed into ecofeminism. In other words the limitless unfolding of the feminist project could be said to depend upon practices of knowing ignorance, undoing the ignorant knowledge of our alibis. We grow in mindfulness of the virtually infinite relations which constitute our bodies, our selves, our worlds.

Here the more recent work of Judith Butler becomes explicit in its joint articulation of relationality and unknowing. This relationality that at its limits and in its multiplicity escapes the net of language, now becomes an insistent theme: '*Moments of unknowingness about oneself tend to emerge in the context of relations to others*, suggesting that these relations call upon primary forms of relationality that are not always available to explicit and reflective thematization' (Butler 2005, p. 20, my emphasis). I am less likely to bump up against the limits of my self-knowledge when left to myself. So our very self is exposed as the crucial fold between *unknowingness and relationality*.

Butler has little interest in cosmology, Christianity or ecology. In relation to nonhuman others, mineral, vegetable, animal or divine, we may nonetheless echo her claim that unknowingness about oneself emerges in relations to others. Indeed I suspect that for those of us who pursue those wider transhuman associations, the unknowing becomes exponentially intensified; the nets of relation approach a cosmological infinity.

Before that infinity we find ourselves willy nilly caught in a feedback loop of theological language.[3] The unknowability of the divine infinite converges – queerly – with unknowingness as to sex, gender, self. And therefore of our finite language about God. Elizabeth Johnson used negative theology in order to negate the exclusively masculine language about God, who thus becomes – in *positively* theological metaphors – spirit Sophia, Jesus Sophia, Mother Sophia.

But in its mystical intensity, negative theology risks losing all bodies, especially our earthbodies, in a great upward disentanglement of the soul from the cosmos. This is pointedly, however, not the case with Cusa. His *docta ignorantia* anticipated and exceeded, in stunningly

---

3 God may not name another entity for us, to whom we relate, but may with Ivone Gebara name the relationship itself; either way, a certain speaking of the unspeakable, drenched now with various current indecencies, is gaining currency. See Gebara 1999.

specific ways, Bruno, Copernicus, Galileo. They would come into conflict with the authoritatively ignorant knowledge of a later, more defensive Church. His creation unfolds – *explicatio* – from God, the infinite, even as it is enfolded – *complicatio* – in God.

How might the enfolding of the universe in God and the unfolding of God in the universe inspire a greater *inter-creaturely* solidarity? The answer lies in the entangled interrelatedness – at once social, ecological and cosmological – of all creatures. Or as Cusa recognizes, perhaps before any other theologian, 'all are in all and each is in each'.[4]

> Since the universe is contracted in each actually existing thing, it is obvious that God, who is in the universe, is in each thing and each actually existing thing is immediately in God, as is the universe. *Therefore, to say that 'each thing is in each thing' is not other than to say that 'through all things God is in all things' and that 'through all things all are in God.'*[5]

I hope to open this premodern fold between negative theology and cosmology as a site of postmodern relationality: the fold between the complication and the explication is discerned only in knowing ignorance. For the complication remains inherently unknowable, the infinite, subject, for Cusa, to conjecture but not to certainty. Surely you are thinking this cosmology of knowing ignorance is terribly antiquated, premodern. But is it? What a precise paraphrase one finds in the mathematical cosmologist Whitehead's *Science and the Modern World*: 'In a certain sense, everything is everywhere at all times. For every location involves an aspect

---

4 In Book One, on negative theology, '[I]t was shown that God is in all things in such a way that all things are in God,' but now 'it is evident that God is in all things, as if, *by mediation of the universe*' (Cusa, *De docta ignorantia*, II.5.117, 140, my emphasis). This is Cusa's key replacement, of Platonic mediation by an abstract multiplicity of forms, with the folding relation. It is not that God is a substance who folds in and out of the world. God is the folding: 'God is the enfolding and unfolding of all things' (II.3.111, 137).

5 Cusa, *De docta ignorantia*, II.5.118, 140, my emphasis.

of itself in every other location. Thus every spatiotemporal standpoint mirrors the world' (Whitehead 1967, p. 91).

Whitehead was reading not Cusa but quantum theory as it was happening. He was riveted to the creative indeterminacy of the quantum event. He began to envision a God who calls forth ever more complex and therefore more free, more uncertain, creatures. These creatures of which the universe is made are events of becoming *internally* related, one creature to another, not externally, mechanically, predictably. They participate in one another and so in God. Process panentheism would decades later flow from his cosmology.

A quantum physicist named David Bohm, who read Whitehead, proposed in the 1980s an implicate order in which all things are internally related: 'In terms of the implicate order one may say that everything is enfolded into everything' (Bohm 1983, p. 177). Bohm was rewriting the wave/particle complementarity: the definitely located particles are the explicate order, the ocean of flowing, interfluent waves comprise the implicate. But he did not read Cusa's echoing explication and implication of all things in one another and in the infinite.

Bohm was trying to make sense of the haunting, one might even say agnotologically repressed, phenomenon of quantum nonlocality. It had been called by Schrodinger entanglement. I concur with a recent book, *The Age of Entanglement*, that only now might the cultural paradigm be shifting enough to accommodate the eerie data of quantum entanglement (Gilder 2008). Experiments have verified what Einstein hoped would go away: spooky action at a distance. It affords a stunning glimpse of a synchronistic relationality that unsays classical and mechanical notions of matter separated by time and space.

Suffice it to say for now that the emergent theory of the undivided universe seems to be affording tantalizing intimations of an intimately relational cosmos. The quantum principles of uncertainty and indeterminacy situate the theory of quantum entanglement within a sea of unknowing. This *complicatio* of a universe winks at us from behind the uncertainty divide. It may be rendering a notion of 'matter' so beautifully alien to the stuff we thought we knew – that the panentheistic metaphor of the world as God's body takes on new credibility. As metaphor: here science and religion meet, in a revelatory tangle of unknowing. Perhaps such a meeting will need feminist mediation in order to cultivate the relational sensibility of a new common sense, a new paradigm capable of holding the tension between relationality and uncertainty.

Yet we are barely as feminist theologians – so recently come to voice – able to tolerate the knowing ignorance. As Sigridur Gudmansdottir has written on the conjunction of feminism and apophatic mysticism, its 'becoming is fuelled by the divine inexhaustabilities of abysmal negations and affirmations, a trembling praxis of opening, touch, withdrawal in language; undoing identities, genders, sexualities, racial, class and heterosexual privileges' (Gudmansdottir 2009, p. 275).

I am hopeful that the attractive power of the new cosmology will help our species to remember and to act responsibly on the best knowledge that is available to us, *despite and because of* the inextirpable uncertainty. That uncertainty is the medium of our collective creativity, and certainly of our risky democracies.

Earlier I noted the low public priority of climate. A recent study sheds light. Humans are apparently not wired for wisdom – as much as for fast reactions to immediate crisis. How can we resist the ignorant knowledges that manipulate short-term crisis? Things look agnotologically bad.

This study claims that climate change can be . . . viewed as a very large 'commons dilemma' – a version, that is, of the textbook situation in which sheepherders have little incentive to act alone to preserve the grassy commons and as a result suffer collectively from overgrazing. The best way to avoid such failure is by collaborating more, not less. 'We enjoy congregating; we need to know we are part of groups', claims the study. 'It gives us inherent pleasure to do this. And when we are reminded of the fact that we're part of communities, then the community becomes . . . the decision-making unit. That's how we make huge sacrifices, like in World War II.' As will be required to avert climate catastrophe.

So the ability to make the individual changes necessary for a green shift can only be mobilized through a collectivity that is not only crisis oriented – but that draws *enjoyment from relationality* itself. Since the heaven and earth of relations are precisely what is at stake in global warming, can we somehow in our congregations mobilize that enjoyment? Indeed, can we multiply it by joy in our trans-species associations?

Maybe those of us allied with religious groups can exercise a certain spooky action at a distance by way of the symbols of creation. For the biblical stories that have co-constituted our cultural history still entangle – consciously and unconsciously – our collective life. My earlier experiment in freeing creation theology from the ex nihilo dogma is such an effort. Returning to the biblical metaphors of creation from the *tehom*, the watery, chaotic deep, one discerns something like Bohm's implicate universe of flowing wholeness – not a prim and closed wholeness, but an open *chaosmos*, in which we are called forth from the womb waters. I called it the *creatio ex profundis* – creation out of the depths. From this *tehom* we are called forth good, but only all together *very* good. The *creatio ex profundis* is *creatio cooperationis* (Keller 2003). The commons dilemma for crises like those besetting our species now invites no single orthodox solution, not even that of a feminist orthodoxy. It invites instead the principled polydoxy of multiple collectives entangled together in the creation commons. The body of Christ – where it outgrows its false certainties – finds itself a vulnerable member of a far larger body.

At any rate I for one take no pleasure in relationality when it caves in on me, when it becomes merely church, merely interhuman, interpersonal, feminist or familial – without the open *chaosmos* of strange relations entanglement strangles. I hope at any rate that I have hinted at how the tangles of our unknowing may unfold in the relations of cosmology, Christianity and climate. May we find a joy in those folds that will enfold and exceed all the inevitable loss and mourning. For there lies before us the risky adventure of the relational renewal of the atmosphere and of the earth.

References

Bohm, David (1983), *Wholeness and the Implicate Order* (London and New York: Routledge).

Butler, Judith (2005), *Giving An Account of Oneself* (New York: Fordham University Press).

Gebara, Ivone (1999), *Longing for Running Water: Ecofeminism and Liberation* (Minneapolis: Fortress Press).

Gertner, Jon (2009), 'Why Isn't the Brain Green?', *New York Times Magazine* – The Green Issue, 16 April. http://www.nytimes.com/2009/04/19/magazine/19Science-t.html?%2339;t%20the%20brain%20green=&_r=1&sq=why%20isn&st=cse&scp=1&pagewanted=all.

Gilder, Louisa (2008), *The Age of Entanglement: When Quantum Physics was Born* (New York: Alfred A. Knopf).

Gudmansdottir, Sigridur (2009), 'Feminist Theology and the Sensible Unsaying of Mysticism', in Chris Boesel and Catherine Keller (eds), *Apophatic Bodies: Negative Theology, Incarnation and Relationalty* (New York: Fordham University Press), pp. ????

Kearns, Laurel (2007), 'Cooking the Truth: Faith, Science, the Market, and Global Warming', in Laurel Kearns and Catherine Keller (eds), *Ecospirit: Religions and Philosophies for the Earth* (New York: Fordham University Press), pp. 97–124.

Keller, Catherine (2003), *The Face of the Deep: A Theology of Becoming* (New York: Routledge).

Latour, Bruno (2004), *Politics of Nature: How to Bring the Sciences into Democracy*, trans. Catherine Porter (Cambridge, MA: Harvard University Press).

Mendieta, Eduardo (1997), 'From Christendon to Polycentric Oikonumē', in David Batstone, Eduardo Mendieta, Lois Ann Lorentzen and Dwight N. Hopkins (eds), *Liberation Theologies, Postmodernity and the Americas* (London: Routledge).

Primavesi, Anne (2008), *Gaia and Climate Change: A Theology of Gift Events* (London: Routledge).

Proctor, Robert N. and Londa Schiebinger (eds) (2008), *Agnotology: The Making and Unmaking of Ignorance* (Stanford, CA: Stanford University Press).

Revkin, Andrew C. (2009), 'Industry Ignored Its Scientists on Climate', *New York Times*, 23 April. http://www.nytimes.com/2009/04/24/science/earth/24deny.html?scp=1&sq=ndrew%20revkin&st=cse.

Schneider, Tapio (2008), 'How We Know Global Warming is Real', *Skeptic Magazine* 14.1, p. 35.

Whitehead, Alfred North (1967), *Science and the Modern World* (New York: Free Press).

7

Wanderings in the Cosmic Garden

LISA ISHERWOOD

In 2008 I was invited to give another inaugural lecture and it seemed the ideal opportunity to implement plans that Erna and Michael Colebrook and I had hatched some years ago, for a garden based on their version of *Walking the Sacred Story* (Colebrook 2003). A story that asks us to consider ourselves in relation to the whole cosmos.

So why start theology in a cosmic garden? Well, didn't it all start in a garden for Christians? But as we know it has not been an unproblematic start when placed in the hands of theologians and centuries of dualistic thinking. The problem begins with the tree in Eden and the way that Christians have interpreted it and the events surrounding it. We have been slow to acknowledge the Babylonian background to the story and quick to read it through the lens of Platonic cosmology. The results have been disastrous. It has meant that the story is not seen as male polemic (see for example Long 1992 and Westermann 1974) against a much older and more ecologically sound goddess culture, a point that is much less veiled in the Babylonian tales than in the Hebrew copy. This has led to a disembodied male Word being viewed as the creator of all and the one who sets in place, as divine, the hierarchical ordering of nature ending with humans, the pinnacle of creation. The male, who is given the power of naming, is in fact the pinnacle. However, humans are commanded to subdue the earth (Heb. *kabas* = stamp down) and dominate it (Heb. *rada* = trampling). Man follows the disembodied voice but the woman prefers to explore and engage with the sensuous delights of her surroundings and to respond to the voices she hears within them. The result of this non-hierarchical and sensuous engagement with the world was, according to the storyteller, devastating, it brought about the fall of man! He could no longer be master, namer, of all he surveyed but was to be thrown from this rigid and controlled environment, this walled garden, paradise, into a place where the world would seem more real and uncertain.

Once the Babylonian background is understood the highly polemic nature of this material is crystal clear. Here is a story that wishes to advocate the absolute power of a hierarchical male god over the cosmic body of the mother goddess. This is of course not to be understood as a battle between divine beings but rather as a battle between ways of living in the world. Naomi Goldenberg, Carol Christ, Marija Gimbutas and others have highlighted for us that Goddess consciousness is creative and fertile, has an intensity of engagement, loves paradox, emerges from diversity, has relationality at its heart and embraces the immanence of the cosmic process. This way of being in the world sat at the heart of most of our human history with the above and beyond God being relatively young, emerging perhaps only about 5,000 years ago. It is the beginnings of this emergence that we see in the pages of Genesis, and the battle was eventually won, some would argue, through the lens of Platonic cosmology. Western culture was henceforth doomed to a dualistic understanding of the world and a struggle to subdue it. Under this scheme women and nature are placed at the bottom of the hierarchy of control and Christian salvation is later seen to lie in escape from both. The way we have read this story places us at odds with the world in which we perhaps now only half live and, I would wish to argue, has brought us to the uncomfortable point where we now find that we have exploited the planet to the edge of extinction, we have maimed more than half of humanity and we even find it difficult to live in our own skins, believing our real home is elsewhere and this discontent has made us victims of a genocidal economic system that has hold of us even though we created it.

And why wander? Well, theologians have not always walked, we have preferred to sit in ivory towers clothed in the comfort of elaborate metaphysics removed from the messy realities of life; and from this safe distance we have forgotten that theology based in Christian incarnation is an ever-changing reflection on action instead of a set of fixed abstract codifications that lend themselves to power and privilege. I have for some time argued that incarnational theology can never lend itself to certainty;

the God who abandoned the heavens in favour of enfleshed existence gave up the assurance of good/correct and perfect outcomes and instead embraced risk as central to the divine unfolding. In grounding theology in incarnation I am declaring for the God who we are told, in the Prologue of John's Gospel, pitched his tent among us. A tent, not a house; a moveable dwelling, one fit for the walk, one that expands and changes shape with the winds of change, best understood perhaps as the breath of the Spirit. It was this incarnation who became God in community/God in society/God in creation. The Gospels show us Jesus becoming the Messiah through walking with, being affected by, marginalized communities and individuals. Marcella Althaus-Reid (2005) believes that the life of Jesus presents us with a communitarian reading of rupture, that is, it challenges us to move beyond a nostalgic dwelling-place from where we remember past utopias or promised kingdoms and propels us into an ongoing process of imagination and creative engagement. It is not the task of theologians to heal the rupture that the divine incarnate made in the world we previously knew, rather it is our task to continue the discontinuity. It is this life and this walk that we need to take in the garden, one that embeds itself in the ecological/evolutionary process, itself a process of continual rupture, with eyes wide open and senses available for knowing. This is not a walk in search of perfect origins and the comfort of utopian endings, it is one that moves us out into ever-expanding life and so perhaps it is Eve who is our best companion as we walk.

But what kind of walk did I find myself in as a Welsh woman working in an English landscape? This land did not grow me, these skies did not call me to dream and wonder and there are no mountains to show me that the space between humans and the divine is one step into the mist. I realized very quickly that the kind of theology that this walk would open for me would include, but be more than, one based in the oneness of all creation; as I put my feet on this land I understood that such a view was in itself a potentially dangerous metanarrative. Having been working in theology that requires we each name ourselves, it would I realized be counterproductive to slide into a cosy form of universal belonging that may overlook deeply significant political considerations under the blanket of cosmic connections. So where could my own theological reflections start? Would this be a postcolonial theology from a Celtic perspective exposing the pervasive normality of constructed and co-opted space, an ecotheology focusing on the plight of the planet and calling for just systems of production that empower the marginalized both human and non-human? Yes, it could be both, but above all it is a body theology and this did take me a little by surprise. I want to put lived-in bodies back in the everyday story, back in the garden as sensuous inhabitants, not as those whose reality is told through the pages of Scripture and hierarchical thinking. It is Ada Maria Isasi Diaz who reminds us that radical change fails when we do not pay attention to the everyday and we create the everyday when we 'walk, when we dance, when we work and when we make love. Let us not forget the everyday is an element of liberation' (Isasi Diaz 2004, p. 92). In the everyday in the garden is where I want bodies to be, and I found myself wondering what an uninterrupted engagement with our enfleshed cosmic story would yield in theological orthopraxis.

I believe the full impact of quantum theory and the new cosmology on Christian theology has not yet been felt, but here are some musings.

As I have already mentioned, engaging with our enfleshed cosmic story moves us away from a search for perfect origins and back to beginnings. There is no place from which we were cast out but rather a place that grew us, that nurtured us and generously gave and gives us life. A cosmos that, as Matthew Fox says, has conspired for us or we would not be here – this is not to say it had blueprint human implanted from the start, but rather we are one of the outcomes of its constant and volatile shifting and changing. We are made of the stars and emanate from Tiamat's fiery womb – we could not be more embedded in the cosmos. Yet Christians still tend to build theology around the notion that our home is elsewhere, a place we once dwelt and have had re-bought for us by the redemptive death of Jesus. Engaging with the cosmic story then asks radical questions of this high Christology based in a story of perfect origins. Is there a way through – I believe there is. And strangely it is a journey back to beginnings! Edward Said reminds us that beginnings are always relative, contested and historical, whereas origins are absolute and power-laden. Beginnings then give the Christian theologian the chance to decolonize this space of origins in creation and the inevitable creator who sits apart and to challenge, as Catherine Keller puts it, 'the great supernatural surge of father power, a world appearing zap out of the void and mankind ruling the world in our manly creator's image' (Keller 2003, p. 6). We are thrown back to cosmic beginnings, to void and chaos and we are asked to make our theology from that ground. To understand who we are and who we might be from *tohu vabohu*, the depth veiled in darkness. Once we give agency to void and chaos there can be no creation out of nothing as our power-laden dualistic origin. Creation ceases to be a unilateral act and the theological vista is cosmic! The divine speech in the pages of Genesis is no longer understood as a command uttered by the Lord and warrior King who rules over creation, but as Keller tells us, 'let there be' is a whisper of desire, and what comes forth emanates from all there is rather than appearing from above and beyond. In this shift we also see the possibility for incarnation to be understood as the rule rather than exception of creation, because the whisper desires enfleshment (Keller 2003, p. 56). Keller certainly moves us significantly from creation out of nothing to a place where the divine is more humble and entices ever unfolding acts of becoming grounded in the chaos at the heart of the cosmos. However, she perhaps still leaves that gap between the divine and material order that the cosmic story itself seems to challenge – there is after all nothing outside the unfolding of the multiverse. But can Christian theology engage with the cosmic story in such a way that it too closes that gap?

It is this gap that secular theorists have no difficulty challenging. Val Plumwood, an eco-philosopher, is among those who insist that it is this gap that continues to harm both us and the planet. While we understand ourselves as something other than the rest of the created order we will inevitably see that as 'better' or 'higher' and this false consciousness leads to alienation and destruction. She is quick to point out to us the logical absurdity of such a position; monological relationships will eventually weaken the provider, the earth on which we rely. We need to move to dialogue between mutually recognizing and supporting agents or, as Thomas Berry puts it, we need to realize that we live in a communion of subjects rather than a collection of objects. Plumwood argues that removing agency from the cosmos, a technique we have so often used in our colonial history in relation to the discovery of 'new lands', makes it and all that lives in it an empty space, one that can be used for profit through the maximization of its development potential. She reminds us of the knock-on effect of this way of thinking. Nature is no longer viewed as a creator of our environment, and the land and those who depend most directly on it are relegated to the realm of 'Other'. They are back-grounded, which means that we deny our reliance on both the land and those who toil in it – we live as though they have no impact on our lives and as though we lived outside the biosphere.

Plumwood argues for a return to what she calls the 'heart of stone' in order to overcome the 'sado-dispassionate rationalism of scientific reduction'. This involves a re-enchantment of the realm designated as material, the rematerialization of spirit as speaking matter. She warns that this project should not slide into the world of the romantic and in order to guard against this it needs to be ever mindful of the spirit/matter dualism and resist it at every turn. Western culture has placed speaking matter in the rarefied world of fairy tale and legend, from where it cannot really impact on ethical or philosophical thinking, but it is this world that we need to foreground if we are to return intentionality and agency to matter. By journeying to the heart of stone we have to walk a different path, one that moves stone (the material world of nature) from the back-ground of consciousness to the foreground, from silent to speaking and from the ordinary to the extraordinary, to the wonderful and even to the sacred. This move is needed in order to challenge the false conscious-ness of the western world, so rooted in our Christian heritage, that tells us we live no longer in nature but in culture. Environmental philoso-phy is attempting this through stressing that attention must go 'all the way down', or as Deborah Bird Rose puts it, 'Nothing is nothing.' This move, Plumwood claims, opens the door to a wide range of interspecies dialogues, drama and projects that would otherwise be unimaginable, which free us to rewrite the earth as sacred, earth exploration as pilgrim-age and earth knowledge as revelation. Hard to imagine after centuries of thinking which has confined us to another realm. Where Plumwood and I agree most heartily, is that in order for this way of thinking to be honest it has to be grounded in cultural practices that reinscribe the material with everyday wonder, and this includes the human body and material labour. The political and economic implications of this I think are quite clear. What impact would such thinking have on logging companies, chemical companies and the bodies of those who labour to make our £2.50 T-shirts?

But can Christian theologians truly address the intentionality and re-enchantment of nature in their story? After all, we have a story of speaking snakes and beckoning trees as a cautionary tale in our beginnings. And so we will require a rethink of beginnings, and flowing from that a reimagining of what we understand by redemptive activity. We are not starting from scratch here as we have foremothers in theology who have helped us begin this painful but liberating process. Mary Grey has for example shown us how redemption understood as at-one-ment brings us into a new and exciting world of co-creation and becoming. She argues that if relationality is at the heart of reality then it is at the heart of the creative redemptive process. So entering more deeply into this reality is the kind of 'redemptive spirituality' needed to transform the world. Sin is going against this relational grain. Very early on in our feminist theological journey Mary encouraged us to realize that liberation, while including justice, needed to engage at another level if it was to be seen as redemptive. For her a 'passion for justice' increases our participation in the divine creative ground of our existence – creation and redemption go hand in hand.

I, rather predictably, have total confidence that radical incarnation, that is taking incarnation seriously without the comfort of metaphysics and delayed parousias, is the key to our living this profound reality. Believing that the God Christians speak about did indeed leave the heavens and that the human and the divine dwell in one flesh, ours as well as Christ's. This is an understanding of incarnation based in empowerment and the shared heritage of *dunamis*, that raw energy which is our birthright, the energy that attracts us to the world and those in it. This is the concept spoken of by Jesus in the Gospels when he rejects 'authority over' and urges those who come after him to claim their empowerment to live in vulnerability, mutuality and relationality. In naming those who were around him as friends he was declaring that this *dunamis* lived in all and increased in the free sharing between equals. Joan Casanas also reminds us that those who made an opening in reality as Jesus did want others to make it bigger, in other words the power we see in the life of Jesus is the power we are asked to embrace in order to continue the bursting forth of the divine in the everyday.

The raw dynamic energy that exists between and within us is, according to a feminist reading of Mark's Gospel, the power of incarnation – it can also be seen as the cosmic explosion that still resonates through the universe, that raw dynamism that empowers all that lives. In calling it divine we have perhaps enabled ourselves to shape our understanding of who we are and how we should live, but we also run the risk of disempowering its wild and challenging core by attempting to capture it in systems and dogmas. However, incarnation, as the Christian story illustrates, is a risky business because it throws us into any number of possibilities. It seems then that risk and potentiality go hand in hand in the cosmic story and in radical incarnation.

Those of us who have reflected on *dunamis* and erotic Christology and the power of godding, that is the way we bring one another forth through vulnerable and mutual relationality, have for the most part reflected on how this impacts on humans and their relationships. Carter Heyward has taken this further by acknowledging that this power infuses the whole of creation and as such invites us into mutually empowering and vulnerable relationships with all that exists. When her article 'The Horse as Priest' first appeared, I am sure some of us thought that she had gone too far. Here she was an Episcopalian priest suggesting that a horse performed the same eucharistic function as she did. For Heyward the argument was a logical one, if God is the wellspring of all, if the *dunamis* that enlivens us is the stuff of all life, then a horse can be the one who helps us in our godding and opens us to sacred energy. And horseriding, like the Eucharist, 'can be an occasion of thanksgiving in which creatures and our divine life are united through mutual participation in the holiest of sacrifices – God's giving up of control in order to be with us'. She says that therapeutic riding demonstrates our capacity 'to give ourselves over to one another and other creatures to go together in right, more fully mutual, relationship, in which we move together, more nearly as one, creatures united' (Heyward 2002, pp. 92–5). The sacredness of this action is the sharing, in this case across species – giving an agency to the non-human that Plumwood would applaud. Here is a Christology that is not simply anthropocentric and power-laden, it is a truly liberating narrative that opens us to life in abundance. In my view, it creatively and empoweringly collapses dualisms and finds a way for Christian theology to move with the cosmic unfolding. It illuminates for me a saying of the Christian mystics, which is, 'that which you are looking at is looking back' – and in this case not from above and beyond but as an active and shaping agent embedded within all that is.

Liz Stuart has so often warned me of the dangers of abandoning metaphysics and seeing this realm as the one that gives us the critical distance to create alternative reality. I have always resisted her caution, understanding our birthright of *dunamis* to be the spur for our dreams and our utopian visions. With the new challenge of quantum theory I am ever more aware that we have a much larger and more complex material vista, now re-enchanted, in which to dream and be visionaries. Our Christian stories remain the spur because as Graham Ward shows us, we have within them transformation through a wide range of the material world, from flesh and blood to bread and wine and from human to cosmic spirit – this is a truly complex and enchanted vista. I believe we have, however, narrowed the vision of these stories through a tight-knit working of metaphysics, one that removes their power to transform. We have stopped telling the stories as though they spoke of our birthright and have given them away by interpreting them as tales of hero gods and their power to save us through *their* magical powers and actions. We and the whole of the cosmos are disempowered. Quantum theory gives us a way to look again at these stories of material transformation, and radical incarnation empowers us in the retelling. We are perhaps able to see that the animate and inanimate are all agents in the cosmos and all engaged in redemptive transformation. Christianity does have within it a way to overcome the old dualisms and re-enchant the world, it does not have to cling to the Christ of imperial absolutes who has overcome the earth, it can instead embrace the erotic divine that infuses it.

I think we begin to realize that truly putting bodies back in the garden and allowing their sensuous engagement does not come without its challenges!! But there are more!! If we have the possibility of a Christology that enables us to live in the world rather than imagining that our true home is elsewhere, then we have to keep asking what it means to be alive and embedded in the cosmic story – and, if we are to be authentic, we have to ask what impact this has on the theology we have created so far.

We are creatures made from the stuff of the universe, our brains carry remnants of ancient mammalian structures, every fibre of our being is related to ancient bacteria and our ancestors are the stars. We are members of a symbiotic universe in which nothing stands alone, and so in short we are creatures of belonging and relationality. Our alienation then from this process is entirely a fiction. But what kind of belonging is this; it is belonging to creatively interacting systems, a network of interplay that moves always towards novelty woven from instability and an ever-moving universe. Not the kind of belonging that Christian theology has been used to with its Alpha and Omega point, the unchanging God, the same yesterday and tomorrow. Indeed the One who remains ever constant for our sakes seems rather at odds with a universe that changes and does not have our interests at heart at all – that is to say it is not here for us, it exists for its own growth and becoming. Gaia goes on living and her species come and go – this rather turns on its head the notion that we have a special place in creation and are here to subdue the earth; it becomes crystal clear that the earth can trample us in an instant and that we more complex creatures are utterly dependent on what we regard as the lowest. Do we, then, have to come down on one side or the other here – declare for the cosmic or the traditional Christian story? Or does radical incarnation give us another way of looking? It certainly decentres the anthropocentrism that makes us see the world as here for us, and it assures us that we have as our birthright the embodied knowing to live with change, paradox and constant becoming. Furthermore, to do this with sisterly regard for everything on the planet. Can we argue that it is *dunamis* that propels us and the universe towards greater complexity, creativity and becoming, towards ever new possibilities? I think we can certainly say that a Christology underpinned by this notion allows us to sit easier with the realities of the cosmic story.

The Christian story tells us that we are people of promise. What can that mean if our privileged position in creation is not that promise nor is there an escape to a real and glorious life elsewhere? What then does this language mean? Diarmuid O'Murchu (2004, p. 29) believes an answer lies in not asking it as an anthropocentric question. Promise should be understood as that which we give to honour and promote creation's own wishes, which are to enable a meaningful future to all creatures. It is our promise to come home to the cosmos. In his words, feminist theologians will hear Nelle Morton, who told us that our journey as women was a journey home – interestingly in coming home to the cosmos we also come home to millions of women whose relationship with nature is direct and harsh. Our industrialized world has widened the gap between rich and poor, and women bear the brunt of this since they and their children make up the largest number of the poor. Vandana Shiva has highlighted for us how economic growth has become another form of colonialism that drains the resources from those who need them the most. Many women are actually being removed from the means of growing food through such activities as cash-cropping. This simply highlights how productivity for survival is very different from productivity for the capitalist market. Shiva claims that the connection between women and the earth needs to be honoured and used as a way of critiquing the dominant approach to both. In our coming home to the cosmos we are not propelled into some safe and fluffy existence but rather into ongoing political struggles for economic justice.

Of course in one sense the promise that Christians may be speaking about is the abundance of life all around us – which as we see we misuse. The cosmos itself is one of outpouring generosity and gift for no reason but the giving. As John F. Haught (in O'Murchu 2004, p. 31) explains, there are three persistent elements in cosmic evolution: gratuity, extravagance and surprise. This he believes suggests that we should move to a more humble and receptive mode of being, accepting all as gift and changing our way of living accordingly. When God was understood as

LISA ISHERWOOD

Mother there was less of a problem accepting this fundamental aspect of existence, but under the patriarchal Father God we have rather confused the issues and created a world that cannot possibly sustain us. The body of the Mother was abundant and fertile, nurturing her children with her multitude of gifts; the gift of the Father God of Christianity was to give the life of his son for the forgiveness of our sins. Certainly an abundant gift but one with a price tag. Of course I am aware that there are many ways to interpret this story and not all need to lead to the worst excesses of substitution atonement, but it is worth exploring where this *has* taken us.

Marion Grau, in her book *On Divine Economy: Refinancing Redemption*, lays before us the link between the plan of creation, the divine economy of salvation and modern economic systems. She skilfully shows how modern *homo economicus* (Grau 2004, p. 89) is a variant of the hysterical male who believes scarcity of goods and scarcity of salvation to be at the heart of life. This is the male who has evolved from a mindset where personal salvation is bought in blood and therefore believes that all interactions are based in the same system of debt and repayment; this is the male who walks through the pages of much patristic theology and some contemporary right-wing theology. Grau is of course not the first to point out the close relationship between a debt economy of salvation and a genocidal economic system; Weber highlighted the links between Protestantism and capitalism many years ago. The generous and extravagant outpouring of the cosmos somewhat challenges this view of scarcity and personal redemption and offers challenges to those who would wish to wall-in their God in this way or conduct their economic lives in this way. There seems to be a call here for generosity and hospitality in theology and economics on a scale that we find hard to even imagine. Of course, I cannot be allowed to skip the thorny question of: if there is no personal salvation what happens to reward in heaven? The extravagant life in abundance that the cosmos offers to all does away with a select heaven for the faithful, but it also offers everlasting recycling on a grand scale – each atom of you has been here since the beginning and will be here forever. Is this a comfort – well, the universe is not here to comfort you!

So why would it be necessary to lead a good life if the notion of reward was removed. In part that has been answered by Plumwood's analysis of the irrationality of disregarding the earth that sustains us – if we want to remain as a species we need a planet. Does this then mean developing some perfect life based on cosmic principles rather than the laws of the father? Of course the idea of perfect is itself a human construction. The cosmos did not emerge from Platonic forms but rather from tehomic chaos; there was no blueprint, there is no blueprint, there is instead glorious outpourings of surprise and novelty. Christian theology has been so used to neat packages of divinely laid out intentions that this comes as something of a surprise. Keller offers a proposition for a te-homic ethic and it is this – that we bear with the chaos, neither liking it nor fostering it but recognizing that *there* is the unformed future (Keller 2003, p. 29). This unformed future is made up of repetition, but from very early in cosmic development this repetition always adds something new, in every repetition is a transgression, our bodies and that of the cosmos are in constant flux; as they regenerate they change, they are in essence transgressive. It seems little less than perverse to insert an unchanging God with a worked-out plan into that cosmic picture. If we abandon ourselves to the cosmic, and I would argue incarnational, pro-cess, we may find that we do not need the unchanging rock-like father protector of moral perfection in order to lead holy lives. I suspect we will not disintegrate into moral decline but rather begin to embrace our responsibility for the unformed future we face and slowly understand that we are as Mary Grey says co-creators and co-redeemers; here and now this is the reality of our cosmogenesis. We will of course have to learn to sit easy with more commitment and connection and less di-vinely orchestrated destiny.

Some may argue that God disappears in this picture of the universe; after all what need is there of such a figure if we are all children of the Big Bang and beyond? It may be true that the realist, transcendent and patriarchal arguments for God are weakened, but the biblical divine known as Sophia/Wisdom emerges more clearly on our ever-unfolding and expanding canvas. She is the aspect of the divine found in many parts of biblical literature, and always we are told that her most important feature is relationality. She is the one who weaves the threads of relationality among humans and the rest of the created order. Asphodel Long has placed her before us in all her challenging glory in her wonderful book *In a Chariot Drawn by Lions*, and Elisabeth Schüssler Fiorenza and Elizabeth Johnson both make the case that Jesus was a prophet of Sophia. That is beyond the scope of this essay. What is not, is the affirmation that the Bible holds other alternatives than the dominating God who holds all power to himself and is concerned with lifting us beyond the world to a place of metaphysical safety. There is in our tradition an invitation to counter-cultural living, to new ways of being beyond power and control and to embedding in the world as our emotional, physical and spiritual home. I believe this tradition is grounded in Sophia/Lady Wisdom, who as Grey says 'shouts epiphanies of connection in a broken world' and comes through, I believe, in the orthopraxis of radical incarnation.

Of course embedding ourselves in the universe as spiritual home is pitching our tent on earthquakes and seismic shifts. Cosmology shows us that new reality all emerges from 'explosive volatile exuberance' (David Toolan, quoted in O'Murchu 2004, p. 85) which offers us big dreams as well as dangers and risks. However, I have argued elsewhere that incarnation itself signals to us such uncertain and ever-changing ground and invites us to continue the discontinuity of cosmic ruptures. To commit to flesh is to commit to change and risk, but it is also to dream big. I urge us all to have the courage to dream big, to embrace the fire inside us which is the literal ground of our being, the *dunamis* of creation that resonates through our bodies and the cosmos, to rejoice in making theology on seismic shifts as the only authentic way to embody the life of the divine.

In all this we are asked to face the dark and to take it seriously. Our cosmogenesis is ultimately in the great darkness, the nothingness. We find this perhaps the hardest to face, seeing it as destruction, but actually in our story it is a place/non-place of creative possibility. Christian theology has had no place for the dark in its picture of God, and of course Christ is the light of the world that dispels darkness. It is a well-rehearsed argument how this dualistic split of dark and light has led to the oppression of dark people and dark continents, and this understanding is increasingly entering discourses about projections and repressions of the shadow from and within our own psyches. In short then it can be argued that by banishing something as fundamental to our existence as the dark from our theological frame we have done and do damage to ourselves, others and the planet. There is a great deal of scope for work in this area and perhaps the existence of black holes as one of the most creative realities of our universe will enable Christian theologians to embrace the dark not as negative but as the very substance of our creative/destructive outpouring as our sister thealogians have done.

Miriam McGillis OP, co-founder of Genesis Farm, tells us

We are at a moment where there are no guarantees as to the Earth's future. It is a question of our own critical choices. And I think what we are deeply in need of is a transforming vision . . . a vision that opens the future to hope. (Quoted in E. and M. Colebrook, Spring Equinox Liturgy, 2006)

For this hope to be radically transforming I believe we need our feet on the earth and our hands in the soil as we move in vulnerable solidarity into the divine unfolding together, animal, mineral, animate and inanimate, together in the mutual embrace of fearful/awesome becoming.

References

Althaus-Reid, Marcella (2005), *From Feminist Theology to Indecent Theology* (London: SCM Press).

Colebrook, Michael (2003), *Walking the Sacred Story: A New Ritual for Celebrating the Universe*, Green Spirit Pamphlet (Association for Creation Spirituality).

Grau, Marion (2004), *On Divine Economy: Refinancing Redemption* (London: T&T Clark).

Heyward, Carter (2002), *God in the Balance: Christian Spirituality in Times of Terror* (Cleveland, OH: Pilgrim Press).

Isasi Diaz, Ada Maria (2004), *Mujerista Theology* (Maryknoll: Orbis).

Keller, Catherine (2003), *Face of the Deep: A Theology of Becoming* (London: Routledge).

Long, Asphodel (1992), *In a Chariot Drawn by Lions: The Search for the Female in the Deity* (London, Women's Press).

O'Murchu, Diarmuid (2004), *Evolutionary Faith* (Maryknoll: Orbis).

Westermann, Claus (1974), *Creation* (London: SPCK).

8

How to Relate in a Quantum Universe!

DIARMUID O'MURCHU

> The radical relationality of the Gospel summons has its own backup in the revelatory intensity of globo-electric communications processes. GloboChrist is no longer simply local . . . Forget about the local church as the paradigm of the Christian community. The principle of two or three gathering together still holds firm. But the gathering is simply the high velocity acceleration of the force field of radical relationality. It ceases to be anchored merely in either the charismatic or structural authority of the religious leader, the preacher or the board of elders. It emerges as a set of passionate one-to-one, or two-on-one micro-responses to the revelatory character of the Christian message in its complete kinaesthetic setting, and to its incarnation in the relational matrix of marriages, families, and friends.
>
> (Raschke 2008, p. 121)

As a social scientist I wish to expand the relational vision which Carl Raschke outlines in the above quote; more importantly, I want to highlight the rich complex web – often metaphorically described as *a dance* – that underpins this vision. It is not simply a human phenomenon, nor exclusively Christian, as Raschke seems to intimate. It embraces every organic creature within the planetary web of life and, consequently, it affirms the cosmic interdependence initially highlighted by *Quantum Theory* almost 100 years ago, and confirmed in recent decades in a field of study known as *The New Cosmology*.

When theology embraces this new worldview, the theological endeavour itself takes something of a quantum leap. *Theology* in its conventional setting tends to be described as the science of God's revelatory encounter with humans. Saint Anselm's classic definition of *faith seeking understanding* implies that the human response (seeking understanding) also belongs to the theological endeavour. God's *logos*, often portrayed as a divine patriarchal imperative, which humans either accept or reject, is better understood today as God's *dia-logos*. Within the revelation is an invitation, not merely to dialogue, but to a *relational encounter* far beyond the anthropocentric context we have long taken to be normative.

The anthropocentric tenor of that encounter, often articulated in deceptively intimate language of person-to-person, requires serious re-evaluation. *Person* is conceptualized in the inherited Aristotelian tradition as the self-contained individual, superior to, and separate from, every other organism in creation. This understanding of personhood is proving to be highly destructive, even for humans themselves.

The largely unexamined claim of a personal relationship with God (or with Jesus) also embodies some dangerous projections. Contrary to the spiritual call to be moulded in the image and likeness of God, a great deal of popular religion, and several trends in Christian theology, indulge in creating God in *our* image and likeness. Indeed, the Christological doctrines of Nicaea and Chalcedon embrace quite uncritically the popular Aristotelian definition of what constitutes a human person.

Relationality: a new paradigm

The Age of Enlightenment reinforced a culture of rational consciousness, hierarchical relations and cultural criteria favouring individual difference and isolated distinctiveness. Although the Enlightenment was largely a European development, colonizers took its key values of domination and control to many parts of the planet. Alternative lifestyles, based on egalitarianism and earth-centred values, were either suppressed or destroyed. Western civilization, advocating might is right, became the leading paradigm.

With the dawn of the twentieth century, another paradigm came to the fore. Already in the 1920s scientists were challenging the monopoly of classical science and the mechanistic metaphors on which it flourished. In the wake of the Second World War, the United Nations came to birth, marking the onset of a new international endeavour which in our time translates into globalization with its complex mixture of exploitation and progress. Meanwhile the cultural shifts of the 1960s – a new chaotic and creative destabilizing in several spheres of life – forged new alliances between previously envious or conflicting ideologies. Feminism won worldwide recognition, and our interdependence within the ecological web of life struck home with a clarity and conviction formerly unknown.

Words like *interdependence*, *conviviality*, *mutuality*, *connectivity*, *relationality* entered the cultural dialogue, and various fields of study and research began to adopt an interdisciplinary sense of direction. Theology has already made a substantial contribution to this new interface – via feminism, liberation praxis, multi-faith outreach, dialogue with science, and so on – although largely unrecognized or accepted by formal churches. What I wish to highlight in the remaining part of this essay are some of the distinctive features contributing to this new theological ferment.

The quantum worldview

Everybody in the scientific community acknowledges and affirms the practical usefulness of quantum physics (popularly known as *quantum mechanics*). For many the theory is baffling, but in practical terms it works, and contributes significantly to the several aspects of our technological and electronic empowerment. Philosophically and theoretically, several scientists exhibit a baffling sense of ambiguity around Quantum Theory. One day they hope – and believe – that it will be subjected to the objective criteria of the classical worldview. Then, and only then, will the scientist feel in control of what is happening in the world.

Philosophically, Quantum Theory flourishes on the principle that *the whole is greater than the sum of the parts*. And that greater whole is neither quantifiable nor capable of being humanly manipulated. It is a process rather than a product; it thrives on collaborative endeavour rather than on conflictual competition. It evolves laterally rather than through linear progression; and the entire process flourishes through the dynamic interrelating of its constituent elements rather than merely the interpretative Darwinian lenses of violent and adversarial conflict (more in Chown 2007; Rosenblum and Kuttner 2007).

Cosmology, rather than formal science, embraces this new worldview. Over the past 2,000 years, religion tended to dictate our human understanding of cosmic creation. Despite the cosmogonic elegance of Hinduism (cf. Panikkar 1994) and Taoism (cf. Armstrong 2006), the innate sacredness of creation perceived by many indigenous peoples, or the cosmic vision of Saint Francis and several Christian mystics, religion tended to espouse an anti-creation spirituality, expressed in phrases such as: *flee the world, abandon the world, turn your back on the world*. Few were left in any doubt that this world was a vale of tears in which humans were condemned to abide until they could escape to the everlasting fulfilment of the world beyond.

That petrified, disempowering cosmology eventually began to lose its grip in the 1960s. Interestingly, the alternative worldview began to unfold from those labelled as the great enemies of religion, namely, scientists and cosmologists. It came to be known as the New Cosmology (Swimme and Berry 1992; Primack and Abrams 2006; Dowd 2007).

In fact, it is not new at all. The New Cosmology seeks to reclaim the long-lost, suppressed values and perceptions known to our ancient ancestors over many millennia, promoted by several indigenous peoples today, and warmly embraced by Christian mystics, especially in the Middle Ages. Some of the key features of this new worldview include:

(a) Creation is viewed as a process rather than a series of products. Swimme and Berry (1992) describe the tripartite dynamics as those of *differentiation, autopoiesis and communion*. Everything in creation has a distinctive identity (differentiation); everything is characterized by a quality of 'within-ness' which confers meaning – otherwise known as the capacity for self-organization (*autopoiesis*); and all evolutionary processes flow in the direction of greater communion. The differentiation and *autopoiesis* (interiority) serve the development of communion (that is relationality) throughout the entire spectrum of cosmic and earthly creation.

(b) Michael Dowd (2007) describes five directions in which creation's process unceasingly flows. He names them as *diversity, complexity, awareness, speed of change, intimacy with itself*. Three of these features are self-explanatory: diversity, complexity and speed of change. Awareness describes the controversial sense of innate intelligence which some theorists attribute to creation at large, a type of cosmic immunity system, which Swimme and Berry (1992) include in their understanding of *autopoiesis*. Dowd's fifth direction, *intimacy with itself* refers not merely to the propensity for relatedness; it also re-echoes the biblical notion that love for God and other are postulated on a certain quality of love for self.

(c) I'd like to add four other features not enumerated above, and often understated in several texts relating to the New Cosmology:

- *Story*: Beyond the facts, and scientific details, lies a story without which we cannot hope to capture the grandeur and elegance of cosmic evolution (cf. Cannato 2006). Hence, the popularity of myths-of-origin throughout the ages.

- *Aliveness:* Biologists engage in an ongoing discernment on what precisely constitutes life, and how precisely do we define it. That which comprises the organic modality is assumed to be superior to all other forms. According to the New Cosmology, the essence of life belongs first and foremost to the cosmic life-conferring processes, from which all other life forms, including the human, are derived. This bold claim has enormous implications for every field of learning, including theology.

- *Paradox:* Creation thrives on an unceasing cycle of creation-and-destruction, frequently named as the cycle of birth–death–rebirth. This I consider to be one of the most profound, and least understood, dynamics of the New Cosmic Story. Without earthquakes we cannot have a viable earth. Without death, new breakthroughs are not possible. Death is not the consequence of sin (cf. Romans 6.23), but an essential, organic ingredient of life. And insofar as theology claims God to be the source and sustenance of all that is, we must therefore attribute the destruction and death to that same divine source – which opens several complex questions for theodicy, a subject beyond the remit of this essay.

- *Spirit-endowment*: All energy is endowed with the power of living spirit, infused by what theology calls the Holy Spirit of God. Several contemporary works in pneumatology embrace this expanded understanding (Edwards 2004; Wallace 2005). All energy is endowed with meaning. Energy is not random, as science claims; in fact it flows in patterns (fields), and culminates in processes and structures which express an underlying capacity for order, harmony and relationship – including the complexities of the paradox I described briefly above.

In more recent times, the study of *epigenetics* provides valuable confirmation of the quantum worldview. Every cell in the human body displays interactive dynamics that, on the one hand, verify the truths of quantum physics, while also illustrating its holistic claims. The cell is an open system – according to Quantum Theory, everything in creation is an open system – with the porous membrane serving as a facilitating channel through which energy is exchanged with the wider environment. The power of the cell to empower is not based merely on the genetic powerhouse (the conventional view), but rather on the interactive relational dynamics through which energy flows, and for this process the membrane is the crucial mechanism. One of the leading theorists, Bruce Lipton (2005, pp. 76, 86) describes it thus:

The true secret of life lies in understanding the elegantly simple biological mechanisms of the magical membrane – the mechanisms by which your body translates environmental signals into behaviour . . . In contrast to conventional wisdom, genes do not control their own activity. Instead it is the membrane's effector proteins, operating in response to environmental signals picked up by the membrane's receptors, which *control* the 'reading' of the genes so that worn out proteins can be replaced, or new proteins can be created.

Enter symbiogenesis

The foregoing examples illuminate a recurring logic, boldly articulated by the microbiologist Lynn Margulis. Most of her professional life has been devoted to the study of bacteria, those micro-organisms upon which the entire spectrum of organic life is founded. She adopted the term *symbiogenesis* from the Russian inventor Konstantine Merezhovsky (1855–1921), referring to the formation of new organs and organisms through symbiotic mergers. Margulis (1998, pp. 38ff.) considers this collaborative endeavour to be a fundamental fact of evolution.

Bacteria thrive on co-operation, not on competition. Their dynamic interactivity, even when it involves extinction and elimination, nonetheless witnesses to a thriving communal enterprise, not merely to enhance survival and growth, but to advance their generic activity to the advantage of all other life-forms, humans included.

Describing the research of Lynn Margulis, Nick Lane (2005, p. 196), writes:

> Given the reality of food shortages in bacterial ecosystems, bacteria gain more by living from each other's excrement than they do by fighting over the same raw materials. If one bacterium lives by fermenting glucose to form lactic acid, then there is scope for another to live by oxidizing the waste lactic acid of carbon dioxide; and for another to convert the carbon dioxide into methane; and another to oxide the methane, and so on. Bacteria live by endless recycling, which is best achieved via cooperative networks.

This co-operative strain, innate to the very foundations of organic life, manifests throughout the entire spectrum of creaturely expression. Val Plumwood (2002), in a splendid study, calls to task our excessive rationalistic conditioning through which we both ignore and undermine the relational patterns that adorn our ecological environments. Jane Goodall (2001), Frans de Waal (2005) and Margaret Power (2008) explore its significance in primate and animal behaviour. Sarah Blaffer Hrdy (2009) unearths some of its primal expression in human infant care. John Stewart

(2000) reviews its philosophical foundations in an intriguing study that incorporates legitimate self-interest into the service and development of co-operative behaviour. Remarkably similar to the Christian claim that we cannot love God without first loving our neighbour, which we can only do genuinely in tandem with a true sense of love for oneself.

Despite this substantial body of research, the academic world still favours the rather slanted – and oft misrepresented Darwinian – view based on the survival of the fittest through competition and violence. The New Cosmology in no way seeks to deny the foundational paradox of creation-and-destruction, evidenced throughout the cosmos and operative in all its constituent parts. But the paradox serves a greater whole, namely the maintenance and embellishment of the relational web within which everything emerges, grows and thrives.

Relationality is the primary datum. Nothing makes sense in isolation. Co-operation and collaboration procure the elegance and progress of evolution. Connection and interdependence are inscribed in every domain of creation. Humans are challenged into deeper relationality not merely because it guarantees a more sane and humane world, but rather because it is the collective inheritance for every organism that inhabits planet earth. Relating is the universal blueprint.

Theological implications

These are fertile insights for theological discernment, yet, to date they have received scant attention among theologians. The dualism of the sacred v. the secular seems to inhibit theologians from exploring this enlarged, multi-disciplinary context. There also seems to be a reluctance to take on the inherent richness of the theological tradition itself. For instance, all the religions, in one way or other, embrace the notion of God's unconditional love, yet in practice persist in laying down conditions undermining the very concept that revolutionizes relationality as a core religious value.

Gordon D. Kaufman (2006) urges us to adopt creativity as a foundational metaphor through which the divine life-force engages our world.

God forever co-creates with the novel breakthroughs of cosmic evolution. Creativity is a divine prerogative that informs all forms of divine relationship with the creaturely creation. Humans are invited and challenged to embrace that same relational dynamic, and co-create with the Holy One to bring about a world of greater love and justice for all.

The divine creativity co-creates gratuitously in pure love. Creation is programmed to flourish in and through the power of love. It knows no other trajectory. That mysterious life-force that begets all possibility and sustains everything in being adopts one outstanding orientation: awakening new life in the relational power of unconditional love.

Several theological developments of recent decades adumbrate this enlarged paradigm of divine creativity. I'll briefly outline two strands which deserve to be more widely known. First, I'll address the awakening sense of the role of the Holy Spirit, and second, the revamped theology of the Trinity for our time.

The spirit who blows . . .

Indigenous peoples all over the planet adopt a theodicy that has received little attention, yet may be one of the richest resources for theological discernment at our disposal today. For first nations' peoples, their primary understanding of God is that of *The Great Spirit*, a primal, intuitive insight with far-reaching ramifications for theology and spirituality alike.

According to this ancient perception God is not a person, as conventionally understood. God is a Spirit-force which inebriates and infuses everything in creation, human beings included. Miriam Therese Winter (2009, pp. 122ff.) goes so far as to align the seven gifts of the Holy Spirit with the key features of quantum physics: *relativity, uncertainty, probability, complementarity, non-locality, synchronicity, change*. The Spirit is gift not merely to humans, but to every force adorning the tapestry of creation.

The Great Spirit stirs in the air, blows in the wind, radiates in sunlight and illuminates in stars. The Spirit howls in the storms, feels the pain of creation's destruction, yet co-creates through the complexities which constitute the universal web of life. The Spirit is neither indifferent nor capricious, but engaged and engaging in every energy-flow of creation's unfolding evolution (cf. Edwards 2004; Johnson 2008; Wallace 2005).

The Spirit is personal, but more significantly, trans-personal. She embraces everything that constitutes human sacredness and uniqueness, yet stretches human yearning in the direction of planetary and cosmic wholeness.

The Great Spirit inspires the cosmic flow of universal energy, of which everything in creation is an external manifestation. Energy is the core ingredient of universal life. It is the foundational 'material' upon which all form is postulated. Some scientists refer to it as the *akashic field* (Laszlo 2007), others call it the fifth force, and others, the zero-point of pure possibility (Cole 2001).

This new theological horizon begins with what may seem a rather innocuous question: 'What energizes the energy that gives foundation to everything in creation?' The scientist does not wish to answer – it means an encounter with metaphysics which might dilute scientific objectivity. The theologian may be in an even deeper quandary, with the accusation of pantheism looming in the background. Theologically and spiritually, we cannot avoid the response: it is the *Holy Spirit of God* who animates and sustains the vibrant energy of universal life. Disciplinary boundaries break down; interdisciplinary discernment becomes the only credible option.

Clearly, this is not the Holy Spirit of conventional Christian theology. It certainly has a lot in common with the spirit that broods over the chaos of early creation (Genesis 1.2), but not with the conferring in a greater fullness at the first Pentecost, about 2,000 years ago. The Great Spirit cannot be simply envisaged as the third 'person' in a linear progression from creator Father, through redeeming Son, who together relegate the Spirit into third place. No, *the Spirit comes first*, the foundational empowering source of all life and possibility. Even St Paul seems to agree in declaring that Jesus was raised from the dead in the power of the Spirit.

Individual baptism will also need to be reconsidered. According to popular understanding, the Holy Spirit is not formally conferred until the moment of baptismal initiation. Contradictions begin to pile up at this stage. What energizes the new life in the first place? What energizes the loving procreative interaction through which each person is begotten in the first place? Are we in danger of compromising the Spirit's prodigious creativity to accommodate the questionable theory of a fundamental flaw (original sin)?

Postulating the Spirit as the foundational inspiration of cosmic creation requires us to revise how we understand energy itself. Science has long considered energy to be essentially random – until channelled into useful means whereby it serves utilitarian purposes. However, since the late nineteenth century, scientists have known *energetic fields*, configurations of energy that engage our every connection with the creative universe. The four main fields are known as gravity, electro-magnetism, the weak and strong forces. Several other fields impinge more directly on our human lives, but have not been extensively studied. These include the human aura, one of an estimated seven fields that constellate in and around the human body (Brennan 1988). Without these fields, human life as we know it would neither exist nor flourish.

Fields are best understood as energy-patterns, reminding us that the cosmic energy flow is not random, but manifests in rhythmical patterns, thus illuminating the tendency towards order and structure in the universe.[1] One hears echoes of purpose in the background, but this might be a case of humans rushing in where angels dare not tread! However, we must venture to suggest that *these energy patterns are replete with relational potential*. The web of life is a complex relational matrix. It flourishes through relationality, which in turn is what empowers every living organism to interact, grow and flourish.

In 1972, the German theologian Wolfhart Pannenberg suggested that we view the workings of the Holy Spirit as somehow akin to the scientific notion of a force-field (cf. Pannenberg 1993). Few theologians responded at that time. In our contemporary multidisciplinary culture, Pannenberg's seminal insight enjoys a wider acceptance. In fact, the emerging pneumatology of our time not merely incorporates field theory, but envisions

---

1 Postulating a foundational sense of order in the universe should not be interpreted as an automatic endorsement of Intelligent Design. For a comprehensive overview, see John F. Haught (2006).

the Holy Spirit as the primordial inspiration of all fields (as in Wallace 2005). In this regard we touch into the deeper unity tantalizing scientific research for several years, leading to such groundbreaking ideas as David Bohm's implicate order and the Bose-Einstein condensates popularized by Herbert Frohlich of Liverpool University in the UK.

The conventional theologian and the average reader of these pages is likely to feel alarmed by the impersonal tenor of these ideas. Echoes of dualistic neatness still seem to haunt us: any absence of the personal flavour evokes an allegation of being impersonal. As indicated earlier, the transpersonal dynamic is what helps us through this dilemma. Persons like all other creatures in the relational web of life can only grow and flourish through relationality (cf. Zohar 1991). We are at all times the sum of our relationships and that is what confers our identity as persons. And the sustaining relational web incorporates all the creatures with which we share God's creation. The Spirit who animates and sustains is also the one who holds us as one, thriving on our mutual interdependence.

Trinitarian configurations

As a child, I recall trying to figure out how three could fit into one; as a theology student I realized I could not figure it out. As an adult preacher and teacher, I avoided the subject as much as possible – until I read Catherine LaCugna's classic work *God for Us* (LaCugna 1991). It profoundly changed my understanding of the Trinity; moreover, it alerted me to a significant shift in those writing about the Trinity after 1980. The focus had shifted from the highly metaphysical constructs of Nicaea, and from the catechetical mathematical quagmires that ensued, to a sense of a relational God depicted in a dogma that should be understood in a very different light.

My background in the social sciences proved immensely helpful in re-visioning this material. Anthropologically, I knew that our ancient ancestors had grappled with questions of spiritual meaning long before formal religion ever evolved. Several ancient artefacts, from the Ice Age epoch, point us towards a God who relates intimately and awesomely. I began to intuit that the ancient experience of a God who relates intimately is imprinted in human consciousness across several thousands of years, eventually culminating in a doctrine of the Trinity, parallels for which can be detected in every major religion we know today.[2]

Against this background, we can understand the doctrine of the Trinity as a human attempt to formalize an intuitive insight that evolved over several millennia. The experience led to the dogma; intuitive faith precedes doctrine. The experiential insight is that of an embracing divine presence – both loving and awesome – that forever holds humanity and all created reality in the web of an empowering relational matrix. Relationality is the glue that holds everything in being, but more importantly the facilitating energy that begets all possibility. The God of love is not some awesome figure loving from a distance, but one relationally involved in the web and flow of all creation.

Several other monographs adopted this relational approach to Trinitarian theology. Unfortunately most focus on the human domain and the interpersonal dimensions (as in Fox 2001). As with the new understanding of the Holy Spirit (above), so this revamped theology of the Trinity needs to extend to embrace all reality, and not merely the human realm. In a planet of so many threatening scenarios because of depleted and exploited resources, it is becoming painfully clear that all life forms need each other – and the embracing relational matrix – to realize that fullness of life which God wishes for every creature, human and non-human alike.

Elizabeth Johnson (2008) provides a condensed but informed résumé of this new thinking. Beyond the patriarchal linear construct of Father, Son, Holy Spirit, she collates a range of other more organic and relational terms used by contemporary scholars. For instance, Keith Ward (1998) depicts the Trinity as primordial *depth* and *pattern* and *power* of love

---

2 A trinitarian religious structure is discernible in all the major world faiths. In the case of Judaism and Islam it has been relegated into their mystical branches, namely the Cabbala and Sufism; one wonders if this was a deliberate move to subvert what was perceived to be a threat to dominant power. Prehistoric religions also embody this concept as noted by Abraham (1994). Several years ago, the scientist George Greenstein (1988) claimed that configurations of three predominate the regions of galactic space. The concept of Trinity seems to have several ancient foundations, many of which have not yet been explored.

throughout the universe. Several contemporary namings may convey a sense of the impersonal, but in truth they are transpersonal renderings that liberate rather than hinder what is more authentically human. And all serving the one enduring truth, encapsulated by Elizabeth Johnson (2008, p. 215) in the statement: For God 'to be' means 'to be in relation'.

Relational images of God

In the popular series of greeting cards, *Bridge Building Images Inc.* (www. bridgebuilding.com), the artist Robert Lentz re-images the Celtic Trinity as three women of different ethnic backgrounds, adopting the three female archetypes of the Virgin, the Mother and the Crone. In archetypal terms the *Virgin* is the great birther, bringing into being everything that exists in creation. The *Mother* is the great nurturer, assisting life to reach its full potential. And the *Crone* is the skilled facilitator for negotiating life's transitions, including the passing-over mediated through death. Lentz surrounds the image of the three with the *Serpent*, an archetypal symbol of fertility, the fertile membrane within which all life unfolds.

How creative these images are compared to the rather morbid, moralistic iconography of conventional Judaeo-Christian religion. When religion ignores the archetypal depth of its key symbols, we run a great risk of adopting idolatrous images that serve dangerous and destructive ideologies. And most tragic of all, the deep layers of relational meaning are in danger of being lost entirely.

I hope the present essay contributes to a revamping and reclaiming of the relational foundations of all authentic faith, Christian and otherwise. Multidisciplinary insights enrich this rediscovery. Contemporary science has a great deal to contribute, but so has the age-old archetypal wisdom that artists of our time are illuminating afresh.

References

Abraham, Ralph (1994), *Chaos, Gaia, Eros* (San Francisco: HarperSanFrancisco).

Armstrong, Karen (2006), *The Great Transformation* (New York: Alfred A. Knopf).

Blaffer Hrdy, Sarah (2009), *Mothers and Others: The Evolutionary Origins of Mutual Understanding* (Cambridge, MA: Harvard University Press).

Brennan, Barbara Ann (1988), *Hands of Light: A Guide to Healing Through the Human Energy Field* (London and New York: Bantam Books).

Cannato, Judy (2006), *Radical Amazement* (Notre Dame, IN: Sorin Books).

Chown, Marcus (2007), *Quantum Theory Cannot Hurt You* (London: Faber & Faber).

Cole, K. C. (2001), *The Hole in the Universe* (London and New York: Harcourt).

De Waal, Frans (2005), *Our Inner Ape: The Best and Worst of Human Nature* (New York: Riverhead Books).

Dowd, Michael (2007), *Thank God for Evolution* (San Francisco: Council Oak Books).

Edwards, Denis (2004), *Breath of Life: A Theology of the Creator Spirit* (Maryknoll, NY: Orbis).

Fox, Patricia A. (2001), *God as Communion* (Collegeville, MN: Liturgical Press).

Goodall, Jane (2001), *My Life with Chimpanzees* (New York: Time Warner Audio Books).

Greenstein, George (1988), *The Symbiotic Universe* (New York: William Morrow & Co.).

Haught, John F. (2006), *Is Nature Enough?* (Cambridge: Cambridge University Press).

Johnson, Elizabeth (2008), *Quest for the Living God* (New York: Continuum).

Kaufman, Gordon D. (2006), *Jesus and Creativity* (Minneapolis: Fortress Press).

LaCugna, Catherine Mowry (1991), *God for Us: The Trinity and Christian Life* (San Francisco: HarperSanFrancisco).

Lane, Nick (2005), *Power, Sex, Suicide: Mithochondria and the Meaning of Life* (Oxford: Oxford University Press).

Laszlo, Ervin (2007), *Science and the Akashic Field: An Integral Theory of Everything* (Rochester, VT: Inner Traditions International).

Lipton, Bruce (2005), *The Biology of Belief* (Carlsbad, CA: Hay House).

Margulis, Lynn (1998), *The Symbiotic Planet: A New Look at Evolution* (New York: Basic Books).

Panikkar, Raimundo (1994), *The Cosmotheandric Experience: Emerging Religious* Consciousness (Maryknoll, NY: Orbis).

Pannenberg, Wolfhart (1993),*Toward a Theology of Nature: Essays on Science and Faith*, ed. Ted Peters (Louisville: Westminster John Knox Press), pp. 127–37.

Plumwood, Val (2002), *Environmental Culture: The Ecological Crisis of Reason* (London: Routledge).

Power, Margaret (2008), *The Egalitarians: Human and Chimpanzee* (Cambridge: Cambridge University Press).

Primack, Joel R. and Nancy Ellen Abrams (2006), *The View from the Center of the Universe* (New York: Riverhead Books).

Raschke, Carl (2008), *Globo Christ* (Grand Rapids, MI: Baker Academic).

Rosenblum, Bruce and Fred Kuttner (2007), *Quantum Enigma: Physics Encounters Consciousness* (London: Duckworth & Co.).

Stewart, John (2000), *Evolution's Arrow* (Canberra: Chapman Press).

Swimme, Brian and Thomas Berry (1992), *The Universe Story* (New York: Penguin).

Wallace, Mark I. (2005), *Finding God in the Singing River: Christianity, Spirit and Nature* (Minneapolis: Fortress).

Ward, Keith (1998), *God, Faith and the New Millennium: Christian Belief in an Age of Science* (Oxford: Oneworld).

Winter, Miriam Therese (2009), *Paradoxology: Spirituality in a Quantum Universe* (Maryknoll, NY: Orbis).

Zohar, Danah (1991), *The Quantum Self* (London: Bloomsbury).

9

Even the Stones Cry Out: Music, Theology and the Earth

JUNE BOYCE-TILLMAN

> Praise the Trinity
> Our life-giving music.
> She is creating all things.
> Life itself is giving birth.
> And she is an angel chorus praising
> And the splendour of arcane mysteries,
> Which are too difficult to understand.
> Also from her true life springs for all.

('Hildegard', translated by June Boyce-Tillman 1994)

This chapter will examine the potential role of music within a relational theology frame. It will look at different views of the natural world at different times in differing cultures. It will examine a phenomenography of the musical experience that includes the totality of the experience and will use this as a frame for examining the role of music as a significant phenomenon in the networking of the cosmos. It will use this frame to examine an event held in Winchester Cathedral and finally suggest three interlocking models for the potential of music as an ecological tool.

The music of the spheres

Sophie Drinker in her remarkable book *Music and Women* sees the loss of a relational view of music in the loss of matriarchal religions.

These goddess-mothers were generally represented as giving speech, music and their art of gesture to humanity, and as being themselves dancers and musicians . . . There can be no doubt that women were creative musicians in that age which preceded the epoch of written history. (Drinker [1948] 1995, pp. 68–9)

But this view became subjugated as the patriarchal religions dominated Europe (Boyce-Tillman 2007a). It is the notion of the Music of the Spheres that underpinned a great deal of thinking in the Classical world but became subjugated at the Enlightenment. It is difficult to examine the complexities of the ideas as part of a short essay.[1] The fundamental idea concerns *musica universalis* (or *mundana*) or the music of the spheres. This sees the proportions in the movements of celestial bodies – the sun, moon and planets – as a form of music. It is not regarded as literally audible, but as a mathematical or religious concept designed to represent the essential harmony of the universe. In this ancient view of the cosmos, the planets were thought to ascend from earth to heaven like the rungs of a ladder. Each planet corresponded to a musical note to produce a musical scale that underpinned the universe, and these were related to the rates of rotation around the earth. It originates with Pythagoras, who distinguished between music made by playing instruments, the unheard music of the human organism – the resonance between soul and body – and *musica mundana*, the unheard music of the cosmos itself[2] (James 1995, p. 30).

The importance of the link that Pythagoras established between human thought and nature, for religion, science, mathematics, music, medicine and cosmology, body, mind and spirit were linked in a complex synthesis. Plato, Cicero, Pliny and Ptolemy followed Pythagoras and the theories filtered into medieval Europe via such writers as Boethius (*c.*480–524/5). His *Principles of Music* became the primary textbook for music in the Middle Ages (Godwin 1988, p. 43). Because the fundamental nature of the universe is music then music in their system became an

---

1 For more detail, see James 1995.

2 This is recalled in the Anglican Eucharistic Prayer G in *Common Worship* in the phrase 'silent music of your praise'.

important tool to heal the body and lift the soul (Godwin 1987b, p. 130). From it an associated system of numerology was developed through mystical movements like the Rosicrucians and figures like Robert Fludd (1574–1637) and Johannes Kepler, who wrote in 1619 his *Harmonice Mundi* (Godwin 1988).

These ideas also filtered into the Church and underpinned the design of many of the great cathedrals of medieval Europe producing spaces of unparalleled resonances which are still there to be rediscovered. One theory sees each building having a particular note. I experienced this in 1999 in a piece written for York Minster. The piece centred around a single note. In rehearsal the piece appeared somewhat drab and uninteresting. In the minster the repeated sounding of the note was taken up by the building. What such theories restore is the building itself as an intrinsic part of the musical experience.

The theologians of the Middle Ages drew heavily on these theories. The medieval mystic Hildegard of Bingen (1098–1179) saw it recreating the original harmony of God and the world in the Garden of Eden:

Music expresses the unity of the world as God first made it, and the unity which is restored through repentance and reconciliation. (Van der Weyer 1997, p. 80)

Central to her cosmology is the notion of *viriditas* – a divine creative energy that fills the cosmos, the earth, its creatures and human and heavenly beings. It links the universe together:

No creature, whether visible or invisible lacks a spiritual life . . . the moon and stars flame with fire. The trees shoot forth buds because of the power in their seeds. Water has a delicacy and a lightness of motion like the wind . . . No tree blooms without greening power; no stone is without moisture; no creature is without its own power. (Fox 1987, p. 277)

These ideas were clearly linked with the basic medicinal frame of medieval Europe – the Doctrine of Humours – which saw the human being inextricably linked with the natural world as being made of the same basic elements. Music plays an important part in this greening power:

> Just as the power of God extends everywhere, surrounding all things and encountering no resistance, so too the sound of human voices singing God's praise can spread everywhere, surrounding all things and encountering no resistance. It can rouse the soul lost in apathy, and soften the soul hardened by pride. (Van der Weyer 1997, p. 80)

Hildegard connected singing with embodiment, as an act of incarnation (Baird and Ehrman 1994, p. 79).

At the Enlightenment these ideas gradually moved from being part of the dominant way of knowing to being subjugated (Boyce-Tillman 2007a) by the development of the scientific rationalist paradigm and the centrality of humanity to the cosmic schema. This meant that music lost its central place as the stuff of the universe and the notion of the aesthetic developed. The aesthetic came to be about the highest expression of human achievement. A barrier was set in place between human beings and the natural world, which now becomes 'inanimate' – lacking a soul. What was lost essentially was the connection with the earth, the material world and human beings. The connection of music with the spiritual world persisted. The notion of transcendence as part of self-actualization led people to regard the musical experience as the last remaining place for the spiritual in western society (Hills and Argyle 2000, pp. 61–75; Hay 1982). Some of the ideas, however, survived through such figures as the harmonic astrologer John Addey (1920–82), Gurdieff and Rudolph Steiner and later figures who we shall consider later in a search for a concept that will unite the cosmos.

The development of and centrality to European music of notation systems also led to a process of separating music from context. In the case of indigenous traditions each place and its associated music will have its own soundscape of the natural world with animals, birds and sounds of wind and sea. Songs were reworked for each occasion and were related to particular holy sites and the mineral and animal world:

In North Russia, where the song leaders (stihovoditzi) are particularly musical, the chantress conducts the old rites . . . She knows by heart the ancient portions of the incantations and invocations . . . she improvises new texts and new melodic lines to suit the emergency. (Drinker [1948] 1995, p. 13)

Once notation was developed, music could be conceived of as a separate entity lacking a body or a specific place. The score of the classical piece became 'the music' and music became separated from:

- the body of its creator
- the place of its creation
- the context (time, place, event) of its first intended performance.

Classical music became about the abstraction of dots on a page, and often its connection with anything other than its own internal construction systems became fractured. The composer Leoš Janáček (1854–1928) complained in a musical analysis class that music was not about a page of a score but about life, passion and nature.[3] The other aspects of the musical experience became subjugated in value and Construction became the dominant area of interest for musicologists (see below). The development of recording techniques has enabled this to happen for more improvisatory and non-notated traditions. They too now face a situation where their music can be taken anywhere, by anyone, for any purpose.[4]

To develop a relational theology of music we need to rediscover music theories from

- medieval Europe with its notion of the Music of the Spheres described above;
- indigenous musical traditions often entering the West through the phenomenon of the New Age described below;

---

3 'The Glagolitic Mass', BBC Radio 3, 26 April 2008.
4 This idea is developed further in Boyce-Tillman 2001.

- the area of music therapy, particularly in the area of entrainment when our bodies adjust our heart rate to the speed of the music.[5]
- postmodern feminist theorists in the area of embodiment and music (Isherwood 2000).

Contemporary science is rediscovering the notion of a sound coming from the earth itself:[6]

a relentless hum of countless notes completely imperceptible to the human ear, like a giant, exceptionally quiet symphony, but the origin of this sound remains a mystery . . . unexpected powerful tunes have been discovered in this hum . . . This sound, first discovered a decade ago, is one that only scientific instruments – seismometers – can detect. Researchers call it Earth's Hum.[7]

There is a rediscovery of vibration as the essential stuff of the universe with molecules and atoms circulating in apparently static matter and vibrations of liquid crystal giving the colour to digital displays. However, the fracturing of the link between arts and sciences has meant that this is not extended to see music again as a powerful agent of destruction or creation. It can bring down fragile church spires, but less work has been done on its capacity to build and heal.[8]

The current development of consciousness studies has also entered the area of the interconnectedness of creation with works like Ken Wilber's *The Eye of Spirit* (1997) and *Integral Psychology* (2000); but seldom does music hold a significant place in notions of consciousness. Here the search for the perennial philosophy drawing on a variety of traditions looks at a spectrum of consciousness often called *The Great*

---

5 For further examination of this see Boyce-Tillman 2000a.

6 www.livescience.com.

7 www.praisecharts.com/live/articles/219/1/The-Rocks-Will-Cry-Out/Page1.

8 The development of cymatics has produced claims for vibrations to heal and mend organs of the body. Greater work has been done on music and the mind in the area of music therapy.

Chain of Being (Wilber 2009) to develop a hierarchy of consciousness. E. F. Schumacher set out four great Levels of Being comprising matter (m), life (x), consciousness (y) and self-awareness (z) (Schumacher 1977, pp. 27–8):

'Man' [*sic*] can be written $m+x+y+z$
'Animal' can be written $m+x+y$
'Plant' can be written $m+x$
'Mineral' can be written m
(Schumacher 1977, pp. 32–3)

If in this model we establish the mineral level as vibrating we have a sense that vibration links all these levels.

So in pre-patriarchal and pre-Enlightenment Europe music was considered central to the cosmic schema, but the development of scientific rationalism subjugated these ideas. Although ideas of the interconnectedness of the cosmos remained in subjugated form, the centrality of music became lost as the subjects held together by the notion of the Music of the Spheres were fragmented in contemporary knowledge systems. The development of musical notation and recording weakened the link of music and place and context.

The separation of animate and inanimate

Traditional societies would not subscribe to the animate/inanimate division of contemporary science which colonialism attempted to subjugate wherever it found it. The entire world has its own energy or quality and human beings and the natural world are in constant interplay:

Did you know that trees talk? Well they do. They talk to each other, and they'll talk to you if you listen. Trouble is, white people don't listen. They never learned to listen to the Indians, so I don't suppose they'll listen to other voices in nature. But I have learned a lot from trees; sometimes about the weather, sometimes about animals, sometimes about the Great Spirit . . . I think that Western people who come into an Indian environment and attempt to preach take along their own set of categories and use it to deal with Indian people they meet. Anthropologists, summarizing what they find in the Indian tradition, always calling us animists, and that view is accepted by a great many people in the field of religion. We are put in a cultural evolutionary framework, and then we are supposed to move from animism to some great abstract conception of one god. Science describes things at a level of abstraction, by leaving out of account a whole range of properties that they have (colour, beauty, consciousness. . .) (Tinker 2004)

But some westerners are relearning their connection with the land from traditional cultures. David K. Turner describes how in playing the didgeridoo he realized his own connection not with Australia but with his own land:

I was where my own spiritual stuff was – in Canada where I had grown up, where I always returned and where parts of me were buried. (Turner 2001, p. 49)

This represents a rediscovery of these subjugated uses of music. It is now much more acceptable to sing to plants to encourage growth than it would have been 20 years ago.

The rise of a new interest in paganism and pre-Christian history has led to a renewed interest in sacred sites involving music. For example, the *Clach a' Choire* on Tiree's coast is an Ice Age boulder which produces a metallic clang when struck. There is evidence of current veneration in the form of coins left in a little hollow on the top.[9] Ringing stones are now known to be in Central, Eastern, South-Eastern and Western Asia, Africa, South America and Europe. These could be like indigenous mythic 'points of emergence . . . where the stories begin and end'.[10]

---

9 www.megalithic.co.uk/article.php?sid=17933&mode=thread&order=0&thold=0.

10 www.landscape-perception.com/a_stone_age_holy_land/.

Music sits as a profound power in societies where there is a profound place connection:

> To the western mind music is essentially something created by man [*sic*], although it may be an unconscious process. For the shaman, music is something separate, a form of spiritual power that has an autonomous being apart from human minds. (Frowen-Williams 1997, p. 51)

But writers like Chris Clarke endeavour to merge scientific and indigenous paradigms by weakening the notion of hierarchies of being. If he were to link music with awareness we would have a very helpful paradigm on which to build a theory of the vibrations of the different elements of the cosmos to produce a cosmic symphony. He postulates the notion that the difference between humans and worms is not the degree of awareness but its content:

> *quantum states are aware* . . . if we consider a living, and hence coherent entity, then the entanglement will take over the individual states of the parts, which will no longer be definable, and replace them with the quantum state of the entangled whole. (C. Clarke 2002, pp. 263–6)

Christian theologians like Mary Grey (2007) and Andrew Linzey (1994) are seeing redemption as cosmic and including the environment. This is based on the statement in Revelation 'I am making all things new' (Revelation 21.5) and includes 'every living creature that is with you, the birds, the domestic animals, and every animal of the earth with you, as many as came out of the ark' (Genesis 9.10). I have recently returned to the 1662 version of the Lord's Prayer which includes the line 'Thy will be done *in* earth as it is in heaven.' But now theology is separated from music, and one of the central aims of this essay is to re-establish that link that would have been commonplace in the Middle Ages and traditional societies.

So the indigenous pagan traditions, current philosophers and theologians challenge the division between animate and inanimate matter and have found a variety of frames for seeing the essential interconnectedness on the cosmos, but whereas indigenous frames have included music, the western ones reflect the fragmentation of knowledge that characterizes western culture.

Two ways of knowing

Scientific realism is so dominant that many would see all of the previous sections as simply metaphor and simile. Isabel Clarke in *Madness, Mystery and the Survival of God* sees the necessity of what she calls the transliminal or relational knowing. In her thinking, this way of knowing is to do with our 'porous' relation to other beings and is where spirituality sits. It is in contrast to 'propositional knowing', which gives us the analytically sophisticated individual that our culture has perhaps mistaken for the whole of knowing (I. Clarke 2008, p. 93). To access the other way of knowing we cross an internal *limen* or threshold. She sets out two ways of knowing – the propositional characterized by either–or logic and the relational or transliminal – characterized by paradox and both–and logic;

> I have floated the hypothesis that we are only partly individual; through our relational minds we are part of the whole. This brings responsibility and pain. It also brings wonder and joy . . . And the deepest and widest of those circles of relationship which we both are, and are beyond us, is god or whatever label you choose. (I. Clarke 2008, p. 172)

In this hypothesis she validates the two ways of knowing as of equal worth and value, the relational including the artistic and the religious. The notion of human connectedness with the cosmos is an essential part of human experience, and ignoring it can lead to madness. It validates composers' accounts of the process of inspiration, when the sounds appear to emerge from the universe, just like Michelangelo sees his sculpture hidden in the marble and waiting to be discovered. This experience sits within the relational way of knowing.

Place memory

In human experience certain memories are regularly attached to certain places. Visitors to the Holy Land are often overwhelmed by the fact that they may be walking on the same stones as Jesus walked on. The Wailing Wall in Jerusalem holds the tears of many Jews. Gravestones in a million cemeteries bear testimony to many unanswered prayers. I remember visiting Romsey Abbey and wondering at an Anglo-Saxon crucifix, in which all the devotion from past ages appeared to me to be contained. We can harness and transform these energies. Community drama groups, for example, have performed dramatic rituals to purify places in Serbia where terrible massacres occurred.

Michael Perry in his book on *Deliverance* tells how the memories held in a place can join with later human experience to produce paranormal phenomena. He tells the story of a young father of two children. Three weeks after the cot death of a child he is woken by what he thought was burglars. He opened the bedroom door to find groups of people walking along the landing of the house and disappearing through the far wall. They were dressed in seventeenth-century costume and looked very sad. They were carrying bundles. A young police officer saw the phenomenon as well, and the police dog would not enter the house. He describes how the man's grief and the memory in the place combined to produce the phenomenon and sees the necessity to bless the place as well as counsel the person to deal with the phenomenon (Perry 1987, p. 34).

So places do appear to hold the memory of events that have happened there in the past. It is therefore possible that music can be a way of accessing and redeeming them.

The musical experience

I have developed a phenomenography (Marton and Booth 1997) of the experience (Boyce-Tillman 2004) drawing on the notion of encounter.[11]

---

11 To take Allegri's choral piece *Miserere* from sixteenth-century Italy, in the area of Materials it consists of a choir. In the area of Expression it is peaceful with

This widens the musical experience to include a variety of parameters traditionally ignored by recent music theory and widening it beyond dots on a page. It uses the frame of the 'I–Thou' experience described by Martin Buber (1970) and develops into a number of domains:

- Expression – another self
- Values – another culture
- Construction – the world of abstract ideas
- Materials - the environment

All music consists of organizations of concrete Materials drawn both from the human body and from the environment and is essentially a co-operation between the vibrations of the human being and those of the natural world. And as we have seen, the human body is made of the elements of the environment. These materials include musical instruments of various kinds, the infinite variety of tone colours associated with the human voice, the sounds of the natural world and the acoustic space in which the sounds are placed. Playing and singing are two of the most intimate relationships human beings have with the environment other than eating it. In traditional societies a drummer would reverence the tree and the animal that give the material for his/her drum, all performance being an intimate relationship with tree and animal. Sadly in the West the loss of the connection with the natural world has been reflected in the way we treat and regard instruments. We need to re-establish this reverence in relation to instruments in our western fragmented culture. If every child opened their musical instrument case and reverenced the elements of the natural world and the labour of craft workers, we could transform ecological awareness at a stroke.

---

fluctuations as the plainchant verses come in. In the area of Construction it is an alternating psalm with full harmonic verses and plainchant alternating verses. This is intimately related to its role as a psalm liturgically. In the area of Value it is held as a masterpiece within the western canon of music, is frequently recorded and achieved a place in classical music charts, and it represents an important statement about the Christian's attitude to penitence based on a Jewish psalm, especially as expressed at the beginning of the penitential season of Lent. It has a declared Spiritual intention.

Instruments are a tangible link with the natural world. Science is showing us that the stones – the mineral – do have an energy which has been channelled in our technology. Early radios were called crystal sets because at the heart of them was a crystal which took the incoming signal and helped to convert it into intelligible sounds. Quartz crystals are still part of transmitters and receivers. Some of us will have made a glass sing with a moistened fingertip, and glass is a form of stone. Rock contains iron ore which when crushed with limestone and coal produces steel. So steel, like that used on a steel-string guitar, is made of ground-up stones with some carbon (coal) thrown in and heated up. So it could be said that in both the gong rocks described above and the steel strings, rocks have a 'voice'. In some cases this does not require human agency. There are in history accounts of singing statues, like the two statues of the Egyptian Pharaoh Amenhotep III, split by an earthquake, which emitted a hum at dawn.[12]

The use of natural material unrefined by manufacture is growing, as interest in the environment grows. In a recent piece *Between* in York Minster, I used quantities of stones knocked together. There is a re-discovery of *lithophones* – instruments constructed from struck stones. One example of the construction of a contemporary instrument is by Ela Lamblin and Leah Mann. The instrument is created with 100 river rocks suspended by music wire from a wing-shaped sound box and hanging in a steep arch. The strings (vibrating longitudinally) release their music as the performers dance and, with rosin-covered gloves, stroke, caress, and tug the strings.[13] Stearns and Sunsinger recorded the rocks on a portable digital audio system – equipment that was designed to record vibrations within the earth near volcanoes and recorded the sounds of rocks 'singing'. They discovered that a wide variety of sounds could be produced by striking or stroking rocks with different items, including their hands and other rocks.[14] It is also possible to purchase magnetic Hematite singing power stones which will make 'most

---

12 www.theparanormalreport.com/singing-stones-2.html.

13 www.oddmusic.com/gallery/om25400.html.

14 www.rambles.net/stearns_singston94.html.

mysterious singing sounds' when thrown in the air.[15] Such developments represent a simplification of musical materials in the light of current complex technological systems.

The area I have called Expression is concerned with the evocation of mood, emotion (individual or corporate), images, memories and atmosphere on the part of all those involved in the musical performance. This is where the subjectivity of composer/performer and listener intersect powerfully. The sounds themselves hold some meaning, but the listener will bring extrinsic meaning to the music – meaning that has been locked onto that particular piece or style or musical tradition because of its association with certain events in their own lives like tunes associated with certain special events. This is an area of empathy and imagination. Singing songs from different cultures can, for example, give children a chance to empathize with cultures different from their own. I set a prayer from the black township of Gugulethu in *The Healing of the Earth*, and when I ask children to sing it I tell them the story of how I collected it. One child said: 'When I sing that song to myself, I think that somehow I am part of those people you talked about so far away.'

In the area of Construction, effectiveness often depends on the right management of repetition and contrast within a particular idiom. The way in which contrast is handled within a tradition – how much or how little can be tolerated – is often carefully regulated by the elders of the various traditions – be they the composers or theoreticians of the western classical tradition or the master drummers of Yoruba traditions. It is in this area where many claims for a spirituality associated with order are linked with the ideas of the Music of the Spheres.

The area of Values is related to the context of the musical experience and links the experience with culture and society. The musical experience contains both implicit (within the music) and explicit (within the context) Value systems. However, these two areas of Value interact powerfully. Notions of internal values are a subject of debate in musicological circles (McClary 1991, 2001), but as soon as a text is present – either in the music or associated with it (Blake 1997, p. 7), Value systems

---

15 www.whitemagic.com.au/singingpowerstones.html.

will be declared, like the words of hymns. Music mirrors the structures of the culture that created it and people's ways of being in them (Shepherd and Wicke 1997, pp. 138–9). This is why feminist theologians, for example, fail to get a spiritual experience out of much of traditional hymnody with its non-inclusive language. Here also is the intention of the musicker which reflects their own Value systems. Music has the potential of transmitting love, and in much of western culture we have lost the notion of intention in a musical performance. Kay Gardner explores this as she uses Hildegard's concept of *viriditas* to construct a piece composed for 'people with life-threatening dis-ease' (Gardner 1990, p. 229). One exercise that I do is what is called a 'humming bath', in which a group of people surround two of their number with hummed sounds which are produced with the intention of loving their colleagues. This always produces feelings of great joy and uplift. As the aesthetic and analytical became dominant value systems in western culture, value systems such as connecting with the natural world, healing, peace and reconciliation became subjugated. They are now being rediscovered (Urbain 2007).

Whereas these four domains exist as overlapping circles in the experience, Spirituality, I am suggesting, exists in the relationship between these areas. I am defining it as the ability to transport the audience to a different time/space dimension – to move them from everyday reality to 'another world'. It is in this experience that some would see music as the last remaining ubiquitous spiritual experience in a secularized western culture (Boyce-Tillman 2001). In describing this experience I have drawn literature from many sources – psychological, philosophical, aesthetic, anthropological, ethnomusicological, theological (Boyce-Tillman 2006), including Isabel Clarke's transliminal described above. The Spiritual domain, then, is defined as a time when the experiencer is able to negotiate a relationship with all four domains. It can be represented as in Figure 1.

So the musical experience can be seen to include the natural world both in the instruments used or the human voice and in the venue with its distinctive acoustic and soundscape and in its associations and memories which are released by the act of musicking, and potentially in the

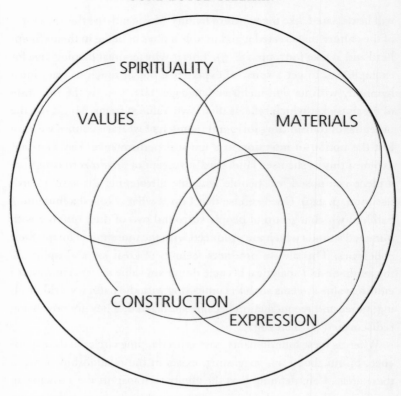

Figure 1   The complete spiritual experience

area of Values the notion of relation between the human, the natural and the Divine.

Acoustic spaces

In my pieces I have been concerned to include the building as an important 'instrument' or player in a musical experience. Traditionally musicians have been placed in the middle of spaces and the walls have been used as places against which the sounds bounce to produce resonance and echo. I have become fascinated by placing musicians around spaces and close to the walls so that the walls support the sounds from behind and are coaxed in resonating. In this I have learned a great deal of the music of John Tavener. In Winchester Cathedral I started with a piece called *The Call of the Ancestors*, where a rock group, Thai gongs and African drums were placed around the cathedral. For Liverpool Metropolitan Cathedral I wrote *Ecological Celebration*, in which small groups of singers were placed around the circular building. This proved immensely successful as they were singing into the widest part of the building rather than from the middle singing into the narrowest part. *PeaceSong* in Winchester Cathedral used twelve different choirs scattered all over the cathedral for the first movement singing fragments of song that might have been sung there in the past, separated by periods of silence. I called it *If These Walls Could Only Speak* and I felt I was making unheard sounds stored in the stones audible. Before the performances of these pieces I go down to the cathedral and sit on the stones and pray that it will play their part in the pieces. It has never failed me, and before *Space for Peace* I saw a gold cloud rise from the floor of the cathedral as if it had responded.

Space for Peace was my most radical piece so far. For this we assembled together local choral groups from a variety of sources – community choirs, schools, the university, the cathedral choristers and quiristers and Rabbi Mark Solomon, who chanted the Hebrew Scriptures. There were some solo singers who wandered around freely singing some Hildegard chants. Some used notation; some had no grasp of it and learned everything orally; some were older and singing for fun, others were skilled musicians in an independent school, some were Jews, some Christians, some secularists, the age range was 7 to 85. It used the cathedral as a resonant meditative space able to contain and merge diversity in a way that accepted it without obliterating it. The groups for one section were situated around the cathedral in various chapels and the transepts. Each had chosen in advance what they would sing – some of their favourite pieces. The musical material included motets, hymns, worship songs, chants and chanting. There were nine shared peace chants (learned by the congregation), which each choir had to sing every 20 minutes. These produced some common threads which threaded through the texture binding the diversity together.

The middle section of the vigil was created by the participants on the basis of choice. Each group chose when to sing and could also be invited by the congregation to sing. The congregation moved around the building, lighting candles, praying, being quiet, as they chose, but also participating in creating the musical sound. It was designed therefore to reflect a new model of peace-making based on the principle that peace will only work if we all do what we want to do but also then have the responsibility of working out how far it fits with what other people want to do. Everyone present (and the stones of the building) had a part in the creation of an experience of beauty and togetherness and experienced intuitive ways of relating to and co-operating with others.

The effect was beyond my imaginings. Children singing *I Think to Myself What a Wonderful World*, merged with plainchant, Jewish cantillation and Taizé chants and motets in a way that saw diversity held in a unity that was not a uniformity.

It was not liturgy as we have known and practised it but it showed the creativity of a diverse group of people given freedom to exercise their own choices – unity without uniformity.

The comments picked up the relational character of the relationship between the sounds and the space

While classic works by Beethoven, Britten and others bear witness to the fact that the pursuit of harmony through music is no mere equivocation, in her *Space for Peace*, June Boyce-Tillman approaches the subject not only as a condition of spiritual grace, to which countless settings of the Mass have aspired, but also as a process. This in turn implies not only musical form, but also dimension and movement . . . its bold yet simple structure, fruit of many years' preoccupation with exploring the perimeters of music and worship, was expertly conceived to turn the venue into a resonant meditative space.

The result was an extraordinary evening of complex soundscapes which nonetheless yielded an uplifting message: that peace might be obtained not from top-down imposition of values, but through collegial pursuit of diversity within a commitment to beauty and the needs of others. (Williams 2009)

Others saw the interaction between space and sound:

> I think the fact that the cathedral had been emptied of chairs was an important factor in the experience. First, it created a root to its past back to a time when cathedrals were masses of movement and diverse activities going on at the same time. Second, it literally created the space for sound and movement . . . I thought this must be what heaven is like, a space where diversity finds its unity and unity blossoms into diversity . . . As the whole event drew to a close I noticed a child near me sitting on the floor in the classic eastern meditation position.

Others described a transliminal way of knowing:

> 'Space for peace' was one of the high points of my life . . . The cathedral was cleared of chairs which was wonderful – one great echoing space. It was all about peace – calls for peace constantly mingling and changing . . . I was able to sit and meditate on the stone floor in the middle of the North Transept, one of the most beautiful parts. It came to me that 'peace is possible'.

It would be not unlike the medieval cathedral with masses being celebrated simultaneously in the chantry chapels. It represented a unique co-operation between stone and human agency.

The biblical view

The title of this chapter is taken from Scripture. The Hebrew Scriptures are filled with the notion that creation makes music in praise of its creator not unlike the ideas taken from indigenous religions above. Isaiah 55 sees creation praising God musically with the mountains and hills bursting into song and the hills clapping their hands. In Psalm 65 the valleys decked in grain sing in joy. Mary Grey shows how the God of the book of Job '[c]Calls from the whirlwind for a total ecology of place; *ecological* rather than exclusively economic objectives must be human priorities' (Grey 2007, p. 40).

It is on this tradition that Jesus is drawing in the account of the Palm Sunday entry. Jesus enters Jerusalem and songs of praise surround him. The Pharisees ask Jesus to stop his disciples singing. To this he replies that if they keep quiet, the stones will cry out.

Music as relational theology

John Chryssavgis (2004, pp. 123–6) sets out three models for ecological prayer which I have adapted here for music as relational musical liturgy, drawing on the ideas in this chapter. The models interface with one another.

The first is the biblical. In this model the universe/cosmos does sing. It is similar to *musica universalis* but includes not only the spheres but the earth and its creatures as well. Listening to these sounds can lead to singing the psalms, hymns and chants alone or together with the intention of joining this cosmic act of praise. Because of the vibrational nature of the universe it is possible for human beings to create or destroy with sound, as in the destruction of Jericho's walls with rams' horns. Here we need to be sure of our own positive and justice-seeking intentions in our music-making.

The ascetic model is a call to simplicity – a return to natural and simpler instruments and an investigation of the sounds of the natural world and the infinite possibilities of the human voice. It involves honouring the earthy origins of the instrument or the voice as well as its spiritual aspirations. The contemplation of a single note, the particular one that is your own note – the one you find easiest to sing – is a re-enchanting experience. In several of my pieces, I have included the 'shalom' procession. A large group of people light candles and on a single note chant shalom freely while moving through a large building. One singer, who had sung all her life (some 45 years) said that for her singing had always been about the pitch and length of the next note (the Construction that has dominated music education). In this simple act it was the first time she had realized that singing was about the breath moving through her body.

This can also re-establish the relationship between music and everyday life as in the re-imagined Celtic spirituality where songs accompanied the lighting of the fire and the baking of bread. Carol Christ calls for the re-establishing of these links in her rediscovery of the goddess traditions, describing a doxology to the goddess which she sings while washing the dishes or swimming (Christ 2003). In the mid-twentieth century people were still generating their own musical material whistling, humming, singing while working, cycling and walking. They were generating their own musical compositions that were intimately related to their bodies and helped them manage their own internal rhythms. The advent of the walkman and MP3 players has deprived people of opportunities for such improvisation and fragmented the relationship between the subtle changes in body, mind and spirit and musicking and put them in the control of the moguls of the music industry. What appears like freedom is actually a constraint on their own creative power. Singing, including wailing, screaming, humming, can provide the profound connection with the earth of which feminist theologians write: 'Linking ourselves as women with body and nature and darkness and moisture and dirt and sex can illuminate the Sacred' (Heyward 1989, p. 103).

It is also possible to harness technology to different ends from the massive amplification of sound that destroys ears and potentially the environment. It involves here contemplating the crushed earth in the technology. New Age recordings are increasingly including natural world sounds in pieces as if the sense of place can be restored by sampled natural sounds. The virtual is replacing the real. Elaine Graham encourages us to embrace technology: 'So just as the boundaries between humans, animals and machines erode; so do the distinctions between the virtual and the real' (Graham 2007, p. 132). So the use of a small digital recorder to record earth sounds for editing later can be a powerful experience of this kind.

The sacramental model treats music as a sacramental tool for reconciliation at all levels. Here we have a profoundly incarnational act where heaven and earth are merged. *Space for Peace* blurred the boundaries between liturgy and concert. Music to be sacramental needs to be inclusive, and traditionally liturgy has embraced only certain musical styles and not in combination, as we perpetuate the misguided division between sacred and secular. The worshippers of the Goddess are closer to this Value system than many Christian churches because of their earth connection. A neo-shaman Maria Mar describes her initiation into the sacraments of the Goddess.

> *Stones are not closed, my child. Stones are open to all that the wind brings them. Dead creatures, dust, sharp objects, knocks and stains . . . it is a work of art that is themselves . . .* Now I am 'Dances the Bones, Sings the Stones'.[16]

The linkage in *Space for Peace* of freedom, choice, diversity, intention and Value in the form of peace-making, inclusion of a variety of abilities and styles, use of freedom and diversity in a resonant space, linked stone and heaven in a transliminal experience:

> My favourite part was . . . sitting in the (then empty) choir whilst the sounds and performances washed in and out. It reminded me of . . . what Heaven must be like!

Conclusion

This chapter has charted the move from music as central to theology to its place in the entertainment industry. It has examined theorists of connectedness and seen how their ideas can be combined with a phenomenography of the musical experience as encounter. It has seen the

16 http://www.shamansdance.com.

rediscovery of subjugated Value systems and attempted to restore a relationship between theology and music, and suggested ways in which music can be used as a tool of a relational theology by blurring the distinctions between liturgy and concert:

[Space for Peace] made me realize that when I go to a concert, I focus on the performers and what is coming from them but last night it was as if the very stone was sounding out itself into that wonderful space . . . as if it was joining in.

It reminds me of a poem . . .

'After a Poetry Reading in Winchester Cathedral' by Doreen Pearce

> These huge Quarr stones
> have stood for centuries
> soaking up sounds, divine and secular,
> thinning the human voice to a mere thread,
> de-thundering the organ, damping down the choir.
> But when the last trump comes
> and graves give up their dead,
> when kings and bishops, saints and noblemen
> rise from their chests,
> sort out their bones, and are re-fleshed,
> will then the transept walls give up their sounds,
> poems re-echo round the arches
> pillars resound with Benedictine psalms?
> Will youth guitars, visiting choirs,
> sermons of deans and Handel's hallelujahs
> all combine with organ notes
> in one triumphant shout of praise
> before the world dissolves?

References

Baird, Joseph and Radd Ehrman (trans.) (1994), *Letters of Hildegard of Bingen* (Oxford: Oxford University Press).

Blake, Andrew (1997), *The Land without Music: Music Culture and Society in Twentieth-Century Britain* (Manchester: Manchester University Press).

Boyce-Tillman, June B. (1994), *Singing the Mystery: 28 Liturgical Pieces of Hildegard of Bingen* (London: Hildegard Press and Association for Inclusive Language).

——(2000a), *Constructing Musical Healing: The Wounds that Sing* (London: Jessica Kingsley).

——(2000b), *The Creative Spirit: Harmonious Living with Hildegard of Bingen* (Norwich: Canterbury Press).

——(2001), 'Sounding the Sacred: Music as Sacred Site', in Karen Ralls-MacLeod and Graham Harvey (eds), *Indigenous Religious Music* (Farnborough: Scolar), pp. 136–66.

——(2006), 'Music as Spiritual Experience', *Modern Believing* 47.3 (July), pp. 20–31.

——(2007a), *Unconventional Wisdom* (London: Equinox).

——(2007b), 'Music and Value in Cross-Cultural Work', in Olivier Urbain (ed.), *Music and Conflict Transformation: Harmonies and Dissonances in Geopolitics* (London: I. B. Tauris), pp. 40–52.

——(2007c), 'Peace Making in Educational Contexts', in Olivier Urbain (ed.), *Music and Conflict Transformation: Harmonies and Dissonances in Geopolitics* (London: I. B. Tauris), pp. 212–28.

Buber, Martin, trans. Walter Kaufmann (1970), *I and Thou* (New York: Charles Scribner's Sons).

Christ, Carol (2003), *She Who Changes: Re-Imagining the Divine in the World* (New York and Basingstoke: Macmillan Palgrave).

Chryssavgis, John (2004), *Light through Darkness: The Orthodox Tradition* (London: Darton, Longman and Todd).

Clarke, Chris (2002), *Living in Connection: Theory and Practice of the New World-View* (Warminster: Creation Spirituality Books).

Clarke, Isabel (2008), *Madness, Mystery and the Survival of God* (Ropley: O Books).

Drinker, Sophie ([1948] 1995), *Music and Women: The Story of Women in their Relation to Music* (New York: Feminist Press at the City University of New York).

Fox, Matthew (ed.) (1987), *Hildegard of Bingen's Book of Divine Works, with Letters and Songs* (Santa Fe: Bear and Co.).

Frowen-Williams, Gareth (1997), 'Between Earth and Sky: Explorations on the Shamanic Path', unpublished dissertation for MA in Ethnomusicology, University of Central England.

Gardner, Kay (1990), *Sounding the Inner Landscape: Music as Medicine* (Rockport, MA, and Shaftesbury, Dorset: Element Books).

Godwin, Joscelyn (1979), *Robert Fludd: Hermetic Philosopher and Surveyor of Two Worlds* (London: Thames and Hudson).

——(1987a), *Music, Magic and Mysticism: A Sourcebook* (London: Arkana).

——(1987b), *Harmonies of Heaven and Earth* (London: Thames and Hudson).

Goehr, Lydia (1992), *The Imaginary Museum of Musical Works: An Essay in the Philosophy of Music* (Oxford: Clarendon Press).

Graham, Elaine, (2007), 'Embodying Technology, Becoming Our Tools: Discussing the Post/Human', in Jonathan Baxter (ed.), *Wounds that Heal: Theology, Imagination and Health* (London: SPCK), pp. 125–48.

Green, Lucy (1988), *Music on Deaf Ears: Musical Meaning, Ideology and Education* (Manchester and New York: Manchester University Press).

——(1997), *Music, Gender, Education* (Cambridge: Cambridge University Press).

Grey, Mary (2007), 'Ecomysticism: A Contemporary Path of Christian Healing', in Jonathan Baxter (ed.), *Wounds that Heal: Theology, Imagination and Health* (London: SPCK), pp. 36–56.

Hamel, Peter, trans. Peter Lemusurier (1978), *Through Music to the Self: How to Appreciate and Experience Music Anew* (Tisbury: Compton Press).

Hay, David (1982), *Exploring Inner Space* (Harmondsworth: Penguin).

Heyward, Carter (1989), *Touching our Strength: The Erotic as Power and the Love of God* (San Francisco: HarperSanFrancisco).

Hills, Peter and Michael Argyle (2000), *Psychology and Religion* (London and New York: Routledge).

Isherwood, Lisa (ed.) (2000), *The Good News of the Body: Sexuality and Feminism* (Sheffield: Sheffield Academic Press).

James, Jamie (1995), *The Music of the Spheres: Music, Science and the Natural Order of the Universe* (London: Abacus).

Langer, Suzanne (1942), *Philosophy in a New Key* (Cambridge, MA: Harvard University Press).

Linzey, Andrew (1994), *Animal Theology* (London: SCM Press).

McClary, Susan (1991), *Feminine Endings* (Minneapolis: University of Minnesota Press).

——(2001), *Conventional Wisdom* (Berkeley: University of California Press).

Marton, Ference and Shirley Booth (1997), *Learning and Awareness* (Mahwah, NJ: Lawrence Erlbaum Associates).

Perry, Michael (ed.) (1987), *Deliverance: Psychic Disturbances and Occult Involvement* (London: SPCK).

Rahn, John (1994), 'What is Valuable in Art, and Can Music Still Achieve It?', in John Rahn (ed.), *Perspectives in Musical Aesthetics* (New York: Norton).

Schumacher E. F. (1977), *A Guide for the Perplexed* (London, Jonathan Cape).

Shepherd, John and Peter Wicke (1997), *Music and Cultural Theory* (Cambridge: Polity Press).

Sullivan, Lawrence E. (1997), *Enchanting Powers: Music in the World's Religions* (Harvard: Harvard University Press).

Tinker, George E. (2004), 'The Stones Shall Cry Out: Consciousness, Rocks, and Indians', *Wicazo Sa Review* 19.2 (Fall), pp. 105–25.

Turner, David H. (2001), 'From Here into Eternity: Power and Transcendence in Australian Aboriginal Music', in Karen Ralls-MacLeod and Graham Harvey (eds), *Indigenous Religious Musics* (Farnborough: Scolar), pp. 35–55.

Turner, Victor (1969, 1974a), *The Ritual Process: Structure and Anti-structure* (Baltimore: Penguin Books).

——(1974b), *Dramas, Fields and Metaphors: Symbolic Action in Human Society* (Ithaca, NY: Cornell University Press).

——(1982), *From Ritual to Theatre: The Human Seriousness of Play* (New York: Performing Arts Journal Publications).

——(1986), *The Anthropology of Performance* (New York: Performing Arts Journal Publications).

Urbain, Olivier (ed.) (2007), *Music and Conflict Transformation: Harmonies and Dissonances in Geopolitics* (London: I. B. Tauris).

Van der Weyer, Robert (ed.) (1997), *Hildegard in a Nutshell* (London: Hodder and Stoughton).

Wilber, Ken (1998), *The Eye of the Spirit: An Integral Vision for a World Gone Slightly Mad* (Boston: Shambhala).

——(2009), *The Great Chain of Being* (London: Arkana).

Williams, Nicholas (2009), Review in the *Church Times*, 27 February.

Part 3

Divine Relationality

10

Monotheism as a Threat to Relationality?

MAAIKE DE HAARDT

Whether or not we call it relational theology, much theology by western feminists is characterized by a specific emphasis on the principal connections, the original relationality between the human and the divine, between the human and the cosmos, the divine and the cosmos and on mutual interdependence as positive and powerful. This approach offers critical and creative ways of doing theology and has deeply informed my own theology. It is from this perspective that I would like to reflect on three questions in this chapter. First, why and how does monotheism, which I understand first and foremost as 'creational mono-generativity', fundamentally undermine relationality or relational theology? Second, is relational theology really free of 'residues' of this kind of mono-creativity and mono-generativity? Finally, do we need different concepts – be it of monotheism, creation or relationality – or do we need different practices? In other words, what – if anything in addition to the pleasure and creativity of theological reflection – will conceptual changes or relational theologies bring us? These are open questions; they are intended to stimulate my own thinking at least on relationality and divinity and, as such, they mirror my intellectual wrestling with these questions. These reflections take place in the context of my general theological project, the developing of a theology of everyday life, by which I mean theological reflection in which 'lived religion', everyday practices and beliefs of 'ordinary' women and men constitute the basis of systematic reflection.

But let me first sketch the background against which these questions arise.

In May 2008, the world was shocked by the discovery of a horrible case of incest in Austria. Josef Fritzl had abused his daughter Elisabeth, since she was 11 years old, and had kept her captive in a specially designed cellar for 24 years – a cellar, for that matter, for which Fritzl had received permission to build. He impregnated her time and again, and she gave birth on her own to seven children in that prison. Three of the children lived with their mother in the cellar and never saw daylight, until they were released. One child died, and the other three were 'found' on the doorstep of the Fritzl home and were adopted by Fritzl and his wife. This situation was finally discovered when Elisabeth's oldest 'cellar' daughter contracted a serious illness, leading Fritzl to take her to a hospital. Linda Fairstein, who has been a prosecutor for 30 years and specializes in violence and abuse against women, stated in an interview on the case that she thought that she had seen it all. It turned out she had not: 'What happened there is beyond imagination in every respect. I cannot even imagine what kept her alive, what she thought, how she handled her children, what she told them.'[1] There was another case in Austria a couple of years earlier of a man who held a girl captive for eight years. And the case of incest and captivity in Bolivia became world news while I was working on this chapter.

Josef Fritzl was convicted for incest, rape, enslavement, coercion and murder by neglect. He denied the murder and slavery charges initially but reversed his plea, so it was said, after watching 11 hours of videotaped testimony from his daughter in court. Nowhere in the Dutch 'quality papers' did I find any reference to the cultural or religious dimensions of this case. No one ever asked how it could be possible that no one in the village became suspicious – not when Elisabeth disappeared nor when the babies were found on Fritzl's doorstep. It was only on some internet sites that I came across questions such as 'Which religion creates such monsters, which culture incubates them?'[2]

---

1 http://in.truveo.com/Linda-Fairstein-on-Elisabeth-Fritzl/id/3965274804.

2 http://www.zimbio.com/Josef+Fritzl/articles/32/religion+creates+these+ monsters+culture+incubates.

Afterwards, the Austrian minister of justice admitted that the authorities had mishandled the case from the start and that the disappearance of Elisabeth in 1984 had not been thoroughly investigated. It would have been different today, she averred. A leading Austrian psychiatrist stated that Fritzl was not insane, as his lawyer claimed, but suffered from an extreme personality disorder, an obsessive exercise of power. Be that as it may, it should not distract our attention from the question how such an obsessive person, how such a man with such an extreme personality disorder, can function as a respected figure in a village for such a long time and that nobody questioned the 'strange' things happening in his family: the eldest daughter had joined a strange 'sect' and three of the children born to her had been found on his doorstep.

In *De Groene Amsterdammer*, a Dutch weekly, I came across an article by Ritchie Robertson (a translation of the original article in *The Times Literary Supplement*, 14 May 2008). The author points to the resemblances this case bears to Austrian literature. As in the Fritzl case, he asserts, there are Austrian novels in which abuse and violence in the family are central. Both novels and reality are about 'power in the family', about patriarchal authority. Austria's pre-1918 civil code sanctioned domestic abuse via the 'rights of chastisement'. Both the actual and the literary abuse of paternal authority seems to fit, according to Robertson, 'into deep-seated cultural patterns and any attempt to investigate them would have to take into account the influence of the Catholic Church in Austria'. The advice given by an priest in an 1877 play is that one should obey one's parents and trust in God. But, so the author continues, the liberal and anti-clerical Freud was no different. In the end, the general effect of his influential and famous case histories has been 'to reinforce the existing family with a conservative bias'. The famous Dora case is perhaps the most illuminating, since 'It looks very much as though Freud is blaming the victims in order to uphold the authority of the father.'

My point is not to indicate the literary adumbration of the Fritzl case, as if paternal abuse in previous times existed only in literature. I also doubt very much that it is a specifically Austrian thing, as Robertson seems to suggest. Rather, my point is that this article put the actual father–daughter/child abuse in a religio-cultural context in which paternal power, as well as paternal abuse, is almost unquestioned by society as a whole. This is not a new feminist theological point. A great deal of work in this field has been done and I will refer here only to the works of Carter Heyward (Heyward 1982), Mary Grey, Rita Nakashima Brock (Brock 1988), Rebecca Parker, Parker Brown and Carole Bohn (Carlson Brown and Bohn 1989) and Annie Imbens and Ineke Jonker (Imbens and Jonker 1992). These authors, notably Heyward, Grey and Brock, emphasize – each from their own perspective – fundamental, ontological and cosmic relationality. From this approach they and others who work in this field are able to criticize 'abusive Christologies', more specifically, abusive interpretations of Jesus' sacrifice, suffering and salvation, and accompanying images of a transcendent divine. These authors also offer inspiring and constructive reinterpretations of these central Christian stories and concepts in which inclusive justice and (inter)relationality are the basic concepts for a Christian theology.

Nevertheless, it is precisely this dimension of absolute power that, so I assume, has everything to do not only with religious cultural views on relations, suffering and salvation, as is demonstrated in much feminist Christological work on this theme, but also with views on creation, procreation and the divine Creator. Gerda Lerner in her classic *The Creation of Patriarchy* already alludes to the urgency of this problem of mono-generativity when she states: 'In the writing of the Book of Genesis, creativity and procreativity are ascribed to all-powerful God, whose epitaphs of "Lord" and "King" establish him as a male God, and female sexuality other than for procreative purposes becomes associated with sin and evil' (Lerner 1986). Again, it is my intuition/conviction that it is precisely in this merging of both creativity *and* procreativity in the one and only – male – God of the monotheistic religious traditions that relationality becomes deeply problematic – that is, if we want to envision a kind of relationality in forms other than unilateral, authoritarian and imperative ones. It is this last intuition that guides and exemplifies my approach in this chapter.

Therefore, it is from the context of patriarchal/paternal power and abuse, not only in families but also in communities and politics, that I want to begin my reflections on monotheism and relationality. Key terms here are obedience, trust, paternal power, creation/creator and mono-generativity as the core of the monotheistic 'problem' with regard to relationality and relations. On what model of faith is monotheism based? I will thus begin with the example of religious faith par excellence, Abraham, and the 'ideal' or exemplary story in this respect, even though it is a highly complicated one: Genesis 22. In short, I am convinced that this story of Abraham's sacrifice still functions as the ultimate prototype of the most perfect form of faith, trust and love with respect to both Abraham and his God. At the same time, and internally related to this proto-type of faith, in the monotheistic traditions Genesis 22 also functions as the prototypical story that equates faith with unconditional obedience and that provides a solid basis for this type of faith in an absolute and authoritarian patriarchal paternal (parental) power. Subsequently, this paternal power is based in the creational, life-giving power of God.

Throughout all centuries many people, women and men, have questioned the wisdom, justice and correct interpretation of Genesis 22, Abraham's sacrifice (the binding of Isaac or the sacrifice of Isaac). And many have found it a complex, horrible, incomprehensible or morally unacceptable story. Nevertheless, all this has not prevented Abraham's unconditional obedience and surrender to his God as demonstrated in this story, however incomprehensible it may be, from functioning in all three monotheistic traditions as *the* 'prototype' of faith. As stated above, many have questioned the meaning of this story. How can a loving God demand such a horrible act from his servant? What kind of obedience is required here? What kind of faith? And in the end, what kind of God would demand this kind of 'proof' of faith from his followers? These questions are similar to those that were posed in the Christological studies mentioned above, although the relation between those two 'prototypical' models was not a point of concern for the above-mentioned authors.

But, regardless of these questions, Abraham's obedience and surrender to the will of God still occupy an important place in the monotheistic traditions, notably in Christianity. From the church fathers onwards, this story is interpreted as prefiguring the central Christian story of Jesus' crucifixion (Brink 2002). What is more, Jesus' sacrifice is an even more pregnant demonstration of both ultimate obedience and the redeeming power of this self-sacrifice (Volf 1996).

According to the philosopher Rudi te Velde, the real question of Genesis 22 is, 'how can one distinguish between an authentic religious attitude where the believer opens himself unconditionally to God and his will, and religious delusion and illusion with possible destructive consequences' (te Velde 2003, p. 8). But is the distinction between authenticity and delusion the real problem indeed? Unconditional openness, according to te Velde, is identical to obedience, and unconditional obedience to the will of God is self-evident and a sign of authentic faith. But is not precisely this – I would say quasi- – self-evident unconditional, absolute obedience as the most authentic religious attitude the core of the problem and the obstacle to any form of mutual relationality? Does this model of faith par excellence imply the classic absolute transcendent God who communicates and relates to his followers through commands and blind obedience? And do not the followers expect the same faith and obedience from their offspring?

I will not conceal that my approach here is deeply influenced by the anthropologist Carol Delaney and her book *Abraham on Trial: The Social Legacy of Biblical Myth* (Delaney 1998). Delaney gives an analysis in this work of the many, many interpretations of Genesis 22 in the monotheistic traditions, and the complicated effects these religious interpretations have on cultural ideas on parenting, fatherhood and the relation between parents and children. To put it bluntly and in an oversimplified way, in speaking of the religio-cultural effects of this biblical story, the case of Josef Fritzl, although very extreme, is just one of the many, and is only the tip of the iceberg. In this light I consider the unasked questions and the failed 1984 investigation of Elisabeth's disappearance to be signs as well of the still present cultural effects of the story, in which the words of the father/God are not to be disputed or mistrusted.

Therefore, I expected feminist interpreters of this story in Genesis 22 to be very sharp and critical about the above-mentioned problems. But, to my surprise, these theologians and exegetes followed other routes. Not only did feminist exegetes seldom explore this specific chapter in Genesis, with the exception of Yvonne Sherwood's counter-readings (Sherwood 2004; 2005), but somehow they always put this specific text into another context and thus found ways to diminish or ignore the obedience and exemplary character of this exemplary faith and trust in God (see, for instance: Fisher 1994; Zorgdrager 2002; but also Brenner 1993, and Newsom and Ringe 1998, who do not mention this specific chapter). My conclusion was that this prototypical and powerful image of Abraham as the ultimate model of faith is hardly challenged by feminist theologians (de Haardt 2003). I find that problematic since it seems to me that this model of faith can influence and has influenced, or at least legitimized, abusive and violent behaviour and reinforces unilateral power relations, perhaps more strongly than the Christological models feminists combat so much and, I would add, so successfully. It also reinforces a kind of mono-generativity in which the father, as generator, has the ultimate power and can demand absolute obedience.

The feminist image of a God-as-Mother giving birth (Grey 2001) and other female images of God (McFague 1987; Johnson 1995), do indeed counteract the image of the male creator. But they leave the mono, singular character of creation and generativity intact. The same goes for all the creative rethinking and reimagining of the Trinity currently going on (McFague 1987; LaCugna 1991; Johnson 1995). The image of the creator God, whether or not feminine, reinscribes the singular, monological character of the act of creation and procreation and, as such, reinscribes a specific kind of unilateral relationality. Also, the many other inspiring images, metaphors and theologies that attempt to go beyond the divine male–female opposition, and at the same time construct a deeply creative, inclusive, empowering and primary *relational* image of God, do not affect this singular creation and generative principle. In my view, that is problematic, since to create, to generate, is not only singular but also strongly male-gendered. Why is it that we only envision the God-She creational act in the image of giving birth, however important, powerful, cosmic and deeply relational that image is? Why do we not have other powerful images of female creativity or female creative power? Are we in a sense reproducing the traditional distinction between creation and reproduction, giving birth?

This deconstructive and constructive work on the predominant masculinity of God and creating is only one side of the problem. The other dimension, the singularity of the Creator and of the act of creation, is still not addressed by these alternatives, since these female divine counter-images of God have not sufficiently undermined the singularity and thus the unilateral dimensions of creation. In fact, they continue this principle. That is why I asked if much of our relational theology still carries these 'residues' of traditional monotheism. There is, of course, much more to say about the problems with or objections to monotheism than those mentioned here, and a great deal has been written on these themes by feminists and many others (see, for example Korte and de Haardt 2009). But for the moment I think that many of these other 'problematic topics in monotheism' have been covered well enough through both critical analysis and constructive proposals.

In my view, the central point of this paper, the focus on *monogenerativity and the monotheistic creator* as *related* to models of faith, obedience and relationality, still needs further critical reflection. It is not only the masculine images of God and the implicit unilateral power relations they generate nor a strict division between God/transcendence and world/immanence that maintain abusive patriarchal power. The concepts and images of creation/creator and creativity are part of the problem *too*. It is not enough, as in relational process theology, to speak of creation as an ongoing process of creativity in which 'God' (or 'Goddess') has to be conceived as an instance of creativity. It is therefore not enough to speak of co-creation or co-creativity, as found in many feminist theology (for example Sölle 1984; Heyward 1982; Christ 2003) and Jewish mystical traditions (Plaskow 1991). These relational approaches neglect the fact that the *act* of creating itself is a highly gendered and singular act, that '*create*' is a gender-specific verb and that 'real' creating is a male prerogative. These gendered images belong to the core images of the religious traditions of the West. According to Carol Delaney, this gendered monogenetic model even dominates most of the so-called 'secular' images of creativity and reproduction in the West – think of Freud – contemporary biological and anthropological findings notwithstanding (Delaney 1998).

The same is true of many theories on creativity and aesthetics in which 'real' creativity or aesthetics often is regarded as 'male', contrary to 'female' reproduction. In the latter instance, according to George Steiner, it becomes clear that if 'reproduction', as in giving birth, is considered 'female creativity', this kind of creativity has nothing to do with 'real creating', let alone with 'real' art (Steiner 1989). In both cases the dominant creation images are male and singular, with all the implications for religious concepts, stories and rituals that tend to reinscribe all kinds of hierarchical dualisms, forms of exclusion and unilateral relationality.

How difficult it is to rethink creation and creativity without getting entangled in these very complex dimensions can be seen in Tina Beattie's recent defence of Christianity against the new atheists (Beattie 2007). The last chapter of her book is dedicated to creativity and the story of God. Contrasting the 'new atheist' art of Ian McEwan in his novel *Saturday* with Zadie Smith's postcolonial novel *On Beauty*, she offers both a critique of the rigidity of the new atheists' (and theologians') model of creativity as 'design' and she grasps the opportunity to propose a concept of creativity in which risk and experiment are fundamental – as she finds to be the case in *On Beauty*. McEwan's *Saturday* is a novel in which the order of 'design' is dominant because its image of creativity lacks any surprise or uncertainty and is based on functionality, construction and control. According to Beattie, McEwan ignores Steiner's argument that all good art reflects a 'wager on transcendence' (Beattie 2007, p. 162; Steiner 1989, p. 214). Her verdict is that, as a thoroughly constructed novel in which there is nothing coincidental, *Saturday* lacks creative genius. Beattie continues by considering God's creation and human functioning in it as the work of a creative genius. Creation is real creativity, in the Steinerian sense of the word, because of the risks God is willing to take with creation. Beattie claims that 'Christian theologians have continued to project images of virile masculinities onto God in the language of omnipotence and omniscience, but at the heart of the Christian story is a different story about God' (Beattie 2007, p. 169). For Beattie, this story is to be found in the Gospels, in the ultimate risk of a God incarnate, thereby surrendering 'all claims of divine power by becoming the child in Mary's womb and the tortured man on the cross' (Beattie 2007, p. 169). But here again, this new path that Beattie chooses diverts us from the actual problem of creation, creativity, and the singularity and masculinity of the creative genius. It leads us from creation to incarnation, from God to Jesus, as we saw earlier.

But there is another problem with Beattie's use of Steiner's ideas on creativity and its relation to transcendence and God's presence. She relates them to her image of creative genius as an image for creation. What she does not mention is the fact that, in his reflections on 'great art', 'real' creation and creativity, Steiner makes a strong distinction between male and female creativity (Steiner 1989). For Steiner, creation, as in God's creation, is reserved for males; it is an act of wrestling with the 'other maker'. Creation, 'real creativity' thus has to do with power, jealousy, in which the male artist identifies himself with God. Female creativity is another matter, different from that of males; it is a less 'great' or less 'real' creativity. That is not to say that Steiner does not see creativity in women. 'I am convinced that there is in the poetry, in the novels written by women, as compelling a force of counter-creation, of life-giving repossession and corrigenda of the world as in those written by men' (Steiner 1989, p. 206). And yet Steiner poses the question, although very cautiously: 'Is the biological capacity for procreation, for engendering formed life which is cardinal to woman, in some way, at some level absolutely primordial to a woman's being, so creative, so fulfilling, as to subvert, as to render comparatively pallid, the begetting of fictive personae which is the matter of drama and of so much representative art?' (Steiner 1989, p. 207). In other words, Steiner suspects that the cause of what he considers to be women's 'almost total absence from drama' lies in their biological capacity for procreation. Indeed, real creation is still a male and powerful thing.

My problem regarding Beattie's creativity as presented here is that her creative genius, in line with Steiner's argument on the creativity of great art, is – even if she does not state it as such – distinguished by its maleness. Can that kind of singular creativity, that begetting of great novels, music, art, indeed be a new model of creation and creativity? Because, although it seems that Steiner realizes the dangers of his gendered approach, his views on women and creativity can also be considered to be a kind of 'pedestal' elimination. Why else should the creativity of procreation be considered identical with giving birth, as if the male had nothing to do with it? What does 'engendering formed life' mean? Who 'formed' that life? Why make female procreation the primordial, creative and fulfilling activity, at least for women? Why make a conceptual distinction, or worse, an opposition, between the capacity of giving birth, *'formed life'*, that is 'procreation' in the biological sense, and abstinence from *poiesis* on the one hand, and the 'aesthetic creation', bringing into being of *'life forms'* as a god-like activity?

Luckily, there are other feminist voices. Catherine Keller, in her challenging creation theology elaborated in her *Face of the Deep* (Keller 2003), is engaged in these same creational issues as is, with different accents, Laurel Schneider in her *Beyond Monotheism: A Theology of Multipliciy* (Schneider 2008). I will focus on Keller, since her study is an explicit creational theology. Rejecting the idea of *creatio ex nihilo*, her alternative *creatio ex profundis* counters theism, the power structures of Jewish and Christian orthodoxies and the abstract male potency as found in the interpretations of creation in the first lines of the book of Genesis. Keller is strongly influenced by relational process thinking (Whitehead), feminist religious reflection (as diverse as Daly and Johnson), Jewish and medieval Christian mystical writers, ecological concerns as well as postmodern French philosophers such as Deleuze, Derrida and Irigaray. Bringing these different strands of thinking together in an admirable tour de force, Keller wrote a thought-provoking book in which she reconstructs traditions and thereby draws from the margins and the depths of the Jewish and Christian texts. She calls her proposal a tehomic theology, a reflection from the Deep, out of the feminine, maternally connoted 'chaos', the *tehom* of Genesis 1.2, as a counter-movement to the space of this 'erased' chaos in which classical theism was created. Rethinking creation and 'God' in this theology means reading 'God' as the 'pluri-singularity of the text', as 'a multiplicity of differences-in-relation, the multiple that as such is relation' (Keller 2003, p. 177). In Keller's approach, the grammar of 'God's Creation' stays ambiguous (Keller 2003). It seems to me that her 'divining of the relational and creational multiple' is an important and necessary act for overcoming the mono-generativity of western monotheism in its philosophical and theological forms. In my view it is one of the first and most impressive attempts at breaking through the monological and mono-generative interpretations of creation and Creator.

At least on a theoretical, linguistic level Keller offers possibilities for rewriting a Christian relational creation theology. And precisely here I feel a bit uncomfortable, partly because I am not as convinced as Keller that a different theology needs to be grounded in the *texts* of the tradition, although I enjoyed and admire her postmodern reading of the works of the fathers, seeking and finding radical resistance in their language. For strategic and intellectual reasons, this feminist and postmodern rereading of notably the works of the early Church is undeniable in its offering of fresh and new insights and interpretations of central Christian concepts. But I cannot escape the feeling that her ambiguous, fluid, mystical, multiple and relational theology has a kind of logic that, in a way, 'fits' too 'neatly'. For all its openness, weakness and uncertainty, the model Keller offers is a very *strong* one. Perhaps that is my deepest problem – as it is with Laurel Schneider's *Beyond Monotheism*, as it is with my own relational theology: we are all searching, longing, for models that 'fit', we are searching for strong models that are able to offer convincing theological alternatives that are *not* impregnated with language, images and metaphors that manifest domination and power. These are strong models, making sense intellectually, theologically *and* spiritually, for many contemporary women and men, living in this part of the world. But is not this longing itself and the impressive relational models it produces characteristic of the monotheistic model? Can we, with our sophisticated, inspiring and creative theological models, ever escape this mono-longing or monological longing even if our models are those of difference, ambiguity, multiplicity and relationality?

Let me be clear: I am deeply convinced that relational theology is the best we contemporary theologians have to offer, as I see it, from white women and men who constitute the western context for the most part. More strongly, I am convinced that theologians, and especially the feminist among us, need this kind of theology to keep us 'sane', religiously and intellectually. Without these relational models I fear many of us would not be able to relate in a positive way to the Christian tradition. In other words, relational theology with its strong emphasis on justice, divine presence and the power of relationality offers more than merely a convincing theological model. It offers a model that enables many contemporary believers 'to keep faith'. Relational theology, perhaps in a way, is a contemporary western prototypical, ideal 'model of faith'.

That brings me to my third question: do we need different concepts, models and metaphors or do we need different practices? This, of course, is the wrong question. We need a different, non-dominational, non-exploitive practice of relating to one another and to the cosmos as a whole, that is certain. However, the relation between ideas, concepts and practices is complicated. Sometimes I get the impression that theo-logians expect too much from the influence of both the theology that we reject and our relational proposals. I am not at all sure that the relation between ideas and social reality is *that* strong, that a different *perspective* on relationality, divinity, creation, faith or obedience would be enough to change the still dominant imperialistic, abusive or unilateral relations, language and reality. Human relations and religions, monotheistic or not, are or can be entangled in violent and powerful relations; they are and can be intertwined and deeply involved in injustice and violence, *and* they are and can be engaged in the struggle for right relations, justice, peace or ecological balance. It is not the religious 'system', the concept, the language, the image or the metaphor 'as such' that is the cause of the problem. There are no 'pure' or 'single' causes, not any more as there are 'pure' or 'single' solutions, as Keller and others have so eloquently demonstrated.

Nevertheless, concepts, metaphors and images do play a role and af-fect reality; they form and guide our experiences and our interpretation of reality and vice versa. Also important is that they reflect our hopes and expectations. But I am also convinced that in the end it is neither the consistency nor the attraction of our relational theologies nor our con-structive proposals on cosmology, creation, generativity or a relational divinity that lead to liberating, sustaining or transformative practices. Reimagining, deconstructing and reconstructing of religious images and religious doctrines are very modest tools in these complicated processes. There is more to relationality, to mono-generativity and to divinity than philosophical, biblical and theological reasoning. Concepts, models or metaphors in themselves are not abusive. Only by appropriating reli-gious images and models of dominance to legitimize practices, laws or social and cultural exclusive systems, can concepts and images become part of violent practices. But it is not an inescapable fate, not a necessity. And although many of us relational thinkers would despise traditional masculine, omnipotent, transcendental God-talk, would despise traditional monotheism, this is not to deny that this language not only had the fundamental potential but also the actual effect of generating love, mutuality, solidarity, because of the trust in those images, concepts and doctrines, because of the trust that God offered to many. And that is my point; many relational theologians argue for fundamental ambiguity, vulnerability, fluidity, multiplicity and differences in our theologies. But our models do not provide the simultaneity of both a relational 'model' and a more traditional monotheistic 'model' in the faith of one and the same person at the same time. The simultaneity that at first sight seems contradictory, paradoxical and highly 'queer' from a singular perspective, be it relational or traditional theistic. The contradictions can only be 'caught', in the religious practices and the lived religiosity in either Christian, Jewish or Islamic individuals and their communities. Even the most 'oppressive images' can gain completely contradictory meanings in their processes of appropriations. How else can Christianity, Christian faith, still be such a powerful force in the lives of many women and men? So for some, Abraham can be the prototype of a person who trusts his or her divine power or divine presence and for that reason feels obliged to follow this empowering relational God. But then, probably, it is not the Genesis story to which reference is made.

Religious appropriation – we have hardly any conception in theology of how it works, for whom and under which conditions. The same is true for the actual influences of images and concepts on the religiously motivated practices of women and men. Historians and anthropological-sociologists of religion have recently coined the notion of 'lived religion' (Hall 1997). These scholars are presenting studies in which they 'map' everyday religious practices in their complexities and pluralities (Ammerman 2007). It is up to theologians to engage with this 'lived religion', this everyday life, which, in a sense, I expect to be far more complex, fluid, inconsistent, *and* relational, than our relational theologies.

References

Ammerman, N. T. (ed.) (2007), *Everday Religion: Observing Modern Religious Lives* (Oxford and New York: Oxford Universiy Press).

Beattie, T. (2007), *The New Atheists: The Twilight of Reason and the War on Religion* (London: Darton, Longman and Todd).

Brenner, A. (ed.) (1993), *A Feminist Companion to Genesis*, vol. 2 (Sheffield: Sheffield Academic Press).

Brink, E. v. d. (2002), 'Abraham's Sacrifice in Early Jewish and Early Christian Art', in E. and E. T. Noort (eds), *The Sacrifice of Isaac: Interpretations of the Aqedah (Genesis 22)*, vol. 4 (Leiden: Brill), pp. 140–51.

Brock, R. N. (1988), *Journeys by Heart: A Christology of Erotic Power* (New York: Crossroad).

Carlson Brown, J. and C. R. Bohn (eds) (1989), *Christianity, Patriarchy and Abuse: A Feminist Critique* (Cleveland, OH: Pilgrim Press).

Christ, C. P. (2003), *She Who Changes: Re-imagining the Divine in the World* (New York: Palgrave).

Delaney, C. (1998), *Abraham on Trial: The Social Legacy of Biblical Myth* (Princeton: Princeton University Press).

Fisher, I. (1994), *Die Erzeltern Israels: Feministisch-Theologische Studien zu Genesis 12–36* (Berlin et al.: de Gruyter).

Grey, M. (2001), *Introducing Feminist Images of God* (Cleveland, OH: Pilgrim Press).

Haardt, M. de (2003), 'Abrahams Offer: Prototype van gehoorzaamheid, prototype van geloof? Over gender, monogenese en monotheïsme', in R. te Velde (ed.), *Doen wat God wil: zegen of ramp? Over ethiek en religie in het licht van Abrahams offer* (Budel: Damon), pp. 36–61.

Hall, D. D. (ed.) (1997), *Lived Religion in America: Toward a History of Practice* (Princeton: Princeton University Press).

Heyward, I. C. (1982), *The Redemption of God: A Theology of Mutual Relation* (Washington, DC: University Press of America).

Imbens, A. and I. Jonker (1992), *Christianity and Incest* (Minneapolis: Fortress Press).

Johnson, E. A. (1995), *She Who Is: The Mystery of God in Feminist Theological Discourse* (New York: Crossroad).

Keller, C. (2003), *Face of the Deep: A Theology of Becoming* (London and New York: Routledge).

Korte, A.-M. and M. de Haardt (eds) (2009), *The Boundaries of Monotheism: Interdisciplinary Explorations into the Foundations of Western Monotheism* (Leiden: Brill).

LaCugna, C. M. (1991), *God for Us: The Trinity and Christian Life* (New York: Harper Collins).

Lerner, G. (1986), *The Creation of Patriarchy* (New York and Oxford: Oxford University Press).

McFague, S. (1987), *Models of God: Theology for an Ecological, Nuclear Age* (Philadelphia: Crossroad).

Newsom, C. A. and S. H. Ringe (eds) (1998), *Women's Bible Commentary*, Expanded edition with Apocrypha (Louisville, KY: Westminster John Knox Press).

Plaskow, J. (1991), *Standing Again at Sinai: Judaism from a Feminist Perspective* (San Francisco, CA: HarperSanFrancisco).

Schneider, L. C. (2008), *Beyond Monotheism: A Theology of Multiplicity* (London and New York: Routledge).

Sherwood, Y. (2004), 'Binding–Unbinding: Divided Responses of Judaism, Christianity and Islam to the "Sacrifice" of Abraham's Beloved Son', *Journal of the American Academy of Religion* 72.4, pp. 826–61.

——(2005), 'Textual Carcasses and Isaac's Scar or What Jewish Interpretation Makes of the Violence that Almost Takes Place on Mt. Moriah', *Journal for the Study of the Old Testament* Supplement Series 400 (Sanctified Aggression), pp. 22–43.

Sölle, D. (1984), *To Work and To Love: A Theology of Creation* (Philadelphia: Fortress Press).

Steiner, G. (1989), *Real Presences* (Chicago: University of Chicago Press).

te Velde, R. (ed.) (2003), *Doen wat God wil: zegen of ramp? Over ethiek en religie in het licht van Abrahams offer* (Budel: Damon).

Volf, M. (1996), *Exclusion and Embrace: A Theological Exploration of Identity and Reconciliation* (Nashville, TN: Abingdon).

Zorgdrager, H. (2002), 'The Sacrifice of Abraham as a (Temporary) Resolution of a Descent Conflict?', in E. Noort and E. Tichelaar (eds), *The Sacrifice of Isaac: Interpretations of the Aqedah (Genesis 22)* (Leiden: Brill), pp. 182–96.

11

Transcendence and the Refiguring of God as Male, the Absolute Same

JENNY DAGGERS

Transcendence has emerged as a vital theme in recent philosophical and theological discourse, though this resurgence is driven by differing, often conflicting commitments. In this chapter I investigate this transcendent turn, by attending to the confluence of two distinct currents in the enlivened discourse on transcendence: on the one hand, radical orthodoxy and, on the other, feminist philosophy and theology.

My aim is to argue that reassertion of transcendence – or at least resistance to its collapse into immanence – may be productive in diverting the impetus towards figuring the triune God of Christianity as necessarily male, the Absolute Same. My reflections seek to retrieve the transcendent God of the Christian tradition as capable of furthering humanity in all its variety of gender and sexuality. By rehabilitating divine transcendence as radical alterity to the human, subjectivities of women as well as men may be facilitated: elevation of men at the expense of women is not a necessary consequence of taking seriously the transcendence of God.

In contemporary philosophy, the turn to transcendence takes issue with an uncompromising trend towards privileging of immanence in the disenchanted world of modernity, in even its late or postmodern manifestations. Thus Claire Colebrook draws attention to Deleuze and Gittari's characterization of philosophy, which she portrays as a necessary affirmation of immanence over against religion with its problematic transcendent and enslaving 'notions of a foundation, ground, or presence that would be other than the becomings of life' (Colebrook 2009, p. 79). It is interesting that feminist moves to think transcendence run in parallel with this male repositioning within the space of immanence – but this is to run ahead of my argument.

Taking Deleuze and Gittari as expressive of the secularizing turn to immanence, their project is to render transcendence redundant together with the religion that keeps it in play: 'Whenever there is transcendence, vertical Being, imperial State in the sky or on earth, there is religion; and there is Philosophy whenever there is immanence' (Deleuze and Gittari cited in Colebrook 2009, p. 96).[1] If religion were eliminated, transcendence would be no more. But the expected demise of religion is complicated by the postmodern and postcolonial re-enchantment of the world. Radical orthodoxy, with its new attention to transcendence, represents a renewed contest between secularism and Christianity in the context of this re-enchantment. The first part of the chapter examines this radical orthodox transcendent turn, arguing that a transcendence/immanence dualism is reinforced in the discourse of radical orthodoxy.

Concurrently, feminist philosophy and theology, in struggling to valorize embodiment over disembodied reason, also speak of transcendence while resisting women's assigned confinement in immanence. The male philosophical turn to immanence, to the feminine, does not address feminist concern with women's subjectivity; women's subjectivity necessarily involves escaping women's entrapment in immanence. The second part of the chapter investigates the feminist turn to transcendence, emphasizing the commitment here to dissolving dualist notions of transcendence over against immanence. But there is a danger that transcendence is compromised in pursuing this commitment.

The return of transcendence: radical orthodoxy

Within modernity there is a secularizing current that gradually asserts a valorization of immanence over transcendence. Modern epistemologies

---

1 It is interesting to reflect that philosophical theologians, such as Anne E. Inman, maintain the notion that some horizon to human knowledge must be posited as a way of affirming its own meaningfulness. In Klein's paraphrase: 'When human beings assert that humanity has a future, they reference what believers have always meant by the word "God"' (Klein 2009, p. 505).

that refuse classical Christian reliance on knowing God, through analogy with what can be known in the created order, are instrumental in this shift towards valorization of immanence. Given that secularism arises within the context of European Christianity, its calling into question of transcendence is a calling into question of the triune God of Christianity, and in particular a calling into question of notions of the immanent as opposed to the economic Trinity.[2]

Within the complexity of modernist thought, three options emerge as influential in disconnecting secular discourse from the Christian understanding of God, both transcendent and immanent. First, transcendence is relegated to the noumenal condition of the Deist God, beyond the reach of, and thus irrelevant to, human ethical concern with available phenomenal evidence. In Deism, there is a disconnection with the immanence of God incarnate in Jesus.[3] Second, in contrast, in the alternative Pietist response to modernity, with its focus on Jesus as Redeemer and personal saviour, there is set in motion a tendency which will eventually lead towards disconnection from God's transcendence.[4] Third, Hegel's idealist dialectical movement towards the realization of Absolute Spirit within Christianity maintains a focus on transcendent spirit – but Marx

---

2 Confusingly, in terms of the discussion here of transcendence/immanence, the immanent Trinity in classic Christian theological thought represents the triune God who *transcends* the palpable activity of the economic Trinity within the (*immanent*) world, revealed in the incarnation of Jesus Christ and the work of the Holy Spirit, and so allowing an inadequate yet accurate analogical human appreciation of the (*transcendent*) immanent Trinity. See Collins 2008, especially pp. 52–62, and Tanner 2001, pp. 35–65 for helpful discussions.

3 Though it is also true that the Kantian Deist God maintains a practically and ethically vital God, albeit a God who is theoretically unknowable. I am grateful to my colleague Steven Shakespeare for this point. However, it is important for my argument that Kant resists the analogical form of knowing on which understanding of the (transcendent) immanent Trinity is based.

4 Though Schleiermacher's theology is grounded in Pietism, his thought is thoroughly grounded in a Trinitarian appreciation of God's transcendence as well as God's immanence. But his turn to religious experience sets in train a theological direction which is capable of losing sight of God as Trinity, immanent as well as economic, in favour of theologies that are content to function in the economic realm alone.

cancels Hegel's idealist transcendence in favour of secular materialism, when he returns Hegel from his idealist headstand to a firm stance in the material.

Separately and together, these distinct Deist, Pietist and Hegelian Christian responses to modernity effect a disconnection between the transcendence and immanence which are bound together within Trinitarian Christian theology. Over against the secularizing trend, wherein religion with its transcendent God is predicted to fade away, post-Enlightenment liberal theologies maintain an economic focus on God at work in the contemporary world: where the Trinity was firmly in place for Schleiermacher as the coda of his theology, there was a tendency in the liberal theology which he set in train for Trinitarian thought to vanish from view. Karl Barth's neo-orthodoxy reinstates the Trinity, immanent (and so transcendent) and economic, over against its neglect in liberal theology.

Radical orthodoxy has some resonances with this Barthian tradition, though it is a new impetus whose primary target is secularism, with challenge to liberal theologies as a secondary corollary of the renewal of Christian critique of the secular.[5] Thus John Milbank opens his book, with its telling subtitle, *Theology and Social Theory: Beyond Secular Reason* – the initial expression of radical orthodoxy – with the statement, 'Once, there was no "secular"' (Milbank 2006, p. 1). A core theme within radical orthodoxy is that the secular arises from a change in the doctrine of God within theology. Aquinas forges an intermediate path of *analogy* between the equivocal – divine and human are referred to in completely different senses – and the univocal – divine and human referred to in identical senses; radical orthodoxy seeks to return discourse – both theological and secular – to this path. This intermediate way allows for an analogy between human goodness and God's goodness, whereby

---

5 See Milbank and Oliver 2009, pp. 368–73 for his critique of Barth's hidden 'extrinsicism' – that is Barth's post-Kantian assumption that reason and faith are separate, and that God must be proved before revelation can be shown to be possible (p. 368); evident in his 'failure to embrace the traditional [liturgical] structure of analogy and participation which overarched the faith reason divide' (p. 370).

goodness is attributed to the human by virtue of human relation to God.[6] The same analogical relationship holds for human being itself: 'we only exist or have being *by virtue of a relation with being itself*, namely God' (Milbank in Milbank and Oliver 2009, p. 17). Creatures exist only through *participation* in the gratuity of God's *gift* of being.[7]

According to radical orthodoxy, the secular has its origins in the shift from this intermediate path to univocity of being, which is crystallized in the work of Duns Scotus. The radical orthodox project is to reinstate transcendence – or to be precise, to refuse 'the possibility of indifference to the transcendent [God]' (see Oliver in Milbank and Oliver 2009, pp. 21–4; Pickstock 2009, pp. 116–46; and Milbank in Milbank and Oliver 2009, pp. 379–87). Also reinstated is the claim that faith and reason are inextricably intertwined, over against the rationalism of modern epistemology. The promise of radical orthodoxy lies in the corollary as neatly put by Oliver: '*one cannot be indifferent to immanence and our created nature* to which belongs the reason that is peculiar to our nature' (Oliver in Milbank and Oliver 2009, p. 20, original emphasis).

However, it is this valorization of 'the reason that is peculiar to our nature' that belies the greatest weakness of radical orthodoxy: a tendency to emphasize reason as the primary means of human knowing and to assume an unreconstructed understanding of the body as biological mechanism.[8] The radical alterity of the triune Christian God, incarnate in Jesus Christ, is short-changed in this impoverished economy where reason is the hallmark of the human, which reproduces the Cartesian framework it purports to sweep aside. When Oliver refers to the 'ambitious *sensibility*' of radical orthodoxy, he uses the term to refer

---

6 I draw here on Milbank and Oliver 2009, pp. 12–16. This analogy of attribution is dependent on the *analogia entis*, the analogy of being, namely that human existence is by virtue of relation with being itself, that is God (p. 17).

7 This is to participate in God's substance; only God exists in himself, only God has substance. Creation only has existence and substance through participation in God. See Milbank and Oliver 2009, pp. 16–17.

8 As one example, see Milbank, 'Postmodern Critical Augustinianism', in John Milbank and Simon Oliver (eds), *The Radical Orthodoxy Reader* (London: Routledge, 2009), pp. 49–61, at p. 58 for reference to 'bodily energies and drives'.

to the breadth of 'the bewildering array of subjects' tackled by this theological school wherein reason is rejoined with faith (Oliver in Milbank and Oliver 2009, p. 20, my emphasis). In contrast, for feminist philosophers and theologians, the 'sensible' is deployed to open up embodied forms of thought where reason is rejoined with the body. Radical orthodoxy's inadequate and impoverished understanding of bodily matter leaves in place the longstanding gendered implications of a reinstated transcendent/immanent binary, where the (male) human spirit soars through reason alone while there is no knowing in and through (female) embodiment.

Before turning to the feminist return to transcendence in the second part of this chapter, I wish to sum up my brief discussion of radical orthodoxy by affirming the space it reopens for radical alterity, wherein, as Paul G. Tyson puts it, critique of faulty rationalism may reopen 'ideas of knowable transcendent truth and inherently meaningful reality', so that 'the largely abandoned territory of epistemology and transcendence' may once more be explored (Tyson 2008, p. 246). However, the dangers of reinstating radical alterity between the divine and human, where this is to be understood in terms of the classic 'chain of being', will hardly need rehearsing for feminist readers.

Thus Mary-Jane Rubenstein, in her tongue-in-cheek response to sparring between Milbank and Kenneth Surin, 'Onward, Ridiculous Debaters', resists making a choice between Milbank's hierarchy and Surin's (Deleuzian) univocity (Rubenstein 2009, pp. 125–9).[9] Rubenstein worries that the 'immanentist collapse' of Surin's politics of the multitude, powered by collective '*autopoiesis*', might 'reinscribe the logic of the autonomous, self-fashioning self at the communal level' (2009, p. 126). A similar concern underlies my own argument in this chapter. Yet Rubenstein's reservations about the Milbankian alternative will form a neat bridge to the second part of this chapter: when Christians act as though there is a great chain of being, the result is slavery, genocide and 'the ongoing racism and sexism both sustaining and destroying mainline Christianities' (2009, p. 126). Feminist philosophers and theologians

---

9 Rubenstein is commenting on debate in Davis, Milbank and Žižek 2005.

who turn to transcendence largely share Rubenstein's unease with these possible implications of radical orthodoxy.

The return of transcendence: a feminist theme

In the opening paragraphs of the previous section, I referred to Deist, Pietist and Hegelian Christian responses to modern rationalism, as opening trajectories in which pre-modern notions of immanence as bound up in transcendence are displaced in a gradual decoupling of immanence from transcendence. In parallel with Marx's materialist (immanent) inversion of Hegel's (transcendent) idealism, an important next step is Feuerbach's secularizing assertion that the transcendent God is but a projection in the mind of the foundational transcendental human subject. In Feuerbach, transcendence is reconceived in humanist terms, as a necessary component of (male) human subjectivity; premodern notions of such human transcendence pointing analogically to the transcendent God of the immanent Trinity – the divine as radical alterity – are already banished at this point. Of crucial importance here for feminist philosophy and theology is the perpetuation, in the transcendent human subject, of the classical tradition of western philosophy wherein the male has been identified with transcendent spirit, and the female with the immanent body.[10]

While there is a rising current in (mainly male) philosophy seeking to 'free ourselves from the burden of transcendence' (Colebrook 2009, p. 79), Luce Irigaray, and Simone de Beauvoir before her, are among those who seek to turn transcendence to feminist ends. Both appear

---

10 Though there is a current philosophical discourse attempting to repudiate transcendence in favour of immanence (Colebrook 2009, p. 79.) See Colebrook for a critique of this attempt, and for a robust defence of 'transcendental ethics' including essentialism as transcendence and the claim: 'every relation to an other is a relation to a self who is oriented to a transcendence, who understands their own being through a genre, a mode, a style, or a divine sense of that which is other than their self-present immediacy' (p. 95). Here Colebrook emphasizes Irigaray's suggestion that 'there are at least two sexes' – so opening a way beyond irreducible sexual difference as constraint on subjectivity.

to assume a Feuerbachian reading of religious belief (Hollywood 1994, p. 175), and both investigate the subjectivities of medieval women mystics as sites of transcendence in bodily immanence. As Hollywood puts it: 'For Beauvoir, a transcendence mediated by the immanent body is always feminized, and hence inadequate, while one that surpasses the body entirely is always false and illusory'; Irigaray moves beyond this 'impasse' with her 'sensible transcendental', which she first articulates in her writings on medieval mystics (2009, p. 161).[11]

Irigaray's 'female divine' assumes Feuerbach's projective understanding of a purely teleological transcendence, which she shapes to provide a transcendent horizon for female becoming. Her aim is to enable women's self-transcendence beyond their imposed immanence. Difficulties facing the creation of a female symbolic first turn Irigaray's thoughts in the direction of divine transcendence.[12] The terrain she has opened for emergent female subjectivity, resourced by an incipient female imaginary, is of incalculable significance, and it is a project that has barely begun and deserves development over millennia to come. But, as a theologian who maintains a commitment to the transcendent Christian God, I find Irigaray's 'sensible transcendental' ultimately disappoints.

Irigaray locates us at the crossroad of a vertical and horizontal transcendence (Irigaray 2009, p. 22). She has complete confidence that vertical transcendence refers to the Absolute Same, the Other of the Lacanian symbolic order, appropriately reduced in stature through the critique of Feuerbach: there is no alterity to the human in Irigaray's vertical transcendence. So it is the horizontal transcendence of the 'sensible transcendental' which is of creative significance for Irigaray, the means of escaping fusion, which is the reducing or subjecting of the one to the

---

11 See Linnell Secombe for a persuasive argument that in de Beauvoir's writings there is to be found an inchoate concept of incarnate-transcendence, or fleshy transcendence of Woman, an implicit 'amalgamation of transcendence and embodiment' (Secombe 1999, p. 99). However, despite the fact that Secombe offers a more productive reading of Beauvoir, it is not pursued here on account of Beauvoir's 'explicit atheism' (Hollywood 1994, p. 159); Irigaray's concept of a female divine renders her work of greater relevance to this enquiry.

12 See Daggers 1997, pp. 38–9 for discussion of this point.

other in response to the imperative of vertical transcendence, and in this escape remaining 'two' (sexed subjects) (Irigaray 2009, p. 23). In this chapter, I am concerned to rehabilitate Irigaray's vertical transcendence in Christian terms, arguing the transcendent God of Christianity is excessive to the Absolute Same of the Lacanian symbolic order. To be clear, this is not to resolve to sabotage or dismantle Irigaray's project. Rather, it is to critique a humanist limitation she imposes through it on Christian thinking the divine and human subjectivity in relation to it.

Responding to Irigaray, Pamela Sue Anderson reasserts secular modernity, with its project of historical transformation in gender relations, as articulated by Beauvoir – its quintessential feminist spokeswoman – over against Irigaray's 'pre-modernism' (Anderson 2009, pp. 27–54). Anderson is careful to distinguish her feminist philosophical project from that of feminist theologians who engage with Irigaray, such as Tina Beattie. She is particularly concerned to resist 'the internally and ethically contradictory conception of transcendence, which, in particular, emerges in the Mariology of orthodox theology', and 'the contradiction inherent in the gendered accounts of the Christian God as Father and the Virgin as the Mother of the Son of God' (p. 28). For Anderson, postmodern theologians are 'guided by the implicit ideals of divinity for men and women' and in their rejection of secularism embrace 'a pre-Enlightenment portrait of the Virgin Mother and God the Father' (p. 29). Anderson argues powerfully against 'apotheosis' – becoming divine – as productive of subjectivity: '[t]he danger in the twofold deification of man as God the Father and woman as the Virgin Mother/Lover is the persistent imprisonment of women in their own bodies and psyches' (p. 45). Where I have critiqued Irigaray for being not Christian enough, Anderson is concerned that Irigaray risks reinstating Christianity in its premodern form, including its rigid gender binary, with all its oppressive effects. For Anderson, the problem is that Irigaray is not sufficiently secular.

Patrice Haynes critiques Irigaray on different grounds. For Haynes, Irigaray is among those feminist thinkers who repudiate the divine transcendence of monotheism in favour of what is in effect divine immanence. Thus, for Irigaray, 'the immanence of female and male sexuate belonging (of body and psyche) *is* divine' (Haynes 2009, p. 57).

Haynes gives as examples of other feminist conceptions of divine immanence, Sallie McFague's revisioning of the world as 'God's body', Carol Christ's use of process theology to reimagine God as a divine power at one with the ongoing creation of the world and Sharon Welch's equation of divinity with the 'relational power' of community (Haynes 2009, p. 57). Haynes argues that the repudiated theistic notion of divine transcendence is as capable of affirming materiality and embodiment.[13] For Haynes, divine transcendence lovingly invests the material with 'determinateness and integrity. Indeed, it is by virtue of the transcendence of divine mind that . . . the transcendence of the object in its sensuous particularity cannot be entirely lost to the immanence of the human mind' (2009, p. 72).

My argument in this chapter runs parallel to that of Haynes, seeking a different response to problematics in women's subjectivity, and thus necessarily to the subjectivities of men, and to ethics of relation, from that offered by either Irigaray or Anderson. I maintain that notions of the Christian God – both transcendent and radically other to the human, and immanent in the incarnation of Jesus Christ – are capable of being rethought so that they exceed the confines of the gendered economy of human polities, including the longstanding patriarchal economy of the Christian Church. Critique of modern formulations of divine and human transcendence prepares the way for a reassertion of divine transcendence as radical alterity.

Mayra Rivera's project in *The Touch of Transcendence* bears some resemblance to my preoccupations in this chapter. In her vision of 'relational transcendence', Rivera hopes 'to remobilize the passion and wisdom of a Christian love for the inappropriable divine Other as theological resources for rethinking our relationship with human others' (Rivera 2007, p. 2). Through dialogue between theological and non-theological discussions of transcendence, she aims to uncover both

---

13 Haynes argues that 'the rampant disenchantment of the world effected by modern rationality, is also the "immanentization" of the world' (Haynes 2009, p. 62), hence her turn to a theological materialism which is also a theological idealism (p. 71).

problems and promises of transcendence for theologies committed to social justice (p. x). As in Rubenstein's critique of the outworkings of Milbank's hierarchy, Rivera aligns herself with progressive theologians who object to the validation of hierarchical rule that attends divine transcendence when it is conceived of as superior, immaterial, apart and above (p. 1).

De Beauvoir resurfaces in Rivera's discussion. As she points out, Beauvoir's notion of woman as (immanent) other to the (transcendent) male subject is highly influential on Mary Daly's inaugural texts in feminist theology, where Daly criticizes Christian theology for tending to 'hypostasize transcendence' – that is to describe transcendence as a characteristic of the 'nature' of a being – so objectifying God. Rather, Daly maintains, transcendence is a verb, the unfolding of God, an event in which women participate, thus releasing women from entrapment in immanence. But, Rivera adjudicates, 'Daly's depiction of transcendence (like de Beauvoir's) retained aspects of its prevalent images, namely those of separation and independence, which other feminists have subsequently found problematic' (Rivera 2007, p. 7; see pp. 6–7 for Rivera's argument produced here). [14]

Rivera's own accomplished crafting of 'relational transcendence' reconceives transcendence so that its problematic separation from the 'constraints' of materiality is addressed. She explores the 'beyond' of transcendence, in conjunction with discourses of 'the Other', as 'inextricable from the witness of oppressed communities'; the beyond 'is not a static place of separation, but a dynamic space of encounters and transformation' (Rivera 2007, pp. 13–14). [15] Engaging in turn with radical orthodox texts, Emmanuel Levinas, the liberationist philosopher Enrique Dussell, Luce Irigaray and Gayatri Spivak, Rivera skilfully unfolds her model of relational transcendence whose threads, encountered in the

14 Rivera's mention of 'other feminist theologians' is supported by reference to Ruether, in *Sexism and God-Talk*, and to a recent book chapter by Catherine Keller, where she critiques Beauvoir's notion of transcendence.

15 Thus Rivera takes Beauvoir's notion of woman as Other in different directions, which return transcendence to materiality, and so she overcomes problematics of Beauvoir's and Daly's thought on transcendence.

human Other, within and through a living cosmic space, can be rendered in theological language as proclaiming the divine glory enfolding all (2007, p. 15).

Rivera's *The Touch of Transcendence* is a considerable achievement. It is beyond the scope of my argument here to do justice to her project, but it is helpful to my argument to focus on Rivera's reliance on Irigaray's sensible transcendental, and on the outworkings of this reliance when she turns to theological language to express her refiguring of the transcendent/immanent binary.[16] It is from Irigaray that Rivera draws her motif of touch (2007, p. 88). And in her final chapter, Rivera turns from her explorations of interhuman encounter to investigate her claim that 'Being in relation to the Other is the mark of the beginning of our very life in a reality underived from us' which theology names as God (p. 126).

Rivera refers to an elusive 'third' to the self and Other engaged in interhuman transcendence, which Irigaray – like theology – names as God. Though Rivera refrains from clarifying this point, it is important for my argument that Irigaray's God is clearly a Feuerbachian projection, rather than the Trinitarian God of Christianity. Rivera is concerned to maintain clear water between the vertical transcendence of radical orthodox Trinitarianism and her own third, but she is content to keep company with Irigaray's ambiguous relation to Christian orthodoxy.[17] When she asserts creation as a site of transcendence, and the transcendence of the human Other as the glory of God, when she adds Victoria Burrus's insightful critique of the fixing of theological language in masculine terms in the Nicene Creed, Rivera cedes the 'Trinitarian journey' (Pickstock, cited in Rivera 2007, p. 133) to an orthodoxy which must remain at odds with her own relational transcendence. I suggest,

---

16 To be sure, Rivera draws on Spivak's postcolonial critique to take a step beyond Irigaray's privileging of sexual difference over other sexual, racial, economic and political differences, see Rivera 2007, pp. 109–10.

17 I am, of course, aware that most feminist theologians share Rivera's priorities. My argument is not to suggest I chart a superior course, but rather to redeploy the fruits of feminist theological labours in direct engagement with Christian systematic theology, as a kind of unintended excess to their authors' own vital projects.

on the contrary, that her relational transcendence is capable of addressing longstanding problems in existing Trinitarian formulations, including those of radical orthodoxy.

Conclusion

By way of conclusion, and to make the case for the orthodox potential of Rivera's model, I take issue with some aspects of her critique of radical orthodoxy. Rivera persuasively pinpoints Milbank's positing of transcendence as suspending the world – and thus suspending Rivera's network of relations with the human Other in cosmic space – 'over-against the void', bereft of being except through participation in God, and she draws attention also to Milbank's erection of a universal totem to achieve a single human reality amid multiplicity (Rivera 2007, pp. 22, 23–4, 28–9). Unsurprisingly, Rivera comments on the phallic nature of this image (p. 29), in which the Absolute Same of my subtitle is clearly reflected. Her whole project is to flesh out the transcendent through the density of encounters amid the irreducible multiplicity of humanity within the living cosmos; Rivera's relational transcendence effectively confounds the transcendent/immanent binary.

However, I suggest that Rivera's enriched economy of relational transcendence is capable of being coupled with the radical orthodox return to Trinitarian theology, as a way of addressing Milbank's inadequate and impoverished view of the immanent material body. The incarnation of Jesus Christ contradicts radical orthodox conceptions of the created world as 'purely immanent', in binary relation to the transcendent God. Participation in God involves the density of relations caught up in Rivera's relational transcendence; in Rivera's refiguring, reason is returned to its status as one capacity among others embodied in human beings. Incarnation, as understood through the lens of Rivera's relational transcendence, confounds the transcendent/immanent binary; incarnation does not necessarily collapse Milbank's vertical transcendence into interhuman transcendence informed by a 'third' with some ambiguous relation to (replacement of?) the Trinitarian God.

Hollywood says of Irigaray that her ambivalence with regard to belief and transcendence leads her immediately to deconstruct the very deities she invokes (Hollywood 1994, p. 176). Though Rivera's sense of the divine is far richer than Irigaray's, she runs a parallel risk of crafting a 'third' of human imagination, influenced by modern secular assumptions of a secularized transcendence, in which the triune God is deconstructed. Trinitarian theology would have it that it is, as Patrice Haynes might say, divine transcendence that lovingly invests the material – Rivera's relational transcendence, in all its embodied richness, might fruitfully be relocated as participation in that divine transcendence.

References

Anderson, Pamela Sue (2009), 'Transcendence and Feminist Philosophy: On Avoiding Apotheosis', in Gillian Howie and J'anine Jobling (eds), *Women and the Divine: Touching Transcendence* (New York: Palgrave Macmillan), pp. 27–54.

Clement, Catherine and Julia Kristeva (2001), *The Feminine and the Sacred* (Basingstoke: Palgrave).

Colebrook, Claire (2009), 'Transcendence and Immanence: Coming of Age in Philosophy', in Gillian Howie and J'anine Jobling (eds), *Women and the Divine: Touching Transcendence* (New York: Palgrave Macmillan), pp. 79–98.

Collins, Paul (2008), *The Trinity: A Guide for the Perplexed* (London: T&T Clark).

Daggers, Jenny (1997), 'Luce Irigaray and "Divine Women": A Resource for Postmodern Feminist Theology?' *Feminist Theology* 14 (January), pp. 35–50.

Davis, Creston, John Milbank and Slavoj Žižek (eds) (2005), *Theology and the Political: The New Debate* (Durham, NC: Duke University Press).

Hawthorne, Sîan Melville (2006), 'Origins, Genealogies, and the Politics of Identity: Towards a Feminist Philosophy of Myth', unpublished PhD thesis (SOAS, University of London).

Haynes, Patrice (2009), 'Transcendence, Materialism and the Reenchantment of Nature: Toward a Theological Materialism', in Gillian Howie and J'anine Jobling (eds), *Women and the Divine: Touching Transcendence* (New York: Palgrave Macmillan), pp. 55–78.

Hollywood, Amy (1994), 'Beauvoir, Irigaray and the Mystical', *Hypatia* 9.4, Feminist Philosophy of Religion (Autumn), pp. 158–85.

Irigaray, Luce (2009), 'Toward a Divine in the Feminine', in Gillian Howie and J'anine Jobling (eds), *Women and the Divine: Touching Transcendence* (New York: Palgrave Macmillan), pp. 13–25.

Klein, Terrance W. (2009), 'Review of Anne E. Inman *Evidence and Transcendence: Religious Epistemology and the God-World Relationship*', *Theological Studies* 70.2 (June), pp. 504–5.

Milbank, John (2006), *Theology and Social Theory: Beyond Secular Reason*, 2nd edn (Oxford: Blackwell).

——(2009), 'Postmodern Critical Augustianism', in John Milbank and Simon Oliver (eds), *The Radical Orthodoxy Reader* (London: Routledge), pp. 49–61.

Milbank, John and Simon Oliver (eds) (2009), *The Radical Orthodoxy Reader* (London: Routledge).

Pickstock, Catherine (2009), 'Duns Scotus: His Historical and Contemporary Significance', in John Milbank and Simon Oliver (eds), *The Radical Orthodoxy Reader* (London: Routledge), pp. 116–46.

Rivera, Mayra (2007), *The Touch of Transcendence: A Postcolonial Theology of God* (Louisville: Westminster John Knox).

Rubenstein, Mary-Jane (2009), 'Onward, Ridiculous Debaters', *Political Theology* 10.1 (2009), pp. 125–9.

Secombe, Linnell (1999), 'The Philosophy of Simone de Beauvoir', *Hypatia* 14.4 (Fall), pp. 96–113.

Tanner, Kathryn (2001), *Jesus, Humanity and the Trinity: A Brief Systematic Theology* (Minneapolis: Fortress).

Tyson, Paul G. (2008), 'Transcendence and Epistemology: Exploring Truth Via Post-Secular Christian Platonism', *Modern Theology* 24.2 (April), pp. 245–70.

12

The Place Where Love is Possible: A Feminist Relational Attempt to Rethink the Cross

NATALIE K. WATSON

Ann Loades has been one of the pioneers of feminist theology in Britain. Although her work as a theologian, ethicist and philosopher of religion covers a much wider range of subjects, her three books and many articles in this area are landmarks which deserve much deeper critical appreciation and discussion than has hitherto been offered. Central to *Searching for Lost Coins: Explorations in Christianity and Feminism* (1987), *Feminist Theology: A Reader* (1990) and *Feminist Theology: Voices from the Past* (2001) is discovery, critical engagement and rereading of the Christian tradition. Such engagement offers what she calls a 'wider view', which allows the reader and participant in the tradition to go beyond the immediate concerns of their present-day agenda.

What then is this wider perspective? Is it really just the finding of her-stories alongside the official line of church history, the unearthing of the forgotten work of women marginalized and excluded from the male-dominated spaces of the institutional Church? Or does it indeed enable us to enter into a deeper and critical debate not only with the Christian tradition itself but also with some of the issues of our day and not least the silences within that tradition and those who are silenced and forgotten by it?

Sources for theological reflection are not only to be found in the tomes of academic theologians of the past but essentially in the lives of women and men for whom their faith has become a source for constructive and creative wrestling with the texts they encounter in their engagement with the Christian tradition and the life of the Church.

Loades explores some features of the non-biblical tradition 'in order to find out what might still seem to be positively helpful and what has to be repudiated' (Loades 1987, p. 40). She then reflects on one particular development of the tradition, 'the morbid over-identification with Christ as suffering victim' (p. 41), which she explores with regard to the life and work of the twentieth-century philosopher Simone Weil, who died of self-inflicted starvation in 1943. Subsequently, there has been significant engagement both with the issue of food and starvation in the Christian tradition and in the present (see for example Isherwood 2007) and also with the experiences of women suffering domestic violence and (sexual) abuse who are being asked, often by clergy, to see themselves as imitating the suffering of Christ while suffering such abuse. Ann Loades writes with regard to Simone Weil's self-inflicted suffering:

> It is one thing to employ the metaphors of the 'imitation of Christ' as the context of love and then be sustained by it in a situation of extremity, but quite another to make the bare possibility of being in that situation a focus of attention outside the context of love. Without that context life may be eaten away by metaphor, with those who employ it literally tested to destruction by it. (1987, p. 57)

The key to understanding Loades's view on the significance of the Christian tradition for women is the theological work of Dorothy L. Sayers:

> that the Christian tradition has resources for women still to be worked out, resources that were already identified by Dorothy in the middle of the twentieth century. It is those committed to a sacramental understanding of the world whom we will find most committed to the future for women, rather than those who narrowly focus on biblical texts and attempt what at times seem implausible re-interpretations. (Loades 2001, pp. 167f.)

In *Feminist Theology: Voices from the* Past, Ann Loades challenges the
short-sightedness of much modern feminist theology with regard to its
history and invites a genuine theological critique of our feminist theological endeavours as genuine engagements with the Christian tradition.
It is the latter on which I want to expand here.

In my own book *Feminist Theology* (2003), I offered the following
working definition:

> Feminist theology is the critical, contextual, constructive, and creative
> re-reading and re-writing of Christian theology. It regards women – and
> their bodies, perspectives, and experiences – as relevant to the agenda
> of Christian theologians and advocates them as subjects of theologi-
> cal discourses and as full citizens of the church. (2003, pp. 2f.)

In what follows, I would like to attempt a look at one of the central
aspects of the Christian faith, the significance of the death of Jesus
on the cross, in the light of this definition and the challenge posed
by the work of Ann Loades to engage with the Christian tradition to
find a wider view. I will do so by engaging with one particular text of
the Christian tradition, the Fourth Gospel, which, so I propose, offers
us a way of looking at suffering in the light of the cross and suffering
of Christ that does not endorse victimhood in order to collude with
the perpetrators as the Church has so frequently done in the name
of Christianity.[1] In fact, I will argue that it might enable us to move
beyond the discourse of victims and perpetrators towards an understanding of human and divine relationships that can hold the full complexity of such relationships, including their absence and breakdown,
within it.

Both the Latin *traditio* and the Greek *paradosis* have connotations
not only of that which is lost in translation but essentially also of betrayal. There are elements of the Christian tradition which have been
used to distort, to betray, to interpret aspects of it in a way that means

---

1 I would like to thank David Painter for sharing his passion for John's Gospel
with me and for inspiring me to think about some of the issues discussed here.

the complete and utter betrayal of those to whom it is supposed to give life. Variations of Christian theology have been used to justify slavery, homophobia, violence and incest. Women experiencing domestic violence at the hands of those whom they had trusted with their lives, and children experiencing sexual and physical abuse at the hands of priests and teachers of the faith, have time and time again been told that they are to remember and to imitate the suffering of Christ on the cross.

Some time ago I found myself planning a series of evening classes with a male colleague. I insisted that my colleague, who was after all an Evangelical, should teach the session on the atonement. When I expressed my strong dislike of the atonement as a theological subject, he pointed to the cross under which we were sitting, and said: 'You have to know why he is up there.' Later I realized that indeed he had a point. Although as a theologian I was able to outline the major theories of the atonement, and I could speak of the limitations of penal substitution, I had always found these rather mechanistic and an attempt to explain what was essentially beyond explanation, the complete and utter public, and yet isolated and isolating, suffering of a human being on behalf of others. Yet, I had to know 'why he is up there'. Or at least find a place in my own theology for the fact that he is.

While we have begun to speak theologically about issues such as domestic violence and sexual abuse, very little has so far been said from a theological point of view about the experience of betrayal and bullying, an experience of relentless emotional, psychological and sometimes physical violence that can and does lead to a fragmentation of the self which can be profoundly traumatic, yet remains up to now largely unaddressed by Christian theology.[2] Even some of the Christian churches are beginning to acknowledge that institutional bullying goes on in their ranks, but little I fear has been done to speak (theologically or otherwise) about the experiences of those who are being bullied or neglected,

---

2 A notable exception is Brock and Parker (2008), which offers an extensive piece of narrative theology that includes reflections on the experience of institutional violence and the inadequacy of most traditional theological language to articulate and meaningfully address such experiences.

NATALIE K. WATSON

who will carry their traumatic experiences with them for the rest of
their lives.

As a theologian I insist that there is a wider theological question which
is to be addressed. The fundamental attack on the human self, on human
dignity and self-worth, can lead to excessive detachment and to what is
perceived to be an inability to love. The ability to love, however, is the
most fundamental expression of being in the image of God. If the ability
to love in a human being is marred or appears to have been destroyed,
then so is the ability to receive love, the ability to make oneself vulnerable to the other, to be in a place where the whole of human life, joy and
pain are allowed to exist and can be borne.

My case here is not merely that of adding another issue to the ever-
growing agenda of social concerns which Christians must address, nor
is it that of inviting appropriate pastoral strategies for responding to experiences human beings might face in the modern world. My concern is
a theological one: can the Christian tradition be a framework for a reading of human life that is not merely therapeutic but essentially redemptive? Such a redemptive reading of the Christian life has to acknowledge
the presence and the deep impact of pain felt by the victims of betrayal
and abuse.

To illustrate this, I would like to consider a well-known episode from
John's Gospel, the narrative of the 'woman caught in adultery' in John
8.1–11. The story itself is familiar: Jesus arrives at the town square to find
a group of men about to stone a woman who allegedly has been caught
with a lover who was not her husband. This is after all what their tradition tells them to do. In their challenge to Jesus, it becomes obvious
that they are not really interested in the woman and what she has done
but use her as a means of testing Jesus whether his interpretation of the
law concurs with theirs or whether they might have cause to begin pro-
ceedings against him. Jesus, in the sovereign way in which John's Gospel
portrays him throughout, refuses to engage with them on this level and
appears to be doodling in the sand. We are familiar with the words he
utters when he does speak, inviting those who are without sin to cast
the first stone, thereby exposing their true intentions. Once the crowd
has disappeared, Jesus addresses the woman and tells her that, if no one

condemns her, he will not condemn her either and charges her to 'go and sin no more'.

What is this story about? Who is this story about? Yes, there are the Pharisees, the religious authorities of Jesus' day who are unable to recognize who Jesus is and seek to find a reason to arrest him and take him to trial. Their true intentions are exposed by Jesus' challenge to look at themselves before condemning others, and thereby the woman is, at least for the time being, saved from her fate. On one level, this is certainly right. It exposes the destructive forces of patriarchal religion and points out that an encounter with God must also involve an encounter with oneself.

It would be very easy to read Jesus' encounter with the woman as an acknowledgement of her victimhood. On one level, she is a victim. She is a 'bit on the side', not worthy even to be regarded as someone's property, and she is the one who is caught out, while, possibly, the man, or men, with whom she was caught, walked free or even may be found among those with stones in their hands. There are those who suggest that she may have been set up in the first place, possibly by a husband who saw this as a convenient way of disposing of a wife he no longer wanted (Toensing 2003), possibly having found someone else himself. We could almost imagine him among those in the front row with a stone in his own hand. I will for the purpose of my argument not take this line.

Yet, this is not actually what happens. Jesus makes no excuses for what the woman has done. He does not class her as a victim, someone who didn't know any better, but tells her to 'go and sin no more'. She is after all the victim of what Andrew Lincoln calls the 'patriarchal abuse of what was already a patriarchal legal system' (Lincoln 2005, p. 530). Yet, Jesus tells her to 'go and sin no more'. So, I argue, he does name what she has done as 'sin', as the betrayal of a relationship of trust, as a rejection of God and of other human beings, including herself. Jesus' words are not so much a commandment but a word of trust and encouragement that a different life is possible, that she is worth more than the lies and the cheap and quick excitement involved in adultery, that true life means true and real, life-giving relationships.

Yet, reading this story leaves me, for all my fascination with John's Gospel, somewhat dissatisfied. For there is, in my mind, another person from whose perspective this story could be read, possibly more than one: what about the wife of the man with whom the woman now about to be stoned had been 'caught', the one who truly experienced betrayal by being at the receiving end of the adultery? Jesus recognizes that the Pharisees are not interested in the woman whom they are about to stone, yet we find no reference to either him or anyone else engaging with the one who was actually betrayed. John's Gospel continues and does not resolve the silence about the hidden victims of adultery or any other form of betrayal. Yet, I argue, a feminist theology of relationality and relationships is not credible and lacks integrity if it does not also address questions of what happens when such relationships break down, the question of betrayal. It is only then that we can speak with integrity of love becoming possible.

However, let us speculate for a moment: what would Jesus' encounter with her have looked like? Maybe, she too would have needed to hear that she was not condemned, maybe not condemned for what she had done but condemned by those who refuse to hear and name her pain of being 'replaced', of being betrayed, of being made to feel that she was not 'good enough' so her husband had to look elsewhere, of being told that she had to 'forgive and forget' before she was ready to do so, that she had to 'move on'. If we speak with integrity about love being possible, we also have to address what it means when love is denied, when someone is told by the person they trusted with their life that they no longer matter, that they might as well not exist, that they are 'replaceable'. She may not have been the one at whom actual physical stones were thrown, but being the subject of gossip or being avoided or silenced by those who refuse to encounter the pain of betrayal or bereavement can be just as painful.

Maybe it is here, where the tradition remains silent, that feminist theologians need to speak. And such speaking needs to come as it were from the centre of the Christian faith, the narrative of the death and resurrection of Christ, as told by the author of the Fourth Gospel.

In addition to being told to reflect on the suffering of Christ on the cross, women who suffer violence are often not believed, they are rendered incredible because their experiences either do not fit with or disturb male privilege:

> If pastoral care and counselling pretend to help women to live their lives in a liberated and gracious way, the silencing of women by privileged men has to be taken into account. The changing of systems of privilege will cost men a lot of frustration, status, and worldly goods. There is work to be done by pastors and counsellors: work that requires a great amount of courage to see what was invisible, and to hear what cannot be said. (Storm 1996, pp. 138f.)

However, this work is not merely to be done by pastors and counsellors but essentially by theologians whose task it is to explore the Christian tradition as a source of language that might enable us to articulate that which cannot be articulated, and to hear what cannot be said.

Perhaps it is the telling and retelling of the narrative of Maundy Thursday, Good Friday, Holy Saturday and possibly Easter that will enable us maybe not to make sense of, but at least to hold the experience of betrayal, of the complete and utter fragmentation of the self and to allow it to exist before we rush into 'getting over it' and 'moving on'.

Don't get me wrong, it is indeed encouraging to see the significant changes in the churches' attitude to divorce that have come about in the last few decades. While as recently as 20 or 30 years ago, a blanket condemnation of divorce led to any divorcee, regardless of the reasons for the divorce, being condemned and excluded, some churches have indeed 'moved on' and begun to acknowledge the complex realities of human relationships and of marriage. We have begun to see that there are indeed situations in which a marriage is no longer a marriage or perhaps never was. And therefore, those who entered into it in good faith are indeed quite rightly to be released from the vows which they took before God and the Church. This change of attitude, as well as for instance changes in our thinking about slavery, can and must be seen as the work of the Holy Spirit and a move towards a Christian ethic that is closer to the gospel of love and forgiveness than that expressed by (male, celibate) Christian theologians of earlier generations.

Yet, I would like to argue that this has not inevitably led to a more honest engagement with the theology of marriage or any other human relationship, nor has it resulted in a more appropriate and constructive engagement with the reality of marriage breakdown for those involved in it. We may have achieved a level of tolerance, yet the Christian tradition challenges us to speak of love which goes far beyond tolerance and means the full engagement and embrace of the Other, a true encounter of human beings in all their humanity. A more sophisticated understanding of the complexities of relationship breakdown frequently finds itself expressed in a cavalier attitude to issues such as adultery or other forms of betrayal, expressed for example in the leniency towards clergy caught in adulterous relationships who are no longer defrocked but merely suspended for a relatively short time compared to the pain which they have chosen to cause, and a lack of willingness to engage with the scarred lives of those who find themselves at the receiving end of such a betrayal.

While divorced victims of adultery may no longer find themselves condemned for the mere fact of being divorced (though this has by no means been entirely eradicated), they are now frequently told that 'these things happen' or pressurized into an unreflected rhetoric of forgiveness without any genuine acknowledgement of the reality of their suffering.

Perhaps words are bound to fail in such cases and the first step towards genuine pastoral encounters is to acknowledge our own inability fully to grasp the impact of the suffering of others. Such would be a very different kind of silence, a silence that is able to hold the pain of others without forcing them to explain themselves.

The twentieth-century Mexican painter Frida Kahlo expressed her own experience of the frequent adultery of her life-partner and husband Diego Rivera (culminating in an affair with her own sister) in her painting 'Only a few nips'.[3]

In this painting, the woman's body is covered in scars which spill over on the floor of the room and indeed on the frame of the painting. The man, Diego Rivera, stands next to her, seemingly uninterested with a smug expression on his face. There is no eye contact between the two.

3 I am indebted to Peter Vardy for drawing my attention to this.

The woman's pelvis is turned towards him, while her head is turned away. The woman is lost in her suffering while the husband's head towers in a clean space where her suffering at his hands is belittled into being 'only a few nips'.

It is unlikely that Kahlo intended her painting to be reminiscent of the traditional form of the Pietà, Christ having been taken from the cross being held by his mother, best known in the form of Michelangelo's famous sculpture in the Sistine Chapel in Rome. Here we see a different encounter. Mary, the mother of Jesus, can do nothing other than to hold and to behold the body of her son bearing the scars of his innocent suffering.

The connection is tentative, and yet, it may help us to move towards the constructive theological proposal I endeavour to make. The following poem may help to take us back to the theological reflection in which we are engaged.

Pietà

I stand before you now
as they stood before me
with nothing to say
nothing to give
but these tears that
mingle with yours
Your time has come
I know
and I cry to God
who made man:
will this circle ever be broken?
or will it be the same
forever
that women are held
by the love of women
at the time of their betrayal
as his broken body was

held by his mother
when they had taken him
from the cross where
she had watched him
die
that we may become
like Christ for one another
on a day
like this

It is 'on a day like this' that pastoral encounters take place. They challenge us to engage with the realities of human life in a constructive dialogue with the language of the Christian tradition while constantly facing up to its limitations and our own. And yet, as ministers of Christ, it is this language of the life-giving reality of the gospel that is given to us in facing up to the unspeakable suffering of others, not to judge or gloss over it but to risk pastoral encounters which are genuine. The phrase 'that we may become like Christ for one another' is taken from the theology of Martin Luther and summarizes his understanding of Christian ethics. It outlines and maps out the limitations and the potential of the Christian life together. What does this mean?

Much western Christian theology, even of a more modern or radical kind, is too narrowly focused on victimhood and how it can be overcome, so that there is no room for the agony of Gethsemane and the reality of the cross without which early Christianity's insistence on the reality of the incarnation remains empty and unrealistic.

The image of the Pietà only takes us so far. The Mary of Michelangelo's Pietà, or even of the modern reconstructions of this image I have suggested, essentially remains a lone figure, someone who is also alone with her pain and her grief. She holds a lifeless tortured body, yet she herself remains alone. This surely cannot ultimately be a constructive image of the Church.

The canon of the New Testament chose four Gospels from the many that were extant at the time. It is John's account that I want to highlight here. The writer of the Fourth Gospel says that Christ died, not for our sins, but that we may have life, life in abundance, and as such provides a critical counter-voice, a wider perspective, to those who want to reduce the suffering of Christ to penal substitution, or any theological discourse too interested in overcoming victimhood before the reality of suffering is acknowledged. The Christ of the Fourth Gospel enters into suffering knowingly, willingly and yet triumphantly. When he breathes his last, he gives up, hands over, his spirit (*paredoken to pneuma*). Here, in John 19.31b, we find the Greek word which means 'handing over', 'passing on'. This can be, and is sometimes, read as the beginning of the life of the Church in which God's Spirit is handed on. It is here that the life and mission of the Church begins.

The abundant life, a new quality of life, brought about by the coming (out) of Jesus in the cross and the resurrection, is the life of new and restored relationships, the life of the new community of disciples.

The early Church discouraged those who actively sought martyrdom, although dying for one's faith was seen as the ultimate consequence of following Christ and the highest form of imitating Christ. Yet, the question is whether this is true to a reading of the Christian narrative which takes into account the whole of the Christian story. The beginning of the Christian story is the incarnation, God becoming a human being, God entering the reality of human life and ultimately of human death. Perhaps asking others to imitate Christ, to suffer abuse willingly because Christ did is not the point. Christ entered our reality, faced up to our suffering. The cross is the place where suffering is allowed to exist, to be seen for what it is, completely and utterly meaningless and beyond what human explanation can contain. It is here, in the wider view offered from the cross, that love becomes possible, that it is possible to transcend patterns of abusing and being abused, to break the cycle of treating other human beings as objects of power, to transcend the human need to atone, where new relationships of love and care are possible.

I doubt that it is Jesus as we find him portrayed in the Fourth Gospel whom those who tell abused women to think of Jesus as suffering on the cross had in mind. For the author of the Fourth Gospel, the suffering and death of Jesus on the cross are life-giving, not the justification of the destruction of a human being, they are the ultimate fulfilment of the incarnation (*tetelestai*). The death of Christ is the moment of birth of the Church. Christ enters into the reality of human suffering and thereby makes life and love possible. This is the inversion, the over-coming of violence and death in the place where love is possible. John speaks of the fifth wound being the pierced side from which flow water and blood. This is an image of birth, of new creation and new life amid suffering.

It is another scene from the crucifixion in the Fourth Gospel which may help us to think further. Strangely enough, this is used as the Gospel reading for Mothering Sunday, often perverted into an ecclesiastical celebration of hetero-patriarchal domesticity with occasional patroniz-ing overtures to those who have failed to accomplish this, the highest purpose of any good Christian woman. With one notable exception, the sermons or condescending children's addresses I have heard on such occasions have largely ignored the text. I am referring to John 19.25–27, the encounter between the dying Jesus on the cross, his mother and the beloved disciple. I would first want to note that Jesus does not spare those dearest and closest to him from encountering his suffering. Yet, in his moment of suffering a new relationship is created, that between Jesus' mother and the beloved disciple. 'Woman, behold your son.' 'Behold, your mother.' 'And from that moment on, the disciple took her into his own.' This has frequently been interpreted symbolically as the establish-ment of the new community, the Church which includes both the trad-itional believers (the synagogue) and the disciples. And such integration is not without tensions about birth rights and the alleged superiority of the new.

Others read it as the event that connects Jesus' earthly life and min-istry with his death and resurrection. Yet, at its most basic, what is es-tablished here is a relationship between two people who share a most profound encounter, that of watching someone they love dearly suffer and die. Both will, together and separately, have to go on living with this memory and this encounter.

It would be very easy to go for what I would call a nostalgic reading of this text and simply to say that even in the moment of his suffering and dying Jesus gives birth or creates a new community, or that even at that moment he was prepared to look after those who were dear to him, not least his mother.

On one level, this is of course true, but this creation of a new community, the re-creation of relationships, does not happen without a most profound encounter with suffering and betrayal itself. In his own suffering on the cross, triumphant or not, Jesus literally faces the suffering of those who have to watch him suffer and die, and he cannot and he does not resolve it.

One of the cruellest forms of torture in our own day, employed by abusive partners, by Saddam's torturers in Iraq and in the infamous Villa Grimaldi of Pinochet's Chile alike, is to force parents to watch their children being tormented and abused. It is a fundamental attack on human dignity, on the ability to relate and to love that makes us human.

Or, looking at it from the other side, there are those who are prepared to watch others suffer, parents who do not intervene when their children are being bullied, mothers who allow their husbands to abuse their daughters to give them a break or because they themselves are no longer capable of intervening, or be it society at large that is prepared to turn a blind eye to the existence of violent and cruel dictatorships in other parts of the world.

Our discourse about love and relationality will remain meaningless if it does not also speak with integrity about the reality of sin as betrayal of the human ability to love. The feminist critique of the concept of original sin as associated with (female) sexuality, particularly in Augustine and Aquinas, Saiving's and Plaskow's rereading of women's sin as triviality rather than pride and the reinterpretation of sin as oppression particularly in the form of kyriarchy, sexism and racism, have been important steps on the way towards a feminist re-engagement with sin. Yet, I argue that we cannot speak about forgiveness and reconciliation or indeed the creation of a new community without engaging with the disruption of human relationships.

It is here that the Christian tradition, and particularly a rereading of the suffering and death of Christ, can open up a 'wider view'.

What we find here in John 19 is not merely the restoration of filial piety or some sort of hetero-patriarchal domesticity. The disciple and Mary do not leave the scene to go off and set up home together. This deeply symbolic scene immediately precedes the actual death of Jesus. Even the Gospel that reads the whole of the Jesus narrative from the point of view of the resurrection needs the actual physical death of Jesus for his full humanity.

'From that hour, the disciple took her into his own.' Many have speculated about the identity of the 'beloved disciple'. For the purpose of my argument, I would like to side with those who, in a symbolic reading of John's Gospel, see the disciple as the personification of the new community of disciples embodied in the Church and therefore in each and every disciple through the ages, in other words in each and every one of us. The author of the Fourth Gospel offers us glimpses into the intimate loving relationship between Jesus and the disciple (and for that matter also into the tension between others about this intimate relationship). Christian mysticism through the ages has made much of entering into such a close relationship with Christ, though not without acknowledging the dark and potentially disturbing side of such intimacy. Any form of intimacy, be it with another human being or the divine, holds within it the risk of separation, abandonment and betrayal. Thus the encounter between the dying Christ, Mary and the beloved disciple under the cross is necessary, not only for our understanding of the meaning of the suffering and death of Christ but for the identity of the Christian Church as the community of believers. Here, Christ himself enters into the experience of separation, abandonment and betrayal of the most profound human relationships. It is here that those whose suffering is being silenced, ignored and forgotten can be heard, and we, the Church, are charged to take them 'into our own'. It is only from the cross that such a 'wider view' is indeed possible. The new community of restored, recreated relations is not possible without this moment of the cross, immediately before the moment of accomplishment.

When the disciple takes Mary, the mother of Jesus, into his own, he does not physically provide a new home for her and assume the responsibilities of the oldest son to look after an older relative who would not otherwise be provided for. Nor does he invite her into his 'spiritual space' on his own terms (as a feminist ecclesiologist I am deeply suspicious of the concept of inclusivity). He invites her to participate in his role as the pre-eminent disciple, to share his experience and to share hers as part of their shared discipleship under the cross (Brown 1994, p. 1024). This to my mind enables us to move beyond an understanding of Mary as the embodiment of the Church which takes no account of the real experiences of real women and makes it possible to move towards a wider view of the Church as an actual body which is able to hold the tensions between its actual members and does not disregard the experience of suffering, rejection and betrayal of any of them.

Early Christianity did not initially show much interest in the ordering of family relationships (though there is ample evidence for its subsequent adoption of collusion with patriarchy). Yet the earliest Christian documents also tell us something of the need to engage with such relationships.

This could offer us a framework which takes us further than counselling and therapy can. Here we are not merely speaking about 'getting over a bad experience', about the need to 'move on', about survival, but about theology done with sufficient integrity to allow for the integration of the whole of human life into our reading and rereading of the Christian narrative, about a view of human life which no longer regards the past (and the present) as what defines who we are, and a theology that speaks not merely of survival but essentially of life (although our theology of life will be meaningless if we cease to fight for the rights of those who struggle to survive). The idea of the sacramentality of the word, for example in preaching, is not in itself a feminist one. Yet in a feminist context it is not only the speaking of the word in public worship that is sacramental, but also the listening to and hearing into speech of those who have no voice, whose suffering is unspeakable (see for example Watson 2002 pp. 99f.). Such a sacramental hearing into speech which does not rush into the rhetoric of forgiveness and does not condemn those who struggle to do so is at the heart of the new community of love being brought about by Christ entering into the reality of our suffering and transcending it by doing so consciously, thus rendering it to be no longer the ultimate reality of who we are. Such a sacramental process of hearing and being heard can I think only take place in the gathering of women under the cross, where it is possible to gain a perspective on life that does not reduce our being human to specific issues, where we find exchanges of grace, and where, above all, love is possible.

There are those who read this passage as the event that connects Jesus' earthly life and ministry with his death and resurrection, his earthly family, personified in his mother, with the new community of disciples, represented by the disciple whom Jesus loved. At its most basic, what is established here is a relationship between two people who share a most profound encounter, that of having to watch someone they love dearly suffer and die. Both will, together and separately, have to go on living with this memory and this encounter.

Where does all this take us in our attempt to reread the cross? Perhaps not much further than to say that we are not required to engage in a reading of its significance that is merely concerned with penal substitution, but that in our reading of the cross there has to be room for the complexity of human relationships including their most profound disruptions.

Being a disciple, a follower and imitator of Jesus, does not require a supernatural ability somehow to forget the pain and struggle incurred by ordinary earthly human relationships. In it there is indeed room for the pain and the difficulties caused in such relationships and not least in families. Robert Goss sees the encounter under the cross, the integration of birth family and family of choice re-enacted at the deathbeds of men and women dying of Aids (Goss 2006, p. 562). This involves the acknowledgement that the new 'family of choice' ultimately has to be able to bear the pain caused by birth families.

It is here that our own attempts to atone, perhaps resulting from our own ability to explore the alliance between matter and emotion, must end. Here we can begin to imitate Christ, not by bearing meaningless suffering at the hands of those whom we trusted with our lives, but by allowing our own suffering to be entered into and borne in all its starkness and reality. It is here, in the handing on of his spirit, that the inspiration of his Church to engage in social action which might end violence and victimhood can begin. Here a wider view becomes possible and our thinking about a feminist relational theology of the Church can begin.

References

Brock, Rita N. and Rebecca Ann Parker (2008), *Saving Paradise: How Christianity Traded Love of This World for Crucifixion and Empire* (Boston: Beacon Press).

Brown, Raymond (1994), *The Death of the Messiah*, 2 vols (New York: Doubleday).

Goss, Robert (2006), 'John', in Deryn Guest, Robert E. Goss, Mona West and Thomas Bohache (eds), *The Queer Bible Commentary* (London: SCM Press), pp. 548–65.

Isherwood, Lisa (2007), *The Fat Jesus: Feminist Explorations in Boundaries and Transgressions* (London: Darton, Longman & Todd).

Lincoln, Andrew (2005), *The Gospel According to John* (London: Continuum).

Loades, Ann (1987), *Searching for Lost Coins: Explorations in Christianity and Feminism* (London: SPCK).

——(1990), *Feminist Theology: A Reader* (London: SPCK).

——(2001), *Feminist Theology: Voices from the Past* (Oxford: Polity Press).

Storm, Riet Bons (1996), *The Incredible Woman: Listening to Women's Silences in Pastoral Care and Counselling* (Nashville: Abingdon Press).

Toensing, Holly J. (2003), 'Divine Intervention or Divine Intrusion? Jesus and the Adulteress in John's Gospel', in Amy-Jill Levine with Marianne Blickenstaff (eds), *A Feminist Companion to John*, vol. 1 (Cleveland, OH: Pilgrim Press), pp. 159–72.

Watson, Natalie K. (2002), *Introducing Feminist Ecclesiology* (London: Continuum).

——(2003), *Feminist Theology*, CTRF Guides to Theology (Grand Rapids: Eerdmans).

13

Relational Theology in the Work of Artist, Psychoanalyst and Theorist Bracha Lichtenberg Ettinger

MARY CONDREN

[Bracha Lichtenberg Ettinger] is . . . asking us to reformulate the very relation between the subject and its other, and to ask what precedes this encounter in which the phallus seeks to confirm its status, where the feminine acts only as a faulty mirror in the circuitry of that narcissism?

What form of relationality troubles the distinctness of these terms? I would even claim that, in her view, it is not possible to say 'I am feminine', or that 'You are feminine'. Since the very ontological designations, 'I am' and 'you are', post-date the space of the matrixial. The matrixial is what we guard against when we shore up the claims of identity, when we presume that to recognize each other is to know, to name, to distinguish according to the logic of identity.

(Butler 2006, pp. x–xi)

More radically than anyone else to date, Ettinger proposes that, *beside* and *behind* rather than *before* the phallic castration model, we can discern another model for dealing with the issue of the Other and the formation of a sense of self: subjectivity. She names this supplementary stratum the *matrixial*. As symbol, the Matrix is not an alternative to the Phallus, not a Mothercentred as opposed to Fathercentred model, not an Earth versus Sky alternative. It is a different model because it is nonphallic; it is not based on the logic of on/off, present/absent, pure/

impure. In one sense, it is a theorization of the sacred in the feminine as passage and frontier understood as borderspace and borderlinking. Ettinger draws into symbolic and imaginative effect what she identifies as borderspace, the potential of the shared threshold, the creative partnership of encounter, the joint transmission and its different registration in each sharing element, hence the shared without fusion, the different without opposition.

(Pollock 2007, p. 39)

Introduction

Feminist theologians have long critiqued those aspects of Christian theologies that give rise to dualisms between the sacred and the profane, male and female, heaven and earth, God and the world. Dualistic assumptions undermine our capacity for relationality, give rise to competitive individualisms, instantiate unbalanced gender and ethnic relations, and produce profound ecological consequences (Grey 1997, p. 23; Primavesi 2000).

These dualisms are said to derive from several sources, and Greek and Hellenistic philosophies are variously implicated (Ruether 1983; 1974; Ruth 1987). In addition, in recent years, theologians have critiqued theologies of atonement, redemption, sin, salvation and sacrifice that appear to feed into such violent social and personal relations. They critique what they term *redemptive violence* and argue that the forms *sacrifices* take (at least in the West) are usually gendered, and culturally specific (Brown and Bohn 1989; Brock and Parker 2008). Sacrificial modes of interpretation of the Christian Gospels (and other major religions) have fostered religious elaborations in which individuals and groups achieve their identities at An/Other's expense, thereby undermining the capacity of religions to foster relationality.

Attention needs to be paid, therefore, to those processes – rituals, stories, theologies, symbol systems, hermeneutics – where relatedness is either promoted or disrupted and that serve to legitimate and promote certain forms of religious and political authority, especially those that have issued in the kinds of personal and political violence the West has historically encountered.

In search of relationality, many feminist theologians have turned to various schools of psychology and psychoanalysis but have come up against some serious limitations: the early optimism regarding our capacity for relatedness has proved not to be well grounded.

Finding additional sources to theorize our relational potential in theological terms is now urgent. Finding psychoanalytic theories that do justice to the complexity involved is crucial.

Finding ways to speak of gender relations that do not simply recreate the old phallic oppositions is a parallel task. That imperative occurs alongside the equally urgent task of analysing the capacity of human societies to wreak the kinds of social havoc to which the history of Europe attests.

This chapter proposes that the work of the Israeli-French artist, psychoanalyst and theorist Bracha Lichtenberg Ettinger holds out those possibilities. Her work has major implications for several disciplines: aesthetics, philosophy, psychoanalysis, feminist theory and religious studies. The task of exploring this potential has been greatly aided by the interpretations of Griselda Pollock, and more recently, Judith Butler and Catherine de Zegher. In 2004, the journal *Theory, Culture and Society* devoted an entire volume to her work and to her commentators.

Ettinger is not directly concerned with theology; however, her work has widespread implications for theology and religious studies. This chapter aims simply to provide an introduction to those facets of her thought with immediate implications for developing a relational theology. First, however, a brief review of the current dilemmas is appropriate.

Feminist theology in the USA

In the United States, in an attempt to develop a more relational theology, feminist and other theologians have broadened the traditional sources of theological reflection to include some aspects of psychology and psychoanalytic theory. Carol Gilligan's work on ethics highlighted the possibility of alternative female and male psychic development, thereby introducing a gendered suspicion into traditional ethical and psychological theory (1982). Nancy Chodorow and Dorothy Dinnerstein introduced Melanie Klein's object relations theory into feminist theoretical and theological

discourse (Dinnerstein 1976; Chodorow 1978). Jean Baker Miller identified a specifically female psychic development that appears to confound
classical psychoanalytic and psychological theory to date (Miller 1976;
Robb 2006). The work of each of these theorists held out the possibility
of a greater capacity for relatedness on the part of women in particular,
implicitly challenging the patriarchal hegemony of traditional psychological theories and undermining theological assumptions.

However, critics have arisen both from within those disciplines mentioned
and more widely from ethnic, postcolonial and subaltern societies who had,
to put it mildly, not experienced the benefits of such relatedness in their political or personal lives. Women's capacity for relatedness is not unilaterally
manifest. Nor has it issued in social structures that bear witness to its efficacy.
In many situations, white western women have reaped the benefits of their
class and ethnic backgrounds, often at the expense of their *Others*, including
other women (Spelman 1990; Armour 1998).

In particular, the phenomenon of envy was acutely analysed by
Melanie Klein, but largely ignored in the popularized versions of feminist object relations theory (Klein 1988). The category of 'woman' has
proved to have distinct limitations, since its expression varies across cultures, class and ethnicities.

European theory

These particular theological movements, offering such positive predictions of our capacity for relatedness, arose mostly in the United States
where, until September 11th, theorists had mostly a fairly benevolent
view of religion and theology.

In Europe, however, the optimism for relatedness, especially among
psychoanalytic thinkers, was never shared to the same extent. For most
of the twentieth century, Europe was still disentangling itself (if that is the
word) from its many colonial enterprises that had often left native popu-
lations deeply damaged. In addition, Europe was also still reverberating
from the effects of the two world wars fought on European soil. The
various psychoanalytic schools were deeply pessimistic, to say the least,
about our human capacity to share the planet at any level (Rose 1993).

Especially since the Second World War, critical theorists had already been asking the question, posed in various ways, 'How does one do theology, painting, art, or theory in the light of Auschwitz, Kosovo, Treblinka, or even the Pentagon?' In the two major world wars, whole cultures and societies had reverted to barbarism.[1] Fascist, communist and nationalist movements gave little reason to assume (despite materialists' best efforts) that reason, and not erratic forces such as those sometimes found in religion, would govern human behaviour.

Nor did European theorists, largely speaking, share the general assumptions (and optimism) of a post-religious secular worldview, especially as that view was expressed in the 'Death of God' school in the late 1960s (Altizer and Hamilton 1966). The great marching armies, the mass political rallies, the psychic fantasies that encouraged fathers and mothers to sacrifice the immediate interests of their families and hero worship fascist dictators — all of these spoke of psychic propensities that might one day have taken a religious expression, but were now unleashed on the world in a completely new and uncontained form (except by the force of counter arms). As the poet William Butler Yeats wrote of the rise of fascism:

And what slow beast, its hour come round at last
Slouches toward Bethlehem to be born?

(Yeats 1983, p. 187)

In Europe, therefore, mainstream theorists began to look again at both religion and psychoanalysis with new eyes. Alongside perspectives

---

1 'Bracha Ettinger's work addresses the question: how can we work with this trauma, grieving for others unknown and for ourselves so as to imagine a future not defined by trauma acquiring through its repression and latency the power to become a dominating tendency? The increase in violence, racism and xenophobia we have seen since Auschwitz, combined with both a revival of anti-Semitic and outbreaks of anti-Islamic or communal violence in India for instance, when we would expect that we would have "learned our lesson", shows the desperate need for a radical and creative way to address the persistence of traumatic legacies in ways that open a future beyond them, rather than defined by their unconscious increase of power to claim us again and again' (Pollock 2004, p. 19).

drawn from sociology, anthropology and linguistics, they *bracketed* any ontological claims in favour of analysing religion's capacity to disrupt, repress or mobilize individuals and society in certain directions.[2]

Some strands of the European women's movement, in addition, have often taken a critical stance in relation to such notions as *equality feminism*. For instance, Julia Kristeva argues that we need a much more radical approach to understand *the sacrificial social contract*. Brought up in Soviet-controlled Bulgaria, which practised its own form of overtly militarist secular religion, Kristeva also became convinced of the need to 'speak otherwise' of those social forces that had once taken religious expression. Kristeva, therefore, has made the most systematic attempts to formulate psychoanalytically based theoretical perspectives to understand religion as a social and psychic phenomenon.[3] Her work has been invaluable in enabling theorists to review critically Europe's religious heritage, in both its positive and negative aspects (Kristeva 1982, 1987).

Kristeva's perspectives, however, would not be optimistic about our capacity for relatedness. Kristeva argues that there can be no innocence on the part of women as to their role in the sacrificial social contract. In her widely quoted essay 'Women's Time', Kristeva provides a sophisticated analysis of various strands of feminism that left no one under the

---

2 'Far from dismissing, therefore, what religious thought and practice holds before us through atheistic negation, which remains tied to that which it negates as the mirroring of the same, semiotic psychoanalytical cultural analysis tracks the intensities secreted within, and veiled by, the late accretions of formalized religion. The aim is not to discuss whether there is a deity or not. Instead, we want to know what fuels the imaginaries and the registers of our distinctively human attempts to understand self–other relations which include those of sociality itself, of affection and desire as well as our position vis-à-vis that against which human identity construes itself – the world, and the radical alterity of the nonhuman, animal, plant, planetary and meteorological forces' (Pollock 2007, p. 15).

3 'Challenged at a conference in Leeds in 1996 about her "Catholic proclivity", Julia Kristeva declared: "to continue with the thread of memory: we do not have a choice but to put into practice a history of religion as a demystification. We have to rid ourselves of the history of religion. *We have to say what it spoke of, otherwise* ... We must not allow ourselves to remain ignorant of this heritage. Instead, as before we have to question it ... "' (Cited in Pollock 2007, pp. 12–13).

illusion that women's moral capacity was inherently any greater than that of men. As she wrote at the time:

> the habitual and increasingly explicit attempt to fabricate a scapegoat victim as foundress of a society or a counter-society may be replaced by the analysis of the potentialities of *victim/executioner* which characterize each identity, each subject, each sex. (Kristeva 1986, p. 210)

However, Kristeva's work has also been critiqued on several grounds pertinent to our discussion here. In a recent collection of letters between Kristeva and Catherine Clément on the question of the *sacred*, Clément criticizes Kristeva for the assumptions she brings to her analyses of religion, assumptions largely derived from Freud and Lacan's ethnocentric and patriarchal theories of subjectivity and their Durkheimian lineages (Clément and Kristeva 2001; Condren 2009).

Second, recent theorists have highlighted the extent to which Kristeva still works within a psychoanalytic framework in which the male Oedipal experience and the apparent necessity for radical individuation and repudiation of the mother's body is established as the essential, standard and normative psychic move (Pollock 2006, p. 56).

Kristeva's work has, nevertheless, been groundbreaking in that, although she distances herself from feminism, she has largely initiated the imperative to bring new dimensions to our understanding of female subjectivity and religion, going beyond the old ontological claims in an attempt to understand the social and psychic substrata. In addition, both she and the other theorists mentioned above have continued to develop and refine their perspectives in the light of their ongoing research and reflections.[4] However, the work of Bracha Lichtenberg Ettinger, and

---

4 To speak unilaterally of any of these major theorists, however, is possibly to reduce the complexity of their work. Gilligan, Chodorow, Dinnerstein and Miller's work has been refined, both by themselves and by their critics, leading to a better appreciation of the role that, alongside gender, race, class and ethnicity play in personal and ethical development. Kristeva has recently produced biographies of Melanie Klein, Hanna Arendt and Collette, and the indications are that her psychoanalytic work may be taking different directions (cf. Kristeva 2001).

especially her positing of *matrixial* dimensions of subjectivity along-side the phallic, now has the potential to bring these debates into new dimensions.

Background to Ettinger

Bracha Lichtenberg Ettinger's parents were Polish, and both had experi-enced the concentration camps at Auschwitz. The familial memories of the Holocaust, the challenges of becoming an artist in a postmodern context, and the additional challenge of articulating a potential fe-male subjectivity in a post-Lacanian context – all of these have served in the creation of the *matrixial theory* which she began to publish in 1992.

Ettinger revisits some key texts of Sigmund Freud and has also trans-lated some of the late work of Lacan. Her work is in dialogue with many of the major philosophers, such as Jean François Lyotard, Gilles Deleuze and Félix Guattari, Maurice Merleau Ponty, Emmanuel Levinas and Edmond Jabés.[5] She works critically with the work of Sigmund Freud, Jacques Lacan and Melanie Klein, and dialogues with the work of Julia Kristeva, Luce Irigaray and object relations theorists.[6]

---

5 'Ettinger trained in both art and psychoanalysis in Israel. When she came to London, she trained at the Tavistock Centre with R. D. Laing and at the London Centre for Psychotherapy. In Paris she trained with Piera Aulagnier, Françoise Dolto, Pierre Fédida and J. A. Miller. She also translated some of the late work of Jacques Lacan. In the 1980s she began to work as an artist while simultaneously practising as an analyst. From 1992 onwards she began to publish her work on what she termed *matrixial subjectivity*' (Pollock 2006, p. 25).

6 'as a subtle reader of the later seminars of Jacques Lacan, where he re-struggled with questions of the feminine through a new alertness to the trans-actions between the Real, the Imaginary and the Symbolic through notions of *sinthôme* and the Moebius strip, Bracha Ettinger carefully re-braids, with a Deleu-zian twist and a feminized Merleau-Pontyian swerve, these three levels of the hu-man unconscious in their relation to the transgressive co-emergence-in-difference with the m/Other' (Pollock 2006, p. 59).

Art and Trauma

Ettinger describes herself primarily as an artist and it is through her art practice, as much as her psychoanalytic training, that her perspectives are derived. Much like psychic trauma that is *repressed* only to emerge in a more virulent form, Ettinger considers that the physical landscape of Europe covers over with a thin veneer the atrocities that have taken place on its soil. Therefore she asks this question: How can art, or other aesthetic or disciplinary practices, become a means of *working through* our individual traumas as well as the transgenerational memories of the traumas of the twentieth century, lest they reappear (as they have) in the current generations?[7]

Her aim is to interrogate how our phallic mindsets, where we achieve our identities, usually at the expense of *Others*, have led to the many forms of racist, misogynist and homophobic eruptions.[8]

---

7 'The theoretical propositions of the Matrix and metramorphosis that are elaborated in a complex relation of affiliation to and critique of Lacanian and Freudian psychoanalysis in which she also clinically practises, emerged in an artist's poetic reflections on her daily practice in the studio. Thus, her radical theoretical innovation is based on the experience of art on the one hand and, on the other, a most scrupulous reading of traces in the Freudian and the late Lacanian texts for a potentiality to articulate femininity with difference, moving from Freud's key theorization of the aesthetic in "The 'Uncanny'" on to Lacan's notions of objet a and sinthôme and towards a Relational-psychoanalysis project that is in some aspects Deleuzian, though not anti-Oedipal but clearly beyond *and beside Oedipus*. The book, *The Matrixial Gaze* (1995a), elaborates an extension of the major rupture in Lacan's theoretical project signalled by the phenomenological re-theorization of the gaze in *The Four Fundamental Concepts* (Lacan, 1964/1977)' (Pollock 2006, p. 50).

8 'My immersion in painting . . . has led me to apprehend a matrixial borderspace beyond-the-phallus in the field of experience and of representation and so in turn to enter a dialogue with Lacan, and with Merleau-Ponty whose work on the gaze strongly influenced Lacan. Via the subject's early contact with a woman, I suggest, there emerges a swerve and a borderlinking (connection, rapport) – sexual in the broad psychoanalytical sense – which engraves a kind of unconscious sub-knowledge that is not appropriated by the phallus and which has surfaced for me in painting. I have named "swerve" a differentiating potentiality in the field of affection, analogue, up to a point, to Merleau-Ponty's écart in the field of sensible perception, and "borderlinking" (after Lacan's "impossible feminine rapport") is an operation of joining-in-separating with/from the other. I call these processes

Throughout her work she asks these questions: How do we go beyond the phallic gaze? How do we do art or theory, and practise psychoanalysis in ways that do not recreate the conditions that have brought about the atrocities of the twentieth century?

How do we theorize the formation of subjectivity in ways that recognize our co-emergence as subjects in relation to the maternal container, alongside our specifically female and male Oedipal and pre-Oedipal development?

How do we do justice to those dimensions of human psychic development that are formed in relationship and presence, rather than in separation and absence?

How can we *give a different reading* to traditional sources that might have nourished us but that now need to be interpreted differently? Can we revisit certain biblical passages with a view to *speaking otherwise* of their realities in contemporary terms?

How do we understand the phenomenon of abjection in the practices and discourses of religion, and the parallel incipient mother hatred in psychoanalytic theory and practice?

For our purpose here, however, it is her specific implications for relational theology and religious studies that is immediately pertinent. While psychoanalysis and religion have often appeared to be at polar opposites, psychoanalytic perspectives can offer valuable information both about the prejudiced cultural mindsets that even the most sophisticated thinkers can bring to their deliberations, and also about the liberating potential of such critical tools, even if they are often turned back against their founders.

Limitations of Freud

In a recent seminar in Dublin, paraphrasing Freud, Ettinger commented that 'psychoanalysis sometimes invents illnesses that it then treats'. In other words, she claimed that Freud was aware that some assumptions

and operations metramorphosis' (Ettinger, 'Matrixial Gaze and the Screen: Other Than Phallic, Merleau-Ponty and the Late Lacan', *PS* 2.4, pp. 3–39, p. 4, cited in Pollock 2006, p. 50).

or modes of interpretation could actually exacerbate or produce *new illness*, *symptoms* and *addictions*. However, Freud was not immune from the disorder that he described. Just as Europe's landscape conceals and apparently erases crucial moments in its history, so too psychoanalytic theory has concealed crucial moments in the acquisition of subjectivity that also threaten to erupt.

Ettinger's main departure from traditional psychoanalytic theory can be summarized simply. Freud had held that subjectivity proper arises with the discovery of missing parts of the anatomy (in the case of girls) or threat of such loss (in the case of boys). The womb was hardly at issue. The object-relations tradition, based on the work of Melanie Klein, does address the importance of the womb, but primarily in order to theorize the psychic consequences of our being ejected at birth. In the Kleinian tradition, subjectivity begins with the loss of *objects* (the womb, symbolized by the breast). What actually happens in the womb is of little apparent consequence since genuine subjectivity only begins once the womb is left behind.

According to Ettinger, however, subjectivity arises in the *presence* of An/Other rather than in the *absence* (of penis or breast).[9] Subjectivity is formed *in relationship* rather than *in opposition*, or in *loss*.[10]

Ettinger makes it clear, however, that her perspectives are neither pre-Oedipal nor Oedipal, but non-Oedipal. According to Griselda Pollock,

> Bracha Lichtenberg Ettinger situates her interests not in this pre-Oedipal, pre-symbolic domain, but in what she calls the sub-symbolic – a stratus of subjectivity that is not at all orchestrated in relation to the phallus, though it exists side by side with it. This is not alternative

---

9 'No pure presence, no pure absence, no pure schize, and their price to pay, but transmissions and transgressions, impurity and hybridisation, fragmentation, partialisation and pluralisation, and their special price to pay' (Ettinger [1996] 2001, [p. 97] p. 107).

10 'Psychoanalytic theory has struggled to overcome the limitations imposed on the understanding of the formation of subjectivity because of the reliance on the Freudian theory of the unconscious which privileges the phallus as signifier of the dynamic between lack and desire, and which supports the model of repression based on the castration complex and its male perspective' (Ettinger 2006a, p. 216).

feminist theorisation; rather the opening up of the symbolic field to extended possibilities which, in a non phallic logic, do not need to displace the other in order to be. (Pollock 1994, p. 16)

Relationships rather than objects

Ettinger emphasizes that her theories should not be used for any new valorization of the womb.[11] As she said in Dublin: 'We must not replace one object with another. The point is not the organ, but the mode of connection and relating.'[12] Her work is 'rigorously psychoanalytical in formulation'.[13]

---

11 'In building subjectivity-as-encounter upon the borderlinking between the subject-to-be and the becoming-mother, between the fetus and the female body-and-psyche, we should avoid the mistake of looking for the sense of the matrixial encounter in nature (just as the phallic structure and the castration mechanism do not represent father/son relations as endangering the real male organ). Yet anatomy makes a difference that we should open to conceptualization. The matrixial sphere is modelled on intimate sharing in *jouissance*, trauma, and phantasy in the feminine/prebirth sphere, and the womb stands for a psychic capacity for shareability created in the borderlinking to a female body – a capacity for differentiation-in-co-emergence that occurs in the course of separation-in-jointness, where affects and mental waves are continuously reattuned' (Ettinger 2006a, p. 181).

12 'Within what Bracha Ettinger proposes, using the Latin term Matrix, the womb ceases to be mere organ. The investment in any organ, male or female, falls within the phallic model in which its presence or absence becomes a determinant of meaning. Nor is it merely an archaic, non-subjective space, an envelope, Chôra, a vessel, Nirvana, undifferentiatedness, autism. The Matrix refers to a structure, a logic, a process of sub-jectivization and meaning-making that traverses all the registers Lacan proposed. The Matrix is a signifier, like the Phallus, between thought, phantasy and its corpo-Real which is never anatomy or nature' (Pollock 2006, p. 58).

13 According to Pollock, 'we are not talking about phantasies of fusion, symbi-osis, nirvana, and thus not about the death drive. The Matrixial stratum concerns the theorization of that trace Freud readily perceived and regularly discovered in his subjects, of a certain kind of phantasy of space, a space that we must strictly understand as always already being a *borderspace* shared by mutually, co-affecting becoming, partial subjects, registering a minimal difference in the most intimate proximity imaginable, gleaning separateness-in-jointness in a non-specular situa-tion' (Pollock 2003, p. 147).

According to Ettinger, the mother and baby in her womb are co-emerging subjects in process and in relationship, but the almost exclusive phallic concentration has prevented us from theorizing the importance of this time.

In the relational intersubjective perspective, after Klein, Winnicott and Kohut many contemporary psychoanalysts with object-relations, intersubjective, and self tendencies are increasingly developing our understanding of the intersubjective field that is opened in the relations between the caring adult (mother) and the baby and revealed between analyst and analysand.

In my work, I have tried to think about a model that breaks with both the Freudian-Lacanian paradigm and the intersubjective as a field of communication, rethinking desire and the unconscious by reference instead to the transgressive encounter between I and non-I grounded in the maternal womb/intra-uterine complex and a notion of affective economy that avoids phallocentrism. (Ettinger 2006b, p. 218)

Ettinger's perspectives enable us to 'understand the passage into the symbolic kingdom outside the paradigm of castration'. Her aim is to open up

a non-psychotic connection between the feminine and creation, and thus points to an artistic practice that reconnects with an enlarged symbolic in which the feminine (neither male nor female) is fully active and informing knowledge and the ethical realm. (Ettinger 2006b, p. 218)

For Ettinger the *Other* does not necessarily have any ontological connotations (in a theological sense) but, in line with liberation theology, she is attentive both to our attitude towards *Otherness* and to the process by which *Others* are created.

For instance, throughout the recent Israeli incursions and bombing of Gaza, Ettinger has worked with the group Physicians for Human Rights, Israel, bringing medical and other supplies to the besieged Palestinians.

Someone asked her, given the danger, whether she went in with an armed escort, and her reply was as follows: 'What kind of *Other* would I create if I went in armed?'[14] In other words, Ettinger sees the creation of subjectivity as an ongoing ethical and political process, the outcome of our choices as much as of our gendered psychic inheritance.

Theories of repression

One of the fundamental tenets of psychoanalysis is that our unconscious is formed through repression and that what is repressed constantly threatens to erupt and disrupt even the most developed forms of personal and social consciousness. All psychoanalytic schools aim to bring to consciousness material that has been radically repressed in the processes involved in our emergence as subjects. Otherwise, unconscious material threatens to erupt in bodily symptoms, or through projecting our own unresolved psychic struggles onto our *Others* with acute personal and social consequences.

A key question then arises immediately relevant to theology: what exactly is repressed in our emerging subjectivities? Does the form that such repression takes vary across cultures, and what role do particular cultural forms and systems of representation play in these developments?

According to Freud, the Oedipal complex constitutes the primary focus of repression. In his key work, *Totem and Taboo*, Freud argues that the primal father is murdered because of his exclusive access to the women. Towards the end of his life Freud reiterated these views and argued in his work *Moses and Monotheism* that this murder is repressed only to return and take a more virulent form in the murder of the Son, in Christianity.[15]

As many of Freud's critics have pointed out, however, there is scant anthropological evidence of such parricides. However, unlike the scant mythological evidence for the Oedipus complex, there is no shortage of evidence relating to matricide in mythology, and in cultural lore regarding place

---

14 Oral presentation at the Dublin seminar, April 2009.

15 Sigmund Freud, *Totem and Taboo*, SE XIII; Freud, *Moses and Monotheism*, SE XXIII.

names. In the Irish tradition of *Dindshenchas* (the stories of how places got their names), there is systematic erasure of women. Although place names are called after women, the stories now recount their overthrow for pride or disobedience. In the discourses that accompany such major cultural transitions, the women who previously inhabited such mythological spaces are ritually raped, murdered or otherwise slain, even though their subterranean symbolic presence continues to haunt such sites to the present day.[16]

Increasingly, therefore, psychoanalytic anthropology is exposing the relativity of such Oedipal perspectives, forcing a radical review of the universality of such claims and calling for a more wide-ranging study of the relationship between the psychic and social orders. Such a review will also have major implications for theology and religious studies, exposing the relativity of western theological symbols and its major assumptions (cf. Mimica 2007).

However, in mainstream psychoanalytic circles these phenomena remain largely untheorized, possibly because such radical individuation, separation or abjection of the maternal body, as attested in so many mythological systems, is regarded as the *sine qua non* of psychic development and, indeed, of human evolution.

For these reasons, when Luce Irigaray wrote her major critique of Freud and Lacan, she argued cogently that:

The problem is that when the father refuses to allow the mother her power of giving birth and seeks to be the sole creator, then according to our culture he superimposes upon our ancient world of flesh and blood a universe of language and symbols that has no roots in the flesh and drills a hole through the female womb and through earth in order to mark out the boundaries of the sacred space in many patriarchal traditions. It defines a meeting place for men that is based upon an immolation. Women will in the end be allowed to enter that space, provided that they do so as non-participants.

The fertility of the earth is sacrificed in order to establish the cultural domain of the father's language (which is called, incorrectly, the

---

16 Some of these materials are discussed in Condren 1989, p. 29. See also Jacobs 2007.

mother tongue). But this is never spoken of. Just as the scar of the navel is forgotten, so, correspondingly, a hole appears in the texture of the language. (Irigaray 1993a, p. 16)

If Irigaray was concerned with forgetting the *scar of the navel*, Ettinger takes that work further. For Ettinger, subjectivity begins in the relationship between two subjects, mother and baby, in the matrixial web. However, the exclusive emphasis on castration and the failure of classical psychoanalysis to theorize the matrixial web has had fatal consequences undermining its potential to deconstruct misogynist attitudes towards women, and to effect ethical gendered relationships. In brief, classical psychoanalysis has reinforced rather than deconstructed some primal mother fantasies. In making this claim, Ettinger is also making a major departure from the work of Kristeva on religion.

Matrixial repression

Ettinger's work highlights the extent to which major facets in the development of human subjectivity are missing from such classical perspectives and raises the question as to whether such is due either to cultural conditioning or to active repression. For these reasons, Ettinger returns to one of Freud's key texts, 'On the Uncanny' (1919).[17]

Freud had encountered unusual psychic phenomena on his couch which he described as the *Unheimlich*. He considered such phenomena, at once strange but familiar, as the *return of the repressed*. For Freud, however, such *return of the repressed* referred primarily to the repression of castration, a repression that returned usually in frightening forms.

Ettinger argues that in 'routing the unconscious object into the aesthetic realm of the mysterious splendour of the artwork', Freud's original essay opened up the possibility of differentiating between the castration complex and what she calls the *maternal womb/intrauterine complex* (2006a, p. 47). However, given Freud's dismissal of the womb in psychic development, this was not followed through.

---

17 Sigmund Freud, 'The Uncanny' (1919), SE XVII.

Freud did not deny *the denial of the womb* as a female bodily specific-ity, nor did he deny its implications. On the contrary, he insisted on *the importance of such a denial* on its necessity! The magnitude of the denial gives us the measure for what is at stake *for the male person.* For the (universal neutral) child (who happens to have a penis) the idea that the womb belongs to the woman would be a catastrophic blow to narcissism, inasmuch as the child believes that he owns every possible organ of any value. The child *must* therefore, says Freud, deny the womb and take up the belief that children come from the anus (even if, so the theory goes, the child happens to be a girl who has a womb).[18]

Following Freud, Jacques Lacan contributed even further to the repres-sion of analysis of the effects of our origins in the womb. In Ettinger's words:

> Lacan warned that whosoever dares deal with the matter of the pre-natal could not be called psychoanalyst and would have to be excommunicated . . .[19]

For Ettinger such *uncanny* experiences had additional origins, specifi-cally, our experience of originating in a maternal womb. Ettinger does not romanticize this time; she is aware that traumatic psychic traces can be left. However, if we fail to acknowledge this time, or if we lack the analytic apparatus to analyse it we contribute to its active repression. As she said in Dublin: 'If we think subjectivity only post-natally we are missing and rejecting a huge part of ourselves.' Unlike Freud, therefore, she returns

---

18 'Thus, the infantile scenario of childbirth without a womb (from the anus) preserves "neutral" narcissism and in the same move saves univocal, "neutral" psychoanalytic theory' (Ettinger 2006a, pp. 54–5).

19 'because for Lacan, the field of psychoanalysis itself depends on the fore-closure of procreation. Against this position, the concept of the matrix moves the womb from nature to culture, making it the basis for another dimension of sense, for another sense, and for a supplementary feminine difference that is the human potentiality for a shareability and a co-poïesis where no "hero" can become cre-ative alone' (Ettinger 2006a, p. 181).

to such *uncanny* traces in an attempt to broaden our understanding of the development of human subjectivity and also to mitigate the *mother hatred* inherent in some of the founding tenets of psychoanalytic theory.

She argues that the effects of such womb fantasies differ from those derived from castration and she distinguishes between the frightening aspects of castration fantasies and womb traumas:

> The intrauterine or womb phantasy is not to be folded retroactively into the castration phantasy but must be considered as coexisting with it, contrary to other pre-Oedipal – postnatal – phantasies based on weaning or on separation from organs as part-objects. (2006a, p. 48)

In other words, our original experiences in the womb (unlike the fears of castration) may not have been frightening. They appear frightening only when they have been repressed. In other words, their repression *causes* anxiety. Furthermore, whatever is repressed gains strength over time and comes back to haunt us, usually in very unpredictable ways.[20]

While *castration phantasy is frightening at the point of the emergence of the original experience before* its repression, the *matrixial phantasy*

---

20 'Denied such recognition, these traces, will, nonetheless, since logically they must occur, haunt the subject in a variety of symbolically foreclosed but affectively pressing ways such as hallucinations or displaced phantasies: moments of the uncanny. These Freud acknowledged in his germinal essay, "The 'Uncanny'"', when he posited at the foundations of the aesthetic both castration phantasies and phantasies of the mother's body: *Muttersleibphantasien*, translated with his approval as "inter-uterine phantasies". He thus recognized the possibility of other tracks than castration and the phallus as foundations of human subjectivity and its unconscious (Freud, 1985: 368). Thus the invocation of the pre-natal must be understood as a means of posing a supplementary stratum and potentiality for our ways of thinking the fundamental questions of human subjectivity – self and other – but in terms that allow us to think about the sexual specificity of our intimate beginnings in relation to a feminine, desiring subject experiencing her own transformation by this event of another's becoming within her corpo-Real but always-also imaginary body/subjectivity space that is lined with the as-yet-unthought sensuate memory of being on the other side of this shared threshold of the several in becoming' (Pollock 2006, p. 28).

(from *matrice*, for womb) is not frightening at the point of its original emergence, but becomes frightening when the experience is repressed. (Ettinger 2006a, p. 47)

Ettinger points out that psychic trauma, therefore, does not necessarily begin with the actual mother, but with archaic anxiety projected back into the mother. She hopes that it might be possible to explore how psychoanalysts, by failing to take account of these *matrixial* dimensions, might not collude with these repressions or contribute to the potential hatred such anxieties might generate.

Primal mother fantasies

Ettinger identifies three primal *mother fantasies:* the fantasies of *abandonment*, *devouring*, and *not-enoughness*. Ettinger claims that rather than *interpreting* such fantasies analysts have *believed* fantasies of mother trauma.

Ettinger claims that for Freud and Klein the object is phantasmatic. As she said in Dublin, 'What we have to reintroduce is the phantasmatic traces. This is sometimes your own trauma; sometimes your mother's trauma.' What we cannot do is to continue to repress the trauma of the matrixial web, or fail to theorize our emerging subjectivity from that context. A matrixial approach to subjectivity, in other words, radically challenges those psychoanalytic theories that assume that a healthy subjectivity requires and is evaluated by means of the capacity of subjects to abject or cut away from the matrixial web, and mothers in particular.

In Ettinger's work, given the co-emergence of two subjects in pregnancy, she argues that '[a] different affective economy then emerges by which one is able to think of an-other kind of loss or separation which is not attributed to rejection, "castration" or abjection' (Ettinger 2006b, p. 218). As Ettinger formulates the issue:

I am categorically opposed to the classical psychoanalytic claim recurrently emphasized by Lacan, Kristeva and others, according to which the womb can appear in culture only as psychosis; that is, that it can only be the signifier for the crazy unthinkable par excellence, and that whatever is thinkable has to pass through the castration mechanism, by which it is separated from its Real-ness, making the womb that which must be rejected as the ultimate abject, and making this ab- ject the necessary condition for the creation of the subject and the psychoanalytic process. It is precisely this mechanism that establishes the mother as an abject or a lack, scarified to the creation of meaning and to the meaning of creation, whose elimination is the basis for the creative process and the Birth of the Hero. This hero perhaps naively ignores the fact that he eliminates and forecludes the begetter-mother (and also kills the father, only to resurrect him) and takes upon himself his own birth. (2006a, pp. 180–1)

Such heroic mythologies are also replete with images of heroic spiritual or military warriors, desperate to establish new religious or political orders and imbued with elaborate schemes promising *seed for ever* or various forms of immortality. One way or the other, death is defeated, overcome: the bodies of women serve as mere portals to an enlarged and heroic existence, and can be left behind, or repressed. Such theories fos- ter the kinds of heroic individualisms that shatter the matrixial web. As Ettinger formulates the problem:

From the phallic point of view, the elimination of the archaic m/Other is the sacrifice necessary for heroic male sexuality to become pro- ductive. Such a Hero-Genius-Artist corresponds to the Canon that Griselda Pollock (1999) proposes to differentiate in her reading of art history. Anyone, male or female, who takes upon him or herself this hero configuration becomes by definition a man who eliminates the archaic Woman-m/Other. The price to be paid for this is very high if you are a female artist whose sexuality fits badly into Oedipal father–son circulation. (2006a, p. 175)

Through Ettinger's work, therefore, we can see that the *repression* of our relationship to maternal origins actively contributes to the cultural elabor- ation – in myth, theology and popular culture – of the *fear of women*, and mothers in particular. From a theological perspective, it is, therefore, vital that we recuperate the matrixial dimension in a cultural context.[21]

The question of abjection

The significance of Ettinger's work in relation to theology is nowhere more evident than in the contrast between her perspectives and those of Kristeva, especially in relation to abjection.

In *Powers of Horror* Kristeva speaks of the phenomenon of *abjection* and relates this through the death drives, to the rites of sacrifice. In simple terms, she argues that systems of abjection are the ways that societies structure consciousness between clean/unclean, pure/impure. The anthropologist Mary Douglas, in her work *Purity and Danger* had categorized these systems as a form of language. However, Kristeva argued that she had 'naively rejected Freudian premises' (1982, pp. 73–4). In other words, Douglas had not considered that such systems had deep psychic roots, beyond any social functions they might be serving.

One of these assumptions is that of the universality of *abjection* primarily experienced in relation to the mother's body. According to Kristeva,

[t]he various means of purifying the abject . . . make up the history of religions, and end up with that catharsis par excellence called art,

---

21 'The validity or not of what happens in the last months of infant post-maturity in the womb is not the question here. But if we allow ourselves to introduce in to culture another symbolic signifier to stand beside the phallus (signifier of difference and division, absence and loss and orchestrating these either/or models) could we not be on the way to allowing the invisible feminine bodily specificity to enter and realign aspects of our consciousness and unconsciousness? This will surely be good for women, who as subjects in the feminine under phallic law are irredeemably other, without signifiers for their sexuality, desire, their bodily specificity? It will surely extend, as do all these metaphors of sexual difference, to other others – issues of race, immigration, diaspora, genocide are tangled at the moment around the lack of means to signify other possible relations between different subjects – I and non-I. The matrix as symbol is about that encounter between difference which tries neither to master, nor assimilate, nor reject, nor alienate. It is a symbol of the coexistence in one space of two bodies, two subjectivities whose encounter at this moment is not an either/or' (Pollock 1994, p. 16).

both on the far and near side of religion. Seen from that standpoint, the artistic experience, which is rooted in the abject it utters and by the same token purifies, appears as the essential component of religiosity. That is perhaps why it is destined to survive the collapse of the historical forms of religions. (1982, p. 17)

The rites of abjection, according to Kristeva, play a major part in the rites of sacrifice, where one's relationship to the mother's body is often re-enacted, through immersion and repudiation. As Kristeva argues:

A whole facet of the sacred, true lining of the sacrificial, compulsive, and paranoid side of religions, assumes the task of warding off that danger. This is precisely where we encounter the rituals of defilement and their derivatives, which, based on the feeling of abjection and all converging on the maternal, attempt to symbolize the other threat to the subject: that of being swamped by the dual relationship, thereby risking the loss not of a part (castration) but of the totality of his living being. The function of these religious rituals is to ward off the subject's *fear of his very own identity sinking irretrievably into the mother.* (1982, p. 64, emphasis added)

Sacrifice is, as we know (at least in the West) the most active culturally elaborated form in which identity is achieved at the expense of *Others*, *Scapegoats*, or whoever does not conform to the physical or moral purities established by those exerting hegemonic control. As Kristeva goes on to argue:

The sacred – sacrifice – which is found in every society, is then, a *theologization of the thetic*, itself structurally indispensable to the positing of language. This theologization takes on different forms depending on the degree of development of the society's productive forces. (1984, p. 79, emphasis added)

Kristeva's work on abjection and sacrifice derives from her understanding of the *death drives*, which she assumes are cross-culturally constant.

Abjection and sacrifice are one of the ritualized forms that the death drives take as we engage in repeating early psychic traumas *for the sake of mastery*.

However, each of these statements explicates Kristeva's attachment to her Freudian, Lacanian and Kleinian heritage, and her failure (so far) to go beyond western ethnocentrism.

Historically such approaches both *describe* certain cultural phenomena and then, through legitimating them as psychically or culturally normative, *prescribe* such practices into the future. In brief, as I have argued elsewhere, such definitions of the sacred and sacrifice serve to legitimate particular social orders and take little account of alternative approaches to the sacred or sacrifice with very different connotations (Condren 1995 and 2009).

Kristeva's claims would be challenged by anthropologists, and by postcolonial scholars. For instance, the anthropologist Nancy Jay considered some sacrificial rites to be the legitimating rites for male paternity superseding birth from a mother's body (Jay 1992).

Implications for theology

The net effect of such uncritical appropriation of anthropological data and their effective legitimation through psychoanalytic theory is that of undermining the potential of both these disciplines to offer resources towards developing a constructive relational theology. In particular, the inherent gendered biases reinforce theological misogyny.

For instance, Ettinger points out that Freud's work has enabled us to understand the sources of Oedipal fantasies. If such fantasies of paternal seduction were literally and always 'true', professionals would be obliged to 'call in the police'. While not denying the possibility of parental abuse, psychoanalysts must interpret such fantasies and place them in the context of emerging subjectivity in relation to one's father or father figure, thereby dissipating their power over the subject, as well as dissipating the hatred of the father.

However, if Freud's work has helped to dissipate the hatred of the father, nothing similar has been done for the mother. The fact that we have been left without the apparatus to touch all those dimensions is, according to Ettinger, nothing short of 'tragic'. If anything, where psychoanalysts have colluded with or promoted such fantasies they might have actively contributed to the denigration of mothers.

For instance, at the Dublin seminar, Ettinger cited Heinz Kohut, who said that the one thing we need is the notion that 'the other should be wonderful'. When the object is wonderful, the analyst thinks, 'This is me!' When the object is dreadful, however, the analyst thinks, 'This is the mother!'[22] Such positions contribute to the further splitting of subjects rather than their healing.

Likewise, cultural symbols and theologies can reinforce such mother hatred. Feminist theologians have queried to what extent particular theologies have been cultural elaborations of male oedipal struggles: sons killing fathers in totemic rituals, or fathers killing sons in a Freudian *return of the repressed*? In different ways, these theorists question the necessity of sacrifice and the universality of its claims. They ask about the significance of the fact that in the major charter texts of the three main monotheistic faiths the sacrifice of sons to fathers is culturally elaborated (Delaney 1998; Miller 2003).

For those reasons, some feminist theologians have turned to the work of Luce Irigaray. Irigaray takes a critical distance from the Freudian/ Lacanian traditions and is also intimately aware of how systems of representation and religions have served to subjugate real women. Irigaray also writes of the death drives, arguing that both men and women experience dereliction, but she goes on to say that men symbolize their death drives, usually at women's expense.[23]

Irigaray goes so far as to relate sacrifice to a specific expression of male morphologies.[24] In other words, she opens up the question as to how

22 Cited in the Dublin seminar.

23 'Unmitigated mourning for the intrauterine nest, elemental homesickness that man will seek to assuage through his work as builder of worlds, and notably of the dwelling which seems to form the essence of his maleness: language' (Irigaray 1993b, p. 127).

24 '[René] Girard shows how each social era is reconstructed on the basis of a sacrifice, of some cathartic immolation that is essential to the return of the

any early psychic trauma is culturally elaborated: this is also the question of theology or representation.

A broad sweep of western cultural mythologies, both secular and religious, would indicate that major cultural labour has been expended in dealing with psychic trauma in relation to mothers' bodies. The constant *abjection* of women, and bodies in general, which is testified to in major religious texts, represents a specific way in which such trauma has been mediated and culturally elaborated (Lederer 1968; Hays 1964).

In the western world, cultural elaborations – myths, symbols, theologies, rituals – have systematically and successively erased female-centred symbols, stories, myths and theologies from the major symbolic arenas. Irigaray points out that there are no mother/daughter representations and this absence feeds into (rather than deconstructs) any potential mother/daughter hatred (1993a, pp. 7–21).

However, the fact that such erasure of women, and that such rites of abjection and sacrifice are by no means universal across cultures, relativizes such cultural elaborations and demands that such mindsets and practices be further explored in relation to how they are serving particular social structures and relations of power, and as to why they have been taken for granted rather than explored in the major psychoanalytic traditions.

Furthermore, the fact that male Oedipal struggles (fathers and sons sacrificing one another) have been almost exclusively culturally elaborated in the main monotheistic faiths has radically shaped their theologies in the direction of separation, splitting, and scapegoating rather than in fostering relationality. Such struggles have theologically elaborated and psychically prescribed a phallic morphology as a condition of holiness or sanity. This morphology has brought us to crisis-point in human culture where military might and domination, rather than the human capacity for coexistence, compassion and relationality, form the current grammar of human relationships.

---

relational order. This type of explanation, of functioning, seems to me to correspond to the masculine model of sexuality described by Freud: tension, discharge, return to homeostasis, etc.' (Irigaray 1993a, p. 76, n. 1).

These emphases have not only shaped particular religious communities internally, but also have radically undercut their capacity for inter-relatedness in that the interpretation of sacrifice, or the claim to superior sacrifices, have become the battlegrounds on which the interminable Reformation and post-Reformation ecumenical and interreligious struggles have been fought.

In sum: when theological images, symbols, practices and doctrines reinforce rather than deconstruct the abjection of women they radically undermine that religion's capacity for relationality. Furthermore, if psychoanalytic theory endorses the necessity for sacrifice and, implicitly, the consequent theologies of atonement and redemption, this can have very serious consequences. One immediate such consequence is that of undermining the possibility of taking seriously the prophetic injunction to be found in both the Hebrew and Christian Scriptures: *I desire mercy not sacrifice*. That possibility is created anew in the work of Ettinger.

Mercy not sacrifice

Kristeva focused on *abjection*, and on what appears to be a necessary *sacrificial social contract*, and she continues to valorize the importance of *sacrifice*. Ettinger identifies a parallel and equally important dimension of human subjectivity and opens up the possibility of another dimension – *mercy* – understood as *primary compassion* (Hosea 6.1–6; Matthew 9.13; 12.1–8).

> In the Hebrew Bible one of the many names for God is El Harahmim, translated as 'God full of Mercy' or compassion, and also as *misereri*, *misericordiam*, *caritas*, *pietas*, *gratia* and so forth. These are indeed the figurative means of *Rahamim*. But the literal meaning, the signifier is: wombs, uteruses, Matrixes. The text literally signifies a '*God full of wombs*' or (in Latin) full of '*matrixes*'. ([1997] 2000, p. 75)

Alongside the Oedipal complex, therefore (which she does not repudiate) there is also *primary compassion* derived from our early experiences of *compassionate hospitality* in *co-emergence*. The cultural elaboration of this *sub-symbolic* often does take place, but usually (in Roman Catholicism at least) in relation to images of the Virgin Mary. The virgin serves as a refuge from the harshness of the sacrificial social contract, but is never allowed to seriously disturb its fundamentals.

Feminist theologians are, therefore, well aware of the ways in which religious maternal language serves often simply to appropriate sub-symbolic energies in the service of patriarchal relations of power. Ettinger's perspectives, however, are very different. Her *metramorphic* perspectives have much more in common with those processes involved in what the Dalai Lama calls 'educating the heart'.

Ettinger intends such reflections to be interpreted, not as a call to recuperate female gods, or goddesses, but as a radical recuperation of the notion of divinity conceived of as matrixial rather than phallic. It is important to say, however, that this should be seen not as a simple opposition, but as an entirely different way of relating to the *Other*, and *Otherness*.[25]

Ettinger defines the term *metramorphosis* as follows:

Metramorphosis is a *co-naissance* – knowledge of being-born-together – which is not cognitive and does not enter direct representation. We can nevertheless reflect on it, taking into account the errors introduced by Symbolic language. We can also grasp it in painting, if the painting accedes to the appearance of the memory of oblivion, to the blind memory of *I* and *non-I* lodging in me without my self-control. Metramorphic relation is neither Oedipal nor even pre-Oedipal. It is a nonphallic *erotic co-response-ability*: a Eurydician tuning of the erotic aerials of the psyche, always in dangerous proximity to Thanatos. (2006a, pp. 143–4)

----

25 'The Matrix is not the opposite of the Phallus; it is, rather, a supplementary perspective. It grants a different meaning. It draws a different field of desire. The intrauterine feminine/pre-natal encounter represents, and can serve as a model for, the *matrixial stratum of subjectivisation* in which *partial subjects* composed of co-emerging *(I)s* and *non-I(s)* simultaneously inhabit a shared borderspace, discerning one another, yet in mutual ignorance, and sharing their impure *hybrid objet a*' (Ettinger 1996, pp. 25–6).

To be engaged in metramorphosis is to be willing to enter a state of *self-fragilization* for the sake of renewal or transformation, to achieve a *compassionate hospitality* to the Other.[26] In theological terms, we might speak of this as the need for ongoing spiritual and disciplinary practices that, far from shoring up our fragile identities at someone else's expense, open us up to the *Other*.

Ettinger argues for the recuperation of the *feminine*. Given the historical difficulties of that term and its potential for the abuse of women under the guise of women's capacity for *self-sacrifice*, expanding what Ettinger means by such terms requires detailed analysis, impossible in the space here. Suffice now to say that Ettinger has formed this concept based on her own experience in her art practice, and also in critical dialogue with the work of two philosophers in particular: Maurice Merleau-Ponty and Emmanuel Levinas.[27] In a recent essay, however, she has taken a critical distance from Levinas's conception of the *feminine*, probably given the potential misunderstanding and misuse of his original formulations.[28]

Ettinger's work raises a crucial question for theology. Is it possible to *create* matrixial space beyond the confines and limitations of an analytic or artistic space? Could we envisage creating the space for *self-fragilization* at a communal level that would assuage some deep psychic and social needs and at the same time take place not at the expense of

---

26 'The matrixial transsubjectivity of pregnancy imprints both the infant and what I call the *archaic m/Other*. The womb-like compassion is a key to access the Other in its *nude vulnerability*. I see this nude vulnerability as feminine-maternal openness to *fragilizing self-relinquishment*' (Ettinger 2006c, p. 105).

27 Ettinger, 'Que dirait Eurydice?': 'What would Eurydice say?', with Emmanuel Levinas (1991–3), reprint of *Le féminin est cette différence inouïe* (livre d'artiste, 1994), trans. C. Ducker and J. Simas; Ettinger 2005.

28 'Hospitality and compassion (to which we shall return later on) are not only the direct path to the connection between sacrifice and redemption but also the direct path to the connection between grace, solace, care and misericord. It is precisely at this locus that I interpret the Levinasian father/infant relation as feminine-matrixial, twisting by this interpretation the continuity between subjects in terms of time and space (intersubjectivity) beyond time and space (the space of the Other and the time of the future) from the femininity-in-dying perspective to the femininity-in-co-implicated living (transsubjectivity) perspective' (Ettinger 2006c, pp. 114–15).

An/Other? Is it tolerable that we fail to ask such questions in theology or religious studies, given the uses to which religions have been put?

This concern with ritual and communal forms of regression is not evidenced in Ettinger's writings, but theologians concerned with relationality might usefully explore this question. In addition, the communal psychoanalytic practises of the BodySoul Rhythms Programme devised by Marion Woodman, Anne Skinner and Mary Hamilton could provide such a context.[29]

Conclusions

This chapter has merely touched on some of the implications of Ettinger's work for relational theology. She is closest to process theology in that she stresses the ongoing acquisition of subjectivity as never static, forever creative, and always occurring in relationship.

Her work has implications for discerning the difference between a *matrixial* or *feminine sacred* and a *phallic sacred* that would take at least a separate article to develop and that has already been brilliantly explored by Griselda Pollock (2007).

In what could be considered a radical critique of monotheism, Ettinger also maintains that 'The Several comes before the One' (Ettinger 1993, p. 12). By monotheism Ettinger would not be speaking of any positivist conception of god or goddess, nor is she making ontological claims. Rather she is speaking about the extent to which the way we name divinity fosters exclusivist or inclusive approaches to divinity on our part, which also has implications for how we perceive the approach of our *Others*.[30]

---

29 Woodman and Dickson 1996; Woodman 1996; Hamilton 2009. Website: www.mwoodmanfoundation.org.

30 'Right from the moment in which we may speak about the subject, we might also speak of an enlarged subjectivity. In the Matrix a meeting occurs between the co-emerging I and the unknown non-I. Each one neither assimilates nor rejects the other and their energy consists neither in fusion nor repulsion, but in continual re-adjustment of distances, continual negotiation of separateness and distance within togetherness and proximity. Matrix is a zone of encounter between the most

The emphasis on mercy and the matrixial web also has the potential to address what is now emerging as a major difficulty for theology and religious studies: finding an Archimedean point from which to speak in the light of the challenges posed by contemporary epistemologies. Drawing on Hegel, Kant and Kierkegaard, Mark C. Taylor, for instance, suggests that we adopt organic rather than mechanistic metaphors that might do justice to what have now become, of necessity, internal rather than external purposes and teleologies. His outlook, however, is profoundly pessimistic in that he asserts that

> history does, in fact, have a discernible trajectory: everything is becoming increasingly interrelated. As connectivity increases, stability, security and certainty decrease. Growing complexity, uncertainty, and insecurity creates the desire for simplicity, certainty, and security, which leads to foundationalism on the left and the right as well as among those who admit they are believers and those who insist they are not. Every such flight from the present deepens the dangers we face. In an increasingly globalized world, models matter more than ever. If the map does not fit the territory, we cannot navigate the perilous currents surrounding us. (Taylor 2009, p. 117)

The matrixial web could provide such a map, but only if omnipotent fantasies for absolute power, knowledge or access to divinity could be kept in check. In other words, such an Archimedean point could be found not necessarily or primarily in what such traditions *believe*, or in how they legitimate themselves metaphysically, but in their demonstrated capacity for relationality and ethics.

This can only happen when the major faith traditions cease trying to establish their identities sacrificially, that is to say, at the expense of their *Others*. In order to do this they would also have to begin to disavow and disentangle themselves from one of their major agreements to date: the

---

intimate and the most distanced unknown. Its most internal is an outer limit, and the limits themselves are flexible and variable. They are potential or virtual thresholds' (Ettinger 1993, p. 12).

abjection and subordination of women, the primary sacrificial victims of the main monotheistic faiths.

Ettinger's recuperation of a matrixial dimension to subjectivity, and especially the implicit critique of the radically unconscious processes of abjection to be found in all the major faith traditions, opens up the possibility that such traditions could begin to adopt the injunctions of their prophets and founders: *mercy not sacrifice.*

Many other dimensions of Ettinger's perspectives have widespread implications for theology, spirituality and religious studies that cannot be explored here. Suffice to say for now that exploring her recuperation of a matrixial dimension to subjectivity is destined to encourage the development of relational theology in new directions, and also to have widespread implications for the overall study of the relationship between gender, religion and culture.

References

Altizer, Thomas and William Hamilton (1966), *Radical Theology and the Death of God* (Indianapolis: Bobbs Merrill).

Armour, Ellen T. (1998), *Deconstruction, Feminist Theology, and the Problem of Difference: Subverting the Race/Gender Divide* (Chicago and London: University of Chicago Press).

Brock, Rita Nakashima and Rebecca Ann Parker (2008), *Saving Paradise: How Christianity Traded Love of This World for Crucifixion and Empire* (Boston: Beacon Press).

Brown, Joanne Carlson and Carole R. Bohn (1989), *Christianity, Patriarchy and Abuse: A Feminist Critique* (New York: Pilgrim Press).

Butler, Judith (2006), 'Foreword', in Bracha L. Ettinger, *The Matrixial Borderspace* (London and Minneapolis: University of Minnesota Press).

Chodorow, Nancy (1978), *The Reproduction of Mothering: Psychoanalysis and the Sociology of Gender* (Berkeley: University of California Press).

Clément, Catherine and Julia Kristeva ([1998] 2001), *The Feminine and the Sacred*, trans. Jane Marie Todd (New York: Columbia University Press).

Condren, Mary (1989), *The Serpent and the Goddess: Women, Religion and Power in Celtic Ireland* (San Francisco: Harper & Row; and Dublin: New Island Books, 2002).

——(1995), 'Sacrifice and Political Legitimation: The Production of a Gendered Social Order', *Journal of Women's History* 6.4/7.1 (Winter/Spring), pp. 160–89.

——(2009), 'Suffering into Truth: Constructing the Patriarchal Sacred', *Journal of Feminist Theology* 17.3, pp. 356–92.

Delaney, Carol (1998), *Abraham on Trial: The Social Legacy of Biblical Myth* (Princeton: Princeton University Press).

Dinnerstein, Dorothy (1976), *The Rocking of the Cradle, and the Ruling of the World* (London: Souvenir Press).

Ettinger, Bracha Lichtenberg (1993), 'Woman – Other – Thing: A matrixial* touch', in *Matrix-Borderlines*, catalogue, ed. David Eliott and Pamela Ferris (Oxford: Museum of Modern Art).

——(1996), 'Metramorphic Borderlinks and Matrixial Borderspace', in John Welchman (ed.), *Rethinking Borders* (Minneapolis: University of Minnesota Press).

——([1997] 2000), 'Transgressing with-in-to the Feminine', in Penny Florence and Nicola Foster (eds), *Differential Aesthetics* (London: Ashgate), pp. 183–210.

——([1996] 2001), 'The Red Cow Effect', in Juliet Steyn (ed.), *Beautiful Translation*, Act 2 (London: Pluto Press), pp. 82–119. Reprinted in Mica Howe and Sarah A. Aguiar (eds), *He Said, She Says* (Fairleigh: Dickinson University Press, London: Associated University Press), pp. 57–88.

——(2005),'Matrixial Co-poiesis: Trans-subjective Connecting Strings', *Poiesis* 7, pp. 212–17.

——(2006a), *The Matrixial Borderspace* (London and Minneapolis: University of Minnesota Press).

——(2006b), 'Matrixial Trans-subjectivity', *Theory, Culture and Society* 23. 2–3, pp. 218–22.

——(2006c), 'Ethical Compassion to Responsibility: Besidedness and the Three Primal Mother-Phantasies of Not-enoughness, Devouring and Abandonment', *Athena: Philosophical Studies* 2, pp. 100–35.

Gilligan, Carol (1982), *In a Different Voice: Psychological Theory and Women's Development* (London: Harvard University Press).

Grey, Mary (1997), *Prophecy and Mysticism: the Heart of the Postmodern Church* (Edinburgh: T&T Clark).

Hamilton, Mary (2009), *The Dragonfly Principle: An Exploration of the Body's Function in Unfolding Spirituality* (London, ON: Marion Woodman Foundation).

Hays, H. R. (1964), *The Dangerous Sex: The Myth of Feminine Evil* (New York: G. P. Putnam's Sons).

Irigaray, Luce (1993a), *Sexes and Genealogies*, trans. Gillian C. Gill (New York: Columbia University Press).

——(1993b), *An Ethics of Sexual Difference*, trans. Carolyn Burke and Gillian C. Gill (London: Athlone Press).

Jacobs, Amber (2007), *On Matricide: Myth, Psychoanalysis, and the Law of the Mother* (New York: Columbia University Press).

Jay, Nancy (1992), *Throughout Your Generation Forever: Sacrifice, Religion, and Paternity* (Chicago: University of Chicago Press).

Klein, Melanie (1988), *Envy and Gratitude and Other Works, 1946–1963* with a new introduction by Hanna Segal (London: Virago).

Kristeva, Julia (1982), *Powers of Horror*, trans. Leon Roudiez (New York: Columbia University Press).

——([1974] 1984), *Revolution in Poetic Language*, trans. Margaret Waller, with an introduction by Leon S. Roudiez (New York: Columbia University Press).

——(1986), 'Woman's Time', in Toril Moi (ed.), *The Kristeva Reader* (New York: Columbia University Press), pp. 187–213.

——(1987), *Tales of Love*, trans. Leon Roudiez (New York: Columbia University Press).

——(2001), *Melanie Klein*, trans. Ross Guberman (New York: Columbia University Press).

Lederer, Wolfgang (1968), *The Fear of Women: An Inquiry into the Enigma of Woman and Why Men through the Ages have both Loved and Dreaded Her.* (New York: Harcourt Brace Jovanovich).

Miller, David Lee (2003), *Dreams of the Burning Child: Sacrificial Sons and the Father's Witness* (Ithaca, NY: Cornell University Press).

Miller, Jean Baker (1976), *Toward a New Psychology of Women* (London: Penguin).

Mimica, Jadran (ed.) (2007), *Explorations in Psychoanalytic Ethnography* (New York and Oxford: Berghahn Books).

Pollock, Griselda (1994), 'Oeuvres Autistes', *Versus* 3, pp. 14–18.

——(2003), 'Does Art Think?' in D. Arnold and M. Iverson (eds), *Art and Thought* (Oxford: Basil Blackwell).

——(2004), 'Thinking the Feminine: Aesthetic Practice as Introduction to Bracha Ettinger and the Concepts of Matrix and Metramorphosis', *Theory, Culture and Society* 21.1 (February), pp. 5–66.

——(2006), 'Re-thinking the Artist in the Woman: The Woman in the Artist, and that Old Chestnut, the Gaze', in Carol Armstrong and Catherine de Zegher (eds), *Women Artists at the Millennium* (Cambridge, MA: October Books, MIT Press).

——(2007), 'Sacred Cows: Wandering in Feminism, Psychoanalysis and Anthropology', in Griselda Pollock and Victoria Turvey Sauron (eds), *The Sacred and the Feminine: Imagination and Sexual Difference* (London: I. B. Tauris & Co.).

Primavesi, Anne (2000), *Sacred Gaia* (London and New York: Routledge).

Robb, Christina (2006), *This Changes Everything: The Relational Revolution in Psychology* (New York: Farrar, Strauss, and Giroux).

Rose, Jacqueline (1993), *Why War: Psychoanalysis, Politics and the Return to Melanie Klein* (Oxford, and Cambridge, MA: Blackwell).

Ruether, Rosemary Radford (ed.) (1974), *Religion and Sexism: Images of Women in the Jewish and Christian Traditions* (New York: Simon and Schuster).

——(1983), *Sexism and God-Talk: Toward a Feminist Theology* (Boston: Beacon Press).

Ruth, Sheila (1987), 'Bodies and Souls/ Sex, Sin and the Senses in Patriarchy: A Study in Applied Dualism', *Hypatia* 2.1 (Winter), pp. 149–63.

Spelman, Elizabeth (1990), *Inessential Woman: Problems of Exclusion in Feminist Thought* (London: Women's Press).

Taylor, Mark C. (2009), 'Refiguring Religion', *Journal of the American Academy of Religion* 77.1 (March), pp. 105–19.

Woodman, Marion (1996), *The Pregnant Virgin: A Process of Psychological Transformation* (Toronto: Inner City Books).

Woodman, Marion and Elinor Dickson (1996), *Dancing in the Flames: The Dark Goddess in the Transformation of Consciousness* (New York: Gill and Macmillan).

Yeats, William Butler (1983), 'Second Coming', in *The Poems of W. B. Yeats*, ed. Richard J. Finneran (New York: Macmillan).